BILLY THE KID & JESSE JAMES

BILLY THE KID & JESSE JAMES

OUTLAWS OF THE LEGENDARY WEST

BILL MARKLEY

TWODOT®
Helena, Montana
Guilford, Connecticut

A · TWODOT® · BOOK

An imprint and registered trademark of The Rowman & Littlefield Publishing Group, Inc.
4501 Forbes Blvd., Ste. 200
Lanham, MD 20706
www.rowman.com

Distributed by NATIONAL BOOK NETWORK

British Library Cataloguing in Publication Information available

Library of Congress Cataloging-in-Publication Data available

ISBN 978-1-4930-3838-1 (paperback)
ISBN 978-1-4930-3839-8 (e-book)

∞™ The paper used in this publication meets the minimum requirements of American National Standard for Information Sciences—Permanence of Paper for Printed Library Materials, ANSI/NISO Z39.48-1992.

To my wife, Liz Markley, best friend and traveling companion

"Put your sword back in its place," Jesus said to him, "for all who draw the sword will die by the sword."

MATTHEW 26:52, *NEW INTERNATIONAL VERSION*

CONTENTS

ILLUSTRATIONS LIST

INTRODUCTION

Jesse James. Billy the Kid. Say those two names and people immediately think—outlaws. Those names are the gold standard in outlaw lore. All other names don't measure up. Jesse James reigns as the American equivalent of England's Robin Hood—robbing the rich and giving to the poor. Billy the Kid is unsurpassed as the loner waging a personal war against corrupt government in league with big business.

Most Americans know their names. Some may know a few tales about them. They may know that Billy was a twenty-one-year-old outlaw who, legend has it, killed a man for every year he lived. They may have heard that Jesse James was the leader of a gang, robbing banks and trains then supposedly giving the loot to the poor. Most likely, many folks' knowledge of Jesse and Billy may be from watching films such as *Young Guns* (1988), portraying Billy the Kid, and *The Long Riders* (1980), portraying the James boys and Younger brothers. They are not documentaries but entertainment loosely based on the facts.

Who were these men encrusted by myths? What sets them apart from other outlaws to the point that Americans still remember their names today? Were they more fearless, devil-may-care, and audacious, pulling off extraordinary feats of daring? Why were they loved by those who knew them best? Why did many strangers consider them courteous—even those they committed crimes against? We'll take a glimpse at their lives, and maybe you will gain a better understanding of what made them tick.

Much of Jesse James's life of crime is murky. He was protected by many friends and supporters. He never stood trial in a court of law for any of his crimes. He always had alibis when crimes were attributed to him, and many times, he had those alibis printed in the newspapers. It didn't help that dime novels and so-called true histories made up and embellished stories about Jesse. People had no way of fact checking what was printed as true history or printed in the newspapers. The same can be said for the deeds of Billy the Kid. Where there was no concrete information, people made up tales. When there were actual events, people told differing versions of what happened. Memories can play tricks on people.

Jesse James and Billy the Kid were blamed for some crimes they didn't commit. Imagine if you are on a stagecoach or train that's been robbed, wouldn't you want to say you were robbed by the king of the bandits, Jesse James, instead of just some run-of-the-mill thief? Or after Billy the Kid became famous, wouldn't you want to tell people he stayed at your ranch for the night while on the run or maybe even stole your horse?

I began this project not being a supporter or opponent of either Billy or Jesse. I have tried to write this book with no bias, but everyone has one, even if it is subtle.

Where does the truth begin and the legend end? Writers sift through conflicting data and stories trying to separate the wheat of the truth from the chaff of the legend. My problem is that everyone I want to talk to who participated in Jesse and Billy's lives is dead. I do believe many of their stories are true but became embellished. I have reviewed the information on Jesse and Billy and tried to present those stories that have the ring of truth. I like what Robertus Love wrote in his "In Place of a Preface" in his book *The Rise and Fall of Jesse James.* I stand with him and wholeheartedly use his quote as my own, giving him full credit: "Notwithstanding some minor errors which in all probability have crept into the chronicle, the author believes that his book is about ninety-nine per cent accurate; and he knows that it is no less than one hundred per cent honest."

I compare Jesse and Billy side by side through each chapter. Jesse was born September 5, 1847, and Billy the Kid was possibly born November 23, 1859. Jesse was twelve years older than Billy, so the first chapters are heavily weighted toward Jesse. Comparing the two outlaws' lives is similar to comparing astronomical phenomena. Jesse's career was like a comet slowly traversing the night skies while Billy's career was more like the streak of a brilliant shooting star plummeting to earth. Through his illustrations, Jim Hatzell has done an awesome job depicting how major events in Jesse and Billy's lives might have appeared.

So, are you ready? Let's enter the frontier world of Jesse James and Billy the Kid to determine who was the greatest outlaw.

CHAPTER 1
THE EARLY YEARS

Since its beginnings, the United States of America divided itself between those states that allowed slavery and those states that prohibited it. Missouri Territory wanted to enter the Union as a slave state, but northern free states worried if Missouri entered as a slave state, the fragile balance of power would tilt toward slave states. In 1820, Henry Clay from Kentucky along with other members of Congress concocted a controversial agreement, named the Missouri Compromise, allowing Maine to enter the Union as a free state and Missouri to enter as a slave state on August 10, 1821.

Clay County, one of Missouri's western counties northeast of Kansas City and north of the Missouri River, was organized on January 2, 1822 and named after Henry Clay. The Clay County commissioners selected Liberty as the county seat.[1] Many pioneers of Clay County came from slaveholding states: Kentucky, Virginia, North Carolina, Tennessee, and Maryland.[2] These settlers brought slaves with them, and slaveholders and slaves were so prevalent in Clay County as well as other counties along the Missouri River that these counties became known as Little Dixie.[3]

In 1842, twenty-four-year-old Robert James and his sixteen-year-old bride, Zerelda, visited her mother and second husband, Robert Thomason, who had settled in Clay County. Robert and Zerelda liked the countryside; it reminded them of their Kentucky homes, so they decided to stay and moved in with the Thomasons.[4]

Robert James earned a master of arts degree from Georgetown College, a Baptist institution in Georgetown, Kentucky. Robert became the preacher of New Hope Baptist Church. He was a charismatic preacher who increased the congregation from 20 to 280.[5] Robert purchased a 205-acre farm with a log cabin in the hills of northern Clay County, northeast of present-day Kearney, Missouri.[6] The James family's major cash crop was hemp, which was woven into strands and shipped to the Deep South where it was used to bale cotton. Robert began buying slaves to help work the farm. By 1850, Robert owned a thirty-year-old black woman and five black children ranging in age from two to eleven.[7]

Zerelda's first child was born January 10, 1843, and they named him Alexander Franklin James. A second son died soon after birth. The next child was born September 5, 1847, and they named him Jesse Woodson James.[8] Frank and Jesse had a younger sister, Susan Lavenia, born November 25, 1849.[9]

On January 24, 1848, James Marshall had found gold at Sutter's Mill in Coloma, California. The news soon spread like wildfire. People from around the world flocked to California to make it rich.

Clay County, Missouri, was no exception. In April 1850, thirty men, including Robert James, left the county for California. Robert left behind his young wife, seven-year-old Frank, three-year-old Jesse, baby Susan, and six slaves, all but one of whom were children.[10] No one really knows what drove Robert to leave his young family, but plenty of other men did the same. He did have a brother, Drury, who was already in California. Was Robert planning to preach the gospel to sinners? Was he smitten by the gold bug? Or as his brother William suggested, Robert wanted to put some time and distance between himself and Zerelda who William considered a constant complainer.[11]

The California gold camps were notorious health risks. Robert became ill, and on August 18, 1850, he died of fever in Hangtown, California.[12]

When Robert left Clay County, he had lots of debt that needed to be paid off. The probate court appointed an administrator to sell off family property to pay the debts, and several sales occurred over the years. In the end, Zerelda was able to keep the land, some of the animals, tools, and all but one of the slaves. The estate administrator sold at auction twelve-year-old William, the oldest boy.[13]

In an attempt to better her situation, Zerelda married Benjamin Simms on September 30, 1852. Simms was a local well-to-do farmer in his early fifties. Simms did not like Zerelda's children and forced Zerelda to give them to Tilman West, who was her neighbor and the legal guardian of her children and her farm. Zerelda's life was miserable. She left Simms, took back her children, and planned to divorce him. Matters became easier for Zerelda when on January 2, 1854, Simms died.[14]

Somewhere along the way, Zerelda and Dr. Reuben Samuel began courting. Reuben and Zerelda were both from Kentucky and moved in the same circles. Reuben, who was three years younger than Zerelda, had a mild temperament compared to Zerelda's fiery demeanor. They married on September 12, 1855. Zerelda had Reuben sign a prenuptial agreement guaranteeing her ownership of the farm and slaves in the event of his death. Reuben became the legal guardian of Zerelda's children. He agreed to give up his medical practice and concentrate his efforts on the farm. Reuben and Zerelda would have four children together, two boys and two girls.[15]

Frank and Jesse attended school and worked alongside the adults and slaves doing farm chores. They did the same as any farm boy—riding horses, shooting guns, fishing, and exploring the countryside. They easily made friends, but those who knew them during their childhood disagreed on whether they were well behaved or malicious.[16]

Reuben recognized Frank and Jesse's desire to shoot and gave each of them his own double-barreled shotgun. They became expert shots, bringing home small game for the dinner table. The boys saved their money, and Reuben and Zerelda allowed them to each buy a pistol which they soon became proficient at using.[17]

Their grandmother's husband's brother, "Wild Bill" Thomason, came to Clay County. Thomason had fought in the Mexican War and had lived on the frontier. He told the boys tall tales of Indian fights as well as buffalo and bear hunts. He honed Frank's, and possibly Jesse's, riding and shooting skills.[18]

Jesse read the Bible and quoted from it. He carried a well-used Bible with him throughout his life. Frank's ambition was to become a schoolteacher. He also carried a book with him at all times, Shakespeare's complete works, and would quote from it.[19]

Life was good for the Samuel family, and the farm was profitable, but trouble was brewing. Abolitionists were increasing in numbers throughout the country, calling for the emancipation of slaves. The war of words changed to physical violence and death in Kansas, and violence spilled across the border into Missouri. The Samuel family was proslavery. Zerelda, who called herself "a woman of fortitude and resolution," was outspoken for maintaining the status quo. By 1860, there were 3,455 slaves in Clay County and the Samuel family owned seven of them.[20]

While the James boys' early years are well-documented, Billy the Kid's beginnings are shrouded by the mists of time. Other than the US federal ten-year census and before the advent of twentieth-century detailed government records, many people were born in this country, lived their lives, and died without anything being recorded about them. Over the years, researchers have tried to determine what Billy the Kid's real name was, who his parents were, where and when he was born. There are lots of theories. Here is what is known.

Billy the Kid's name was Henry McCarty. His mother's name was Catherine McCarty. It is not known if this was her maiden name or her married name, but she said she was a widow. Henry had a brother, Joseph, who might have been born in 1863 and who might have been a half brother.[21] Catherine is listed in the Indianapolis, Indiana, city directory for 1867 and 1868 as the widow of Michael McCarty, who might or might not have been Henry's father.[22]

Pat Garrett's book, *The Authentic Life of Billy the Kid*, stated Henry was born November 23, 1859, and some of the newspapers at the time of his death reported that he was twenty-one years old, so that would put his birth in 1859.[23]

As to where he was born, Garrett stated Henry was born in New York City.[24] William H. Antrim, who married Catherine in 1873, said Catherine's husband had died in New York City.[25]

The 1880 census taken at Fort Sumner, New Mexico, listed "Wm. Bonny," which was Henry's alias, as being twenty-five years old, his occupation as working cattle, and that he was born in Missouri, as were both his parents.[26] By that time, Billy the Kid was probably attempting to create a new identity.

Researchers continue to hunt for more clues about the early life of Billy the Kid and many theories abound. There is no clear-cut record of the little McCarty family until the 1870s.

CHOOSING SIDES—ABOLITIONIST AND PROSLAVERY

Ever since the Constitution went into effect on March 4, 1789, the United States remained divided on the issue of slavery. The federal government attempted to maintain an equal balance of power between free states and slave states. With the Missouri Compromise of 1820, Missouri entered the Union as a slave state and Maine entered as a free state, continuing the balance of power. One provision of the compromise was that slavery was not allowed in territories north of latitude 36° 30' with the exception of the new state of Missouri.

By the early 1850s settlers were moving westward onto the plains, and railroad companies wanted to open up new territory for their lines and a transcontinental railroad. Congress passed the Kansas-Nebraska Act that would carve up the country's unorganized central-western territory into two new territories. The act was signed into law on May 30, 1854, creating the territories of Kansas and Nebraska. One of the act's provisions was that settlers in the territories would determine if their territory would be free or slave and, when ready, enter the Union as such. Both slave and free-state interests saw this as an opportunity to extend their power.

Many of Kansas Territory's original settlers were proslavery. Northern abolitionists went to work promoting the settlement of Kansas by northern and Midwest farmers. Northerners established several new towns including Topeka, Manhattan, and Lawrence. Large numbers of proslavery Missourians crossed the border into Kansas so that when elections were held for the territorial legislature, the proslavery faction won a majority of seats. The appointed territorial governor was also proslavery.

Antislavery proponents were called free soilers or free staters, and slavery proponents were called border ruffians because they had crossed the border from Missouri. Opponents entered into heated arguments. Arguments escalated into brawls and culminated in murder. Trouble soon spilled across the border into Missouri.

Both slavery and antislavery partisans in Kansas and Missouri formed militia and guerrilla units. Missouri proslavery units were called bushwhackers, and Kansas antislavery units were called jayhawkers, who raided across the border into Missouri.

On December 6, 1855, near Lawrence, Kansas, a proslavery advocate shot and killed free stater Thomas Barber, making him an abolitionist martyr.[27] Then on May 21, 1856, eight hundred border ruffians invaded Lawrence, burning the hotel, destroying two newspaper offices, and ransacking homes and stores.[28]

John Brown led a band of free staters, including four of his sons, to the proslavery settlement at Pottawatomie Creek, Kansas, on the night of May 24, 1856. Pulling five proslavery men from their homes, Brown and his men butchered them with swords. Brown escaped from Kansas and plotted further actions to fight against slavery.[29]

Violence in Kansas would subside and then flare up again, spilling over into Missouri. The violence pitted Missouri neighbor against neighbor even before the Confederates began firing artillery at Union-held Fort Sumter in Charleston, South Carolina, on April 12, 1861.

CHAPTER 2
CIVIL WAR

With the election of Republican Abraham Lincoln as president of the United States in November 1860, slaveholding states began seceding from the Union, and on February 4, 1861, they formed the Confederate States of America. Missouri faced a dilemma—remain in the Union or join the Confederacy. The Little Dixie counties were pro-Confederacy while most of the rest of Missouri's citizens were neutral or favored remaining in the Union. A large German immigrant population in eastern Missouri was abolitionist and pro-Union. Some slaveholders believed it was better to stay in the Union than secede.

Democrat and border ruffian Missouri governor Claiborne Fox Jackson and most of the state legislature were in favor of leaving the Union and joining the Confederacy. A constitutional convention was called to determine whether Missouri should secede. In March, the convention voted in favor of remaining in the Union.[1] Clay County was predominantly pro-Confederacy; not one vote had been cast for Abraham Lincoln during the election.[2]

On April 12, 1861, Confederate artillery began bombarding Union-held Fort Sumter in Charleston Harbor, South Carolina. Two days later, the fort surrendered, and the day after the surrender, President Lincoln declared the country was facing an insurrection and called upon the states for seventy-five thousand troops to put down the rebellion. This infuriated remaining slaveholding states that had not seceded, and some soon did just that.[3]

Missouri governor Jackson called Lincoln's proclamation "illegal, unconstitutional and revolutionary . . . inhuman and diabolical." He further stated, "Not one man will the state of Missouri furnish to carry on such an unholy crusade."[4] The majority of Clay County residents were of the same mind. On April 17, the *Clay County Flag*'s headlines proclaimed, "War Inaugurated by the Abolitionists—the Soil of the South Invaded!!!" Three days later, two hundred pro-Confederates took control of the federal arsenal in Liberty, one of two in Missouri, and removed rifles, cannons, and ammunition.[5]

The Samuel family was pro-Confederate. Zerelda was an outspoken proponent for the Confederacy, creating enemies of those county residents who were pro-Union.[6] She was a great influence on her sons, Frank and Jesse, who became staunch Confederates. On May 4, 1861, eighteen-year-old Frank James joined the pro-Confederate Missouri State Guard.[7]

Events did not turn out well for Missouri Confederates. Union forces took control of the arsenal in St. Louis, and Governor Jackson and his Confederate legislators were forced out of Missouri's capital, Jefferson City. Frank's first battle was at Wilson's Creek south of Springfield, Missouri. On August 10, 1861, a Union force attacked the Confederate camp but was repulsed and retreated to Rolla, Missouri. Frank then fought at the Battle of Lexington, Missouri, from September 12–20, 1861, which also resulted in a Confederate victory. A new Union army advanced from St. Louis and forced the Confederates to abandon Springfield.

Frank traveled with the army into southwest Missouri. In February 1862, he contracted measles and was left behind in a hospital that was captured by Union forces. The Union authorities paroled Frank, and he returned home.[8]

Life had continued as normal as possible on the Samuel farm. Jesse would have continued with the chores, hunting, and horseback riding. The family would have been informed of the latest war news and of jayhawker and bushwhacker raids.

Frank, along with all other eligible men, was forced to enroll in the Clay County Union militia, but he failed to participate. He may have aided and rode with bushwhackers during the summer and fall of 1862. Confederate general Jo Shelby and others claimed that Frank saved his life during the Battle of Prairie Grove, Arkansas, December 7, 1862. Union authorities arrested Frank and jailed him in Liberty in the spring of 1863, but he escaped, heading to "the brush," meaning joining the bushwhackers. Frank said he joined notorious William Quantrill's bushwhacker outfit in May 1863.[9]

Feared by Unionists and well-liked by Confederates, Quantrill claimed he was from Maryland but was actually from Canal Dover, Ohio. He had first fought as an abolitionist jayhawker but then switched sides. Frank said of Quantrill, "He was full of life and a jolly fellow. He had none of the air of the bravado or the desperado about him. . . . He was a demon in battle."[10]

Frank became lifelong friends with one of Quantrill's men, the easygoing Cole Younger. Nineteen-year-old Younger came from a prominent Jackson County, Missouri, family. His father, a pro-Union slaveholder, had been murdered by Union militia, believing he had a large amount of money on him.[11]

Frank was spotted participating in bushwhacker raids under the leadership of Clay County saddler Fernando Scott. The bushwhackers ambushed Union soldiers, murdered surrendered prisoners, and stole from local Unionist farmers. Zerelda acted as an informant to the guerrilla band, and fifteen-year-old Jesse carried her messages to the bushwhackers. He wanted to join them, but they told him he was too young.[12]

The local Union militia began searching for Scott's bushwhackers, and a logical place to visit was the Samuel farm. On the morning of May 25, 1863, Clay and Clinton County Union militia rode up to the Samuel farmhouse. They questioned the family about Frank and the other bushwhackers' whereabouts. Family members answered they had no idea. Jesse was out working in the fields. Militiamen surrounded him and whipped him to make him reveal where Frank and the others were. Jesse refused to talk. They brought him back to the farmhouse where a rope was tossed over a tree limb. One end of the rope was tied around Dr. Reuben Samuel's neck, and two fellow Clay County neighbors hoisted him off the ground, strangling him. The Reverend William James, the brother of Zerelda's first husband, rode onto the scene and later said, "Mrs. Samuel, [was] making such an outcry and giving them [the militia] such a tongue-lashing as only she could give." After letting Samuel dangle, the militia members dropped him to the ground. Some accounts claim they strung him up two more times. He revealed that Frank and the others were camped in a nearby woods to the north of the house. Forcing Samuel to lead them to the bushwhacker camp, the militia spotted Frank and the other bushwhackers lounging, playing cards, and gambling over their spoils. The militia ambushed them, killing two, but the others raced away on horseback. In the running fight, the militia killed three more bushwhackers. The pursuit ended when Frank and the other survivors escaped across the Missouri River.[13]

The militia hauled Reuben to prison in St. Joseph, Missouri, and then returned later for Zerelda and took her to prison as well in St. Joseph. After she took the oath of allegiance, she was paroled on June 5 and allowed to return home. Reuben also took the oath, was paroled, and allowed to return on June 24.[14]

During their absence, Jesse managed the farm and looked after his younger family members. That summer of 1863, with the help of a black man, Jesse raised a large crop of tobacco. It was probably during this time that he was cleaning a pistol when it fired, blowing off the tip of the middle finger of his left hand.[15]

Frank continued his bushwhacking activities with Quantrill. The bushwhackers had been effective terrorizing pro-Union Missourians and Kansans. Union general Thomas Ewing arrested

HATZELL 2019

wives and sisters of known bushwhackers, including cousins of Cole Younger and two sisters of William "Bloody Bill" Anderson. The women were imprisoned in a three-story brick building in Kansas City, Missouri. On August 14, 1863, the building collapsed, killing five of the women including one of Bloody Bill's sisters and one of Cole's cousins, and two women were crippled for life. A rumor spread that the Union authorities had deliberately undermined the building's foundations to create the collapse. The bushwhackers clamored for revenge, and Quantrill determined to retaliate by attacking the heart of Kansas Unionism—Lawrence, Kansas. Leading 450 men, including Frank James and Cole Younger, Quantrill arrived at the outskirts of Lawrence on the morning of August 21, where he told his men, "Kill every male and burn every house." Within three hours, they slaughtered 183 men and boys and burned 185 buildings, then escaped back into Missouri. That October, Quantrill led his men, including Frank, to Texas.[16]

In April 1864, Frank returned to Clay County with the bushwhacker leader, Charles Fletcher Taylor. Fletch had broken with Quantrill and was now on his own. Along with Fletch Taylor's bushwhackers was a vicious killer, eighteen-year-old "Little Archie" Clement.[17]

Jesse was now sixteen years old and joined brother Frank and Taylor's bushwhackers. There were no muster papers for Jesse to sign. There was no pay. There were no weapons or supplies provided. There were no uniforms. There were no barracks or official camp; they lived in the brush relying on the hospitality of family, friends, and Confederate sympathizers or pilfered from pro-Union Missourians. The Confederacy did not officially claim the bushwhackers. Taylor's bushwhackers had no military objective other than create havoc among Union supporters and attack military targets of opportunity. They took their pay by robbery, and obtained their weapons, ammunition, and supplies from gifts and theft.

Zerelda or another family member sewed Jesse's guerrilla shirt with multiple pockets for pistol caps and bullets. He wore several revolvers stuck in a waist belt. Able to fire six rounds, the revolver was the bushwhacker's weapon of choice. Since it took time to reload the powder and bullet in each cylinder and then place a new cap on the cylinder's nipple, the bushwhacker would carry multiple revolvers, pulling a new one when all cylinders had fired. Another standard weapon was a hunting knife.

The bushwhackers gave Frank the nickname "Buck," and after Jesse pinched a finger in a pistol or other piece of equipment shouting "Dingus!" they gave him that nickname.[18] They were a band of brothers who cared for little other than each other. "Take our company and there has never been a more reckless band of men," Frank later said. "Most of them were under 21."[19]

There was unfinished business to take care of in Clay County—it was payback time. Taylor's band began terrorizing and murdering Clay County Union sympathizers. First was Bradly Bond, one of the men who had strung up Reuben Samuel. Bond was shot down after being asked to come outside his house. The next day, Alvis Dagley, another man who had hoisted Samuel off the ground, was murdered while working in the fields near the Samuel farm. Taylor's bushwhackers murdered six more men, including a black slave, during the next several weeks.[20]

Joining with other bushwhacker bands the summer of 1864, they attacked Union patrols and captured and pillaged the towns of Parksville and Platte City, Missouri. After that, Taylor's bushwhackers attacked the home of Methodist minister and abolitionist Charles Morris. They set the house on fire, and when Morris and two other men tried to escape, they were shot down.[21]

The bushwhackers were riding through a Dutch settlement in southern Ray County. Jesse saw a saddle on a fence rail in front of a house and decided he needed it. "I was in the act of picking it up," Jesse later told a friend, "when a Dutchman came to the door and shot me through the breast." Frank held Jesse in the saddle as they rode away. He was taken to his Uncle John and Aunt Mary Mimm's boarding house across the Missouri River from Kansas City where he was hidden. Dr. J. M. Ridge treated his wound, and his nineteen-year-old cousin, Zee Mimms, who had been named for Jesse's mother, took care of him. The bullet had passed through Jesse's chest and out his back without hitting vital organs. After a short recuperation, he was fit enough to hit the brush and join the bushwhackers again.[22]

On August 8, 1864, a shotgun blast mangled Fletch Taylor's right arm, resulting in its amputation and taking him out of the action while it healed. With Taylor gone, an even more ferocious guerrilla leader took command of the bushwhackers—Bloody Bill Anderson. Both Frank and Jesse and their close friend Archie Clement joined Anderson's band. Jesse said Clement was "one of the noblest boys, and the most promising military boy, of this age."[23]

Bloody Bill Anderson, now in his mid-twenties, had been born in Kentucky, lived in Huntsville, Missouri, and later Kansas. His family owned no slaves, but they were staunch proslavery. Anderson began a life of crime that devolved into bushwhacking after a Kansas Unionist murdered his father. After one of Anderson's sisters was killed in the Kansas City women's prison collapse, Anderson exacted revenge, participating in the Lawrence, Kansas, massacre and other atrocities. Later he broke with Quantrill, forming his own bushwhacking band. He was brutal, torturing and killing Union soldiers, militia, and supporters. Anderson scalped the men he killed and hung their scalps from his horse's bridle and reins. In July 1864, he sent a letter to the Lexington, Missouri, newspapers threatening anyone who supported the Union, "I will hunt you down like wolves and murder you." Archie Clement became one of Bloody Bill's chief lieutenants and excelled in scalping his victims.[24]

In August 1864, Anderson and his bushwhackers camped near the Samuel farm and Zerelda gladly fed them dinner. From there they rode into Platte County, where Anderson cut off the ears of a prisoner before shooting him in the head. On August 10, back in Clay County, they shot and killed a young Union man who had been married three days earlier, leaving his naked body alongside a stream bank.[25]

Bloody Bill Anderson impressed Jesse James, and Jesse claimed that he was one of "Anderson's best men."[26] Anderson said of Jesse, "Not to have any beard, he is the keenest and cleanest fighter in the command."[27]

Anderson made Rocheport in Boone County, Missouri, his capital, stopping Missouri River traffic and collecting tolls. The slaughter and atrocities continued on both sides. On September 23, Anderson's men killed twelve Union soldiers and three black teamsters, as Union soldiers captured seven bushwhackers, murdering and scalping six of them. The next day, Anderson combined his men with other bushwhacker bands. Wearing captured Union uniforms, they entered the town of Fayette, Missouri, to surprise and attack the Union troops, but the Union troops rallied, repulsing the bushwhackers.[28]

On September 27, 1864, again wearing Union uniforms, Anderson led eighty bushwhackers, including Frank and Jesse, north to Centralia, Missouri, to gather newspapers and any other intelligence they could acquire. Centralia was a small railroad town with a train station for the North Missouri Railroad.[29]

Trotting their horses into town at 10 a.m., Bloody Bill's men burst into homes, terrorizing the residents. The bushwhackers robbed the town's two stores, confiscating whatever they wanted. They hauled a keg of whiskey into the street, then broke open the barrel head. Anderson and his men began guzzling its contents.[30]

At 11 a.m., the stagecoach from Columbia, Missouri, arrived. The bushwhackers robbed the passengers, not caring if they were pro-Union or pro-Confederate. Fortunately for Unionist congressman James Rollins, the bushwhackers did not discover who he was.[31]

Bushwhackers hauled railroad ties and other obstructions across the train tracks. About 11:30 a.m., the northbound passenger train from St. Louis was pulling into the station. As bushwhackers began shooting at the train, the engineer realized they were trapped; he could not go forward and could not back up as a construction train was approaching from behind. The bushwhackers found twenty-three Union soldiers on the train, all but two unarmed. The bushwhackers considered a German wearing a blue shirt and cap to be a Union man and forced him to join the soldiers being herded off the train. After robbing all 125 civilian men, women, and even children, and after ransacking the baggage car for money and valuables, the bushwhackers abused the soldiers then forced them to undress. Anderson removed a sergeant from among the soldiers, and then made them line up along the tracks. He told Archie Clement to lead twenty-five men in "paroling" the soldiers. They began firing into the soldiers, killing every last one of them as well as the German. They then set the train's passenger cars on fire and sent the train out of town with its whistle blowing. After setting the train station on fire, the bushwhackers were done. Yelling and laughing, Bloody Bill, Frank, and Jesse, and the other bushwhackers rode out of town with their plunder and lone prisoner.[32]

At 3 p.m., Major Andrew Johnson, leading a battalion of the Thirty-Ninth Missouri Infantry US Volunteers, rode into Centralia. Although they were infantry, they were mounted on horses, making them more mobile. These troops were green—having been recruited three weeks previously, they had not yet been in a fight. The murdered soldiers' bodies lay along the tracks, and the charred remains of the station and railroad cars still smoked as the townspeople told Johnson what Bloody Bill's boys had done.[33]

Major Johnson saw bushwhackers riding in the distance. The townspeople said there was a large bushwhacker camp to the south and advised Johnson not to go after them, but he said it was his duty to attack the culprits. He left a detachment of thirty-seven men in town and rode off after the bushwhackers with 120 men.[34]

The bushwhackers knew Johnson and his men were coming and had roughly 225 men in camp ready to attack. Bushwhacker decoys led the Union troops three miles to the southeast, close to the rebel camp. The Union troops rode to an open field and saw mounted bushwhackers waiting at the field's far edge. Johnson ordered his men to dismount and form into a line on top of high ground. Every fourth man was designated a horse holder taking the horses back behind the Union line. Johnson, remaining on horseback, drew his revolver and ordered the men to load their Enfield muskets and fix bayonets.[35]

With a wild shout, the bushwhackers galloped toward the waiting Union line. The soldiers fired a ragged volley. Most of the shots flew over the bushwhackers' heads. "We were laying low on our horses, a trick the Comanche Indians practice and which saved our lives many a time," Frank James said later. "Up the hill we went, yelling like wild Indians. . . . Almost in the twinkling of an eye we were on the yankee [sic] line."[36]

Firing their revolvers, the bushwhackers raced upon the Union soldiers before most of them could reload their weapons. Some soldiers swung their muskets as clubs while others thrust their bayonets at riders and horses. Major Johnson was shot off his horse. Some soldiers asked for mercy and tried to surrender. All were killed—many shot in the head. Some of the mounted horse holders fled toward Centralia. Bushwhackers chased them, shooting many of them out of the saddle.[37]

The bushwhackers killed 108 men on the field and in the chase while losing only four of their own.[38] Frank James and others later said Jesse was the bushwhacker who shot Major Johnson.[39]

The bushwhackers pressed their attack through Centralia all the way to Sturgeon, Missouri, eight miles away. Some Union soldiers were left behind in Centralia. The bushwhackers hunted them. One Union soldier was told to come out of the hotel and surrender. When he did, he was shot down. Another was killed in the bedroom of a girl lying sick in bed. Two hiding in a hotel privy were shot dead.[40]

Arriving at the battlefield's scene of carnage thirty hours after the fight, Lieutenant Colonel Daniel Draper of the Ninth Missouri State Militia Cavalry reported, "Most of them [the Union soldiers] were beaten over the head, seventeen of them were scalped and one of them had his privates cut off and placed in his mouth. Every man was shot in the head. One man had his nose cut off. One hundred and fifty bodies have been found, including twenty-four taken from the train."[41]

News of the bushwhackers' massacre of the Union prisoners at Centralia made its way back to Clay County. Liberty's Unionist assistant provost marshal, William Kemper, learned from local citizens that both Frank and Jesse had participated in shooting the unarmed men. Kemper said he overheard one of Zerelda's neighbors confront her over Frank and Jesse's role in the slaughter of the prisoners. Zerelda responded by saying she was proud of them and "prayed to God to protect them in their work." Kemper further wrote of Zerelda, "I regard [her] as being one of the worst women in this state."[42]

Bloody Bill's bushwhackers continued their rapes, tortures, murders, and mutilations as they rode west to Clay County. There they received hot meals and shelter from Zerelda and other sympathizers.[43]

On October 27, 1864, Unionist Major Samuel Cox, commanding portions of the Thirty-Third and Fifty-First Enrolled Missouri Militias and First Missouri State Militia Cavalry, set a trap for Bloody Bill's bushwhackers in Ray County, west of the village of Albany. The trap was a success. Some bushwhackers were shot out of the saddle, while Jesse and others escaped. The boy Clell Miller, a friend of the James boys, was wounded and captured. Miller claimed the bushwhackers had captured him and forced him to join them. Cox prevented the militia from hanging Miller and sent him off to prison. Other bushwhackers, including Bloody Bill Anderson, were killed. The militia found two fresh scalps tied to his horse's bridle and on his person, a silk scarf he carried in memory of his sister who died in the Kansas City prison collapse. Each time he personally killed a Unionist, he tied a knot in the scarf. It had fifty-three knots. His body was hauled to Richmond, Missouri, where it was photographed. They chopped off his head mounting it on top of a telegraph pole and dragged the body through the streets.[44]

The war was not going well for the Confederacy or its efforts in Missouri. Union forces had forced Confederate troops out of the state and bushwhacker groups were being hunted down. Frank and Jesse returned to Clay County where it was claimed they murdered two Unionists and sent death threats to others.[45] In November 1864, Frank James joined William Quantrill's bushwhackers riding east to Kentucky.[46] Jesse joined George Shepherd's bushwhackers riding south to Texas for the winter.[47]

On January 29, 1865, Union authorities had identified Reuben and Zerelda Samuel, along with nine other families, as leading rebels in Clay County. They were banished from the county and told to travel to Confederate-held territory. Instead, the Samuel family moved one hundred miles northwest to Rulo in southeast Nebraska.[48]

The Confederacy was on its last legs. By April 9, 1865, Union troops had surrounded and cut off the Army of Northern Virginia at Appomattox. Confederate general Robert E. Lee surrendered to Union general Ulysses S. Grant. Other Confederate armies were surrendering. On May 10, Confederate president Jefferson Davis was captured. For all intents and purposes, the war was over. That is, over for most combatants, but not for all the bushwhackers.

Jesse's friend Archie Clement became a bushwhacker leader, and Jesse returned to Missouri with Clement's band in March or April 1865.[49] They fought their way through the state, attacking and being attacked by Union militia. By May, they were in Benton County. There they captured a Union militiaman named Harkness who was said to have killed Clement's brother and burned down Clement's mother's house. Jesse and two other bushwhackers held Harkness as Clement slit his throat then scalped him.[50]

On May 9, wearing Union uniforms, a hundred of Clement's bushwhackers rode into Kingsville, Johnson County, near Clement's family farm. They killed eight men and boys and set fire to five homes. They attacked Union militia member and postmaster Leroy Duncan, who they alleged was a bandit and house burner. Duncan made a stand behind a plank fence as Jack Bishop, Clement, and Jesse galloped toward him. Duncan shot Bishop's horse and then shot Clement's horse before Jesse was on him, firing four shots into him. Duncan clung to life but died on May 18.[51]

Clement's bushwhackers rode north into Lafayette County where they continued their killing spree. On May 11, Clement wrote a letter to Major Berryman Davis, the Union commander at Lexington, Missouri, demanding that Davis surrender the town to him or they would attack and "burn the town and kill the soldiers." The attack never happened.[52]

On May 14, the bushwhackers held a meeting. Many realized the war was over and decided they would surrender. Others were determined to continue the fight and talked of heading to Mexico.[53]

On May 15, 1865, seventeen-year-old Jesse James rode along with Archie Clement and a small group of bushwhackers. Jesse later said he was on his way to Lexington to surrender and carried a white flag of truce. The bushwhackers were attacked by a larger group of Union troops. As the bushwhackers fled on horseback, Jesse was shot in the right side of his chest, the bullet entering close to his previous wound and piercing his lung. His horse was hit and went down. Jesse eluded his pursuers by running into some woods and submerging himself in a stream through the night.[54]

The next morning, Jesse approached a plowman who took him to the Brady home where they cared for him. On May 21, 1865, some of the bushwhackers and the Bradys loaded Jesse into a wagon and drove him to Lexington where he surrendered, took the oath of allegiance, and was paroled.[55]

As to Billy the Kid's life during the Civil War, he would have been a toddler. Currently, there is no reliable information on his early childhood. Catherine McCarty may have moved from New York City to Indianapolis, Indiana. It is not known if she was married. If she was married, no one is sure as to whom. Catherine referred to herself as the Widow McCarty. She would later become involved with William H. Antrim, who was thirteen years younger than she. Antrim was from Indianapolis, Indiana, and there is reference to a Catherine McCarty living in Indianapolis. So, Catherine and Antrim may have met there. Everything is speculation. There is no concrete evidence.[56]

CHAPTER 3

BANKS ARE WHERE THE MONEY'S AT

It was mid-June 1865. The wounded Jesse James had surrendered and had been paroled at Lexington, Missouri. With the approval and assistance of Lexington's provost marshal, Captain Clayton Rogers, Jesse's friends carried him aboard a Missouri River steamboat that took him to Kansas City. He again stayed at his Uncle John and Aunt Mary Mimm's boarding house where doctors and the Mimm's daughter, cousin Zee, cared for him.[1]

In mid-July, Jesse's sister arrived and took him to the James family's exile home in Rulo, Nebraska. Under their care, he made little progress in healing. He pleaded with his mother, "Ma, I don't want to be buried here in a northern state." On August 26, Zerelda took him by riverboat back to the Mimm's boarding house, where for the next several weeks he recovered under the care of physicians and cousin Zee. Jesse and Zee became close and made a secret pact to marry later. During Jesse's convalescence, the Samuel family returned to their Clay County farm. Along with them came Charlotte and other former slaves who would continue to work and live with the Samuel family. At the end of October, Jesse was strong enough to travel home, soon making a full recovery.[2]

Frank James had ridden with Quantrill's bushwhackers to Kentucky where, during a May 10, 1865 skirmish, Quantrill was wounded and paralyzed, dying June 6. Frank and the remnants of

Quantrill's band surrendered and were paroled on July 26, 1865. Frank lingered in Kentucky, returning to the family farm later that year.[3]

Jesse joined the Southern Baptist Church and for all intents and purposes appeared to lead a good Christian life. He was well liked by many.[4]

Jesse and Frank's close friends continued to be their old bushwhacker comrades: Archie Clement; Clell Miller; Dave Pool, a bushwhacker commander at the Centralia massacre; Jim Anderson, brother of Bloody Bill; and others. However, Jesse feared Yankee retribution for his wartime actions and always traveled well armed.[5]

Missouri newspaper editor and former Confederate major John Newman Edwards, who had been adjutant for Brigadier General Jo Shelby, described Jesse and Frank's characteristics. Jesse was tall and well built. His face was "as smooth and innocent as the face of a school girl." His blue eyes were penetrating and restless. He was always smiling, lighthearted, and devil-may-care. Older brother Frank was taller than Jesse. He was the opposite—somber, never laughing. Both brothers were ready to face any danger.[6]

The war taught the James boys many things that would be useful as they grew older. They knew who their friends were and who could be trusted. Even though the North had won, the network of Confederate and bushwhacker supporters was still in place, and the James boys could use it. In 1907, William Allan Pinkerton would say, "As a rule the James and Younger brothers and their associates, after each crime, would return to their home, Clay County, Mo., where they were virtually immune from arrest, either through fear of them by the respectable element or through the friendly aid they received from their admirers."[7]

They had learned the art of disguise to the point of fooling Union troops and supporters into thinking they were Yankees. The tale was told how Jesse had disguised himself as a girl, deceiving an Independence brothel madam who catered to Union officers. He rode up to her house of ill repute claiming he was a girl who would like to return that evening with a few neighbor girls for "a good time." The madam consented, telling him to come back with his friends. Jesse and fellow bushwhackers returned that night and had their good time by ambushing waiting Union officers.[8]

Jesse and Frank would create aliases and new identities for themselves, fitting into communities and acting as model citizens. For sixteen years, Jesse and Frank would elude law enforcement and private detective agencies. Jesse successfully used the alias John Davis Howard to the end of his life, and Frank went by B. J. Woodson.[9]

After the war, former Confederate soldiers, officials, politicians, and supporters were disenfranchised throughout the South. They could not vote or hold office. In some areas, the government was run through military districts. In June 1865, Missouri had passed and enacted the Drake Constitution, which stated before someone could vote they had to take an oath that they did not fight against the federal government or provide aid or support persons who did. The Drake Constitution also stated that clergy, businessmen, teachers, and lawyers had to take the same oath or they could not work at those professions.[10]

Republicans controlled the State of Missouri and Clay County governments. On January 29, 1866, the Republicans held a mass meeting at the Clay County courthouse in Liberty. They were in control and planned to implement their reforms. Former Confederate sympathizers were not pleased.[11]

Two banks conducted business in Liberty. Many Republicans had their money in the Clay County Savings Association run by a Republican board of directors. Missouri Republican governor Thomas Fletcher called James Love, the bank president, "a good Union man." The other bank, the Liberty Savings Association, did not have any strong Union supporters in its management.[12]

On Tuesday afternoon, February 13, 1866, a group of ten to twelve men wearing federal greatcoats rode into Liberty and stopped in front of the Clay County Savings Association building.[13]

Cashier Greenup Bird and his son William, who was the clerk, were working inside the bank building. At 2 p.m., two men entered the front door; one man stopped by the stove to warm himself while the other asked for change for a ten-dollar bill. As William began to make change, the two men pointed revolvers at his father and him and then jumped over the counter. The men told the Birds not to make any noise or they would be shot. Then they demanded all the money in the bank.[14]

William was slow to move so one of the robbers struck him on the back with his revolver saying, "Damn you, be quick!" William entered the vault and handed over bags of gold and silver to one robber while Greenup opened the box with greenback currency and bonds which the other robber took and put in sacks they had brought with them. The robbers forced the father and son into the vault and, closing its door on them, supposedly said, "All Birds should be caged." The vault's door was not locked, and they were out as soon as the robbers left.[15]

The two bank robbers mounted their horses and the waiting riders fired their revolvers as they galloped east down Franklin Street. Greenup Bird opened a front window and shouted the bank had been robbed. Nineteen-year-old George Wymore and his friend Henry Haynes were walking to their college classes and stood on the opposite side of the street from the bank. George started yelling, "Robbers! Robbers!" One rider's horse reared as the rider fired and other robbers aimed and fired their revolvers at George who died with four gunshot wounds. Henry ducked behind a tree and was unharmed.[16]

The robbers escaped with over $60,000 in gold, silver, cash, and bonds. A posse lost track of the robbers as a snowstorm hit, obscuring the robbers' tracks. Bank president James Love offered a $5,000 reward for the recovery of the stolen money. It was never

HATZELL 2019

recovered, and no one was ever convicted of the robbery, considered the first peacetime, daytime, bank robbery in United States history.[17]

Even though no one was caught, people began to have their suspicions as to who the robbers were. Most people believed the same as bank president James Love that the robbers were Clay and Jackson County bushwhackers. Then people began suggesting a long list of names, adding to it Archie Clement and the James boys, but there was never any proof and the robbers weren't talking. B. S. Minter told neighbors Frank James and Bud Pence obtained two sacks of meal from him before the robbery and that the sacks used in the robbery looked like the same ones Pence and Frank had taken. Minter later changed his story, claiming he did not know the men. There is a story handed down through the James family that Jesse was the one who developed the plan to rob the bank.[18]

On October 30, 1866, four men robbed over $2,000 from the Alexander Mitchell and Company bank in Lexington, Missouri. Dave and John Pool, former bushwhacker comrades of Frank and Jesse James, led a citizen posse made up of former bushwhackers in a chase after the bank robbers. They claimed they were stopped when the robbers fought back and escaped. Folks were suspicious that the Pools and their posse might have been in on the heist. Again, people speculated the James boys could have been involved, but there was no evidence, and no one stepped forward to identify them.[19]

As the November 1866 elections approached, former bushwhackers, Confederates, and their sympathizers, who were barred from voting, began intimidating Republican and black voters, especially in Clay and Lafayette Counties. Trouble was brewing in Lexington, Lafayette County's seat, where bushwhackers were harassing voters. On Election Day, one hundred former bushwhackers, led by Archie Clement, and Lexington resident bushwhackers, led by Dave Pool, took over the town, intimidating anyone who planned to vote. Lafayette County Sheriff Thomas Adamson sent a telegram to Governor Fletcher stating he and his officers were outgunned and requesting help. He wrote that former bushwhackers had fired over two hundred shots in the streets. The message was forwarded to the army which did not do anything for weeks.[20]

Election Day in Clay County was contentious. Sheriff James Jones had to call upon federal troops to help make an arrest as he faced "an armed mob consisting of the most dangerous men in the county numbering more than a hundred." Judge Philander Lucas related that Frank and Jesse James had sent a message to Deputy Sheriff Joseph Rickards saying they were coming to Liberty and "no d__ed Republican could arrest them." After the election, the James boys, Clell Miller, and two others rode into Liberty shouting and cursing as they fired their revolvers in the air. After they entered Fred Meffert's saloon, Deputy Sheriff Rickards and another deputy got the drop on them, disarmed them, and arraigned them before Judge Lucas, but since they had done nothing that they could be charged with, they were admonished and let go.[21]

Back on March 12, 1866, Governor Fletcher had placed a $300 reward for the capture of Archie Clement for creating mayhem in western Missouri. On December 13, 1866, Clement rode into Liberty with a twenty-three-member contingent of former bushwhackers including Dave Pool and the James boys. They claimed they wanted to join the militia. Bacon Montgomery, the militia commander, played along. He was sure the real reason they wanted to join was to continue their acts of violence under the guise of being militia. He signed up the bushwhackers then sent them home. Clement remained in town, drinking at the City Hotel's bar. Montgomery stationed men inside the courthouse at the windows as he sent three men to arrest Clement. Shots were fired as Clement broke out of the hotel. He attempted to ride past the courthouse on his way out of town but died in a hail of militia bullets.[22]

On the afternoon of May 23, 1867, ten men rode into Richmond, Missouri, where Bloody Bill Anderson's body had been dismembered and displayed. They robbed the Hughes and Wasson Bank of $3,500 and in their getaway killed the mayor and two other men. Seven bushwhackers accused of being members of the gang were hunted down and killed on the spot or removed from jail and lynched. It was rumored that Frank and Jesse James were involved in the robbery, but again there was no hard evidence, and no one would testify against them.[23] Whether they took part in the Richmond bank robbery or not, the demise of some of the alleged robbers would have been an additional lesson to Frank and Jesse to be careful before, during, and after a robbery.

Jesse claimed he was in Nashville, Tennessee, in June 1867 under the care of former Confederate surgeon Dr. Paul Eve who treated his chest wound and damaged lung. After three weeks of treatment, Eve told Jesse there was nothing he could do for him and that he should go home to die.[24] However, Jesse continued to live an active life.

In March 1868, Frank and Jesse traveled to Kentucky staying at a hotel in Chaplin. There they rendezvoused with five old bushwhacker friends, including Cole Younger and George Shepherd, who Jesse had traveled to Texas with in 1864.[25]

On March 10, a man calling himself Thomas Colman or Colburn, most likely Thomas Coleman Younger, entered the bank of Nimrod L. Long and Company in Russellville, Kentucky, one hundred miles south of Chaplin. The bank was known to have lots of Unionist depositors. Colman asked Long if he was interested in buying a mature $500 US bond. Long refused. Colman returned on March 18 to change a hundred-dollar bill, but Long refused, suspecting the bill was counterfeit. Two days later, on Friday afternoon, March 20, Colman was back in the bank with two other men. He demanded Long make change for a fifty-dollar bill. When Long refused, Colman leveled his revolver at him demanding cash. Long refused and tried to escape. One robber shot at him, the bullet grazing Long's head. He was then pistol-whipped but managed to run out the door and sound the alarm that the bank was being robbed. As the three robbers inside the bank gathered up the money, two accomplices stationed outside shot at anyone attempting to stop the robbery. The five men galloped out of town with between $9,000 and $14,000 in cash and gold. A posse followed but was unable to catch them. Louisville detectives Delos "Yankee" Bligh and John Gallagher were on the case. They learned of the James boys' meeting with the other bushwhackers and apprehended George Shepherd. One of his cousins, Oliver Shepherd, was shot and killed while resisting arrest. However, the detectives could not determine if Frank and Jesse were in on the robbery.[26]

After the bank robbery, Jesse traveled to New York City where he had sufficient funds to pay for ship passage to Panama, cross the isthmus, and continue by ship to California. Whether Frank traveled with him or by the overland route is unknown, but they both stayed with their father's brother, Drury Woodson James, who was a successful cattleman and one of the founders of Paso Robles in San Luis Obispo County. There, Jesse soaked in the hot sulfur springs, hoping it would help him recover from his wounds.[27]

By October 28, 1868, twenty-one-year-old Jesse had returned home to Clay County, and Frank joined him later. They were always concerned about the militia. Jesse claimed he had chased away militia members who had come after him in the night back in February, and so he made sure he always had three revolvers on hand. In September 1869, Jesse requested to be removed from membership with the Mount Olive Baptist Church, his wish being granted in November 1869 "for the stated reason that he believed himself unworthy."[28]

Gallatin, Missouri, lay roughly fifty miles north of the Samuel farm. Shortly after noon on Tuesday, December 7, 1869, Frank and Jesse rode into town. Jesse dismounted from his mare, Kate, and entered the Daviess County Savings Association building, while Frank tended to the horses.[29]

Inside the bank was William McDowell, a lawyer, and sitting at a desk in front of a large safe was bank owner and operator John W. Sheets, prominent local Democratic leader.[30]

Entering the front door, Jesse stared at Sheets's face then held out a hundred-dollar note as he asked for change. Frank walked in the door and said, "If you will write out a receipt, I will pay you that bill." Sheets began to write at his desk as the James boys stared at him. They must have believed Sheets was Samuel P. Cox. Cox was the Union major who had ambushed and killed their friend and leader Bloody Bill Anderson. Cox was known to be living in Gallatin.[31]

Jesse cursed as he pulled out his revolver, saying, "Cox, I am bound to have my revenge." He shot Sheets in the chest and then the head. McDowell dashed out the door shouting, "Captain Sheets has been killed!" Jesse fired at McDowell twice, one shot hitting him in the arm.[32]

They grabbed a portfolio off the desk, raced out the door, and mounted their horses. Someone fired a shot, and Jesse's mare, Kate, reared, tossing Jesse out of the saddle, but one of his feet was caught in a stirrup. Kate dragged Jesse thirty to forty feet before he could extract his foot. More people were firing at them as Frank returned and hauled Jesse up behind him and they raced out of town leaving Kate behind.[33]

Outside town, Frank and Jesse came upon Daniel Smoote, a wealthy farmer, riding a good horse which they took from Smoote at gunpoint. A Gallatin posse chased them as they rode in the direction of Clay County, but the James boys eluded it. Stopping to open the portfolio, they found nothing of value to them. As they rode home, they bragged to people they happened upon, including the Reverend John Helm, that they had killed Major Samuel Cox in retaliation for the killing of Bloody Bill Anderson.[34]

Sheets had been popular in Gallatin, and the citizens were determined to find his killers. By December 11, they were able to establish that Kate's owner was Jesse James and that one of the robbers appeared to be Frank James. Two men rode from Gallatin to Liberty where they enlisted the aid of Deputy Sheriff John Thomason to arrest the James boys. Thomason was a nephew of Wild Bill Thomason, who had taught Frank and Jesse how to ride and shoot.[35]

Taking along his son Oscar, Thomason rode with the two Gallatin men out to the Samuel farm. He stationed the two Gallatin men in woods north of the house, and then he and Oscar dismounted and walked toward the front door. The door opened and out ran thirteen-year-old former slave Ambrose. Reaching the stable, Ambrose opened the door. Frank and Jesse, mounted on fast horses, burst out of the stable, jumped the fence, and galloped away. Thomason and the others fired at the James boys, who fired back. Thomason and the others mounted their horses to follow. Thomason's horse was the only one to jump the fence; the others balked. Alone, he chased after the brothers who shot back at him. Stopping his horse and dismounting, Thomason took aim at them with his revolver. His shots missed but startled his horse, which took off after and caught up with the James boys' horses. One of the brothers fired his revolver at the horse's head, killing it.[36]

Thomason walked back to the Samuel farm where he took one of their horses to ride back to Liberty. Ten minutes later, the James boys returned to the farm, armed themselves, and rode to the nearby new town of Kearney where, in a rage, they raced through its streets.[37]

They declared their innocence in the murder of Sheets. They harassed store owner John Groom and told him they had killed Thomason and his posse. Leaving town, they threatened two men they met along the road and told them they would not be taken alive and they would kill anyone who came after them.[38]

Thomason stayed on their trail for three weeks, but never caught up with them. The town of Gallatin and Daviess County citizens, including Sheets's widow, offered rewards totaling $3,000. On December 24, 1869, Missouri governor J. W. McClug offered a reward of $500 apiece for Jesse and Frank, dead or alive. In addition, he authorized the Platte County and Jackson County sheriffs to raise posses to help Clay County in the hunt for the James boys, but the brothers eluded all attempts to find them.[39]

Daniel Smoote, whose horse the James boys had taken at gunpoint, hired a young lawyer, Henry McDougal, to file a civil lawsuit against Frank and Jesse in Daviess County on January 10, 1870. Smoote wanted $223.50, the full value for his horse, saddle, and bridle. The James boys hired one of the best lawyers in Missouri, Samuel Richardson, who had the case dismissed on a technicality—Frank and Jesse had not been personally served notice, even though the Clay County sheriff had delivered the papers to the Samuel farm.[40]

In June 1870, the *Kansas City Times,* edited by John Edwards, printed a letter from Jesse to Governor McClug. Edwards was a diehard Confederate who had crossed into Mexico with General Jo Shelby at the end of the war rather than surrender. By 1867, Edwards and Shelby were back in Missouri, and by 1868, Edwards was co-owner and editor of the new *Kansas City Times*, through which he continued to fight for the Confederacy, now using his pen instead of the sword.[41]

In Jesse's letter to the governor, which may have been touched up by Edwards, Jesse stated his innocence in the murder of Sheets and that "some of the best men in Missouri" could prove his alibi. He claimed he would turn himself in when he knew he would be safe from mob violence.[42]

In July, the *Times* published a brief note from Jesse to the governor, stating people would provide alibis for him. Three Kearney residents said he had been in Kearney the evening before Sheets's murder and the day after the murder. Storekeeper and former Confederate soldier John Groom, whom the James boys had harassed in Kearney, wrote Jesse had been in his store on December 6. Groom added Jesse was "respectful" and "I have never known a more honest person in all his business transactions."[43]

Frank and Jesse's family declared the brothers' innocence. They said Frank and Jesse were home the day of the murder of Sheets and that Jesse had sold his horse, Kate, to a man from Topeka, Kansas.[44]

Daniel Smoote and his lawyer, Henry McDougal, were not finished trying to recover Smoote's horse, saddle, and tack, or payment for their value. The court allowed them to file a notice of service in the classified section of the *Gallatin Weekly Democrat* for four consecutive weeks over the summer of 1870. Jesse and Frank's lawyer, Samuel Richardson, filed a motion to dismiss, claiming the James boys weren't in Gallatin when the notice was published. However, at the next court hearing, Richardson stated Frank and Jesse authorized him to allow a judgment to be entered against them. The court awarded Smoote $223.50 and ordered that Jesse's horse, saddle, and tack, left behind in Gallatin, be sold to pay him.[45]

Heavily armed, Jesse and Frank rode through Kearney in early August 1870, and later that month they left for Texas. While in Texas, they ran into, of all people, Oscar Thomason, who was traveling through with some other men. Jesse gave Oscar fifty dollars, possibly in payment for his father's horse, which the James boys shot. The brothers traveled through Indian Territory, returning to Missouri in February 1871.[46]

Jesse continued his secret courtship of cousin Zee. Frank met Annie Ralston at a Kansas City horse-racing track, and he began to pay her visits at her home in Independence, Missouri.[47]

On Saturday afternoon, June 3, 1871, the famous orator Henry Clay Dean stood in Corydon, Iowa's Methodist church, speaking to a large audience, which overflowed into the churchyard. His topic was the merits of contributing to a fund to help bring the railroad to Corydon. Almost everyone in town was there.[48]

Several days earlier, residents of Wayne County encountered four strangers wearing linen dusters and riding good horses. When asked their business, the strangers' answers ranged from they were buying sheep to none of your business. The four men were the James boys, Cole Younger, and Clell Miller.[49]

The gang had learned that the Wayne County Treasurer's Office had $40,000 in cash and tax receipts. Their plan was to rob the treasurer's office while everyone was preoccupied with Dean's speech, but when they entered the office, they learned the safe was locked and the treasurer had the key. He was in the crowd listening to Dean.[50]

The gang rode down the deserted street toward the crowd at the church. They planned to try to find the treasurer, but instead they saw the Ocobock Bank had only one person inside it. Two gang members guarded the entrance as the other two entered the bank building. Drawing their revolvers, they ordered the lone cashier, Ted Wock, not to speak or they would shoot him. They began loading loose cash into a saddlebag and demanded Ted open the safe.[51] The robbers took a total of $5,242.07 in cash and tied up Ted. As they left the bank, one of them said to Ted, "Good day."[52]

The bandits rode westward to the edge of the spellbound crowd and joined in listening to Dean. One of them interrupted the orator, announcing they had just robbed the bank and defied the crowd to come after them. Irritated at the rider's interruption and believing it was just a ploy to break up the gathering, the people turned back to listen to Dean. The four men cursed the "damned Yanks" for being cowards, turned their horses away, and galloped out of town whooping and shooting their revolvers in the air. One shouted, "We've robbed your bank! Catch us if you can!"[53]

A few individuals in the crowd thought they better check the stranger's story and discovered Ted trussed-up in the robbed bank.[54] The Corydon citizens quickly formed a large posse to chase after the gang. Many were former Union soldiers, carrying a variety of weapons; some were not armed at all. The gang shouted to people they passed that they had plenty of money and were the lords of creation. They would taunt the posse, letting them get close, and then spurring their horses, leap ahead. The posse realized the pursuit was futile and gave up after losing the gang's trail near Eagleville, Missouri.[55]

Meanwhile, Wayne County Sheriff J. Nelson Wright formed a four-man posse as the bank officials sent a telegram to the Chicago, Illinois, headquarters of Pinkerton's National Detective Agency, requesting assistance. Allan Pinkerton, the founder of the detective agency, immediately sent his son Robert to Corydon to investigate the crime.[56]

Robert joined Wright's posse as it followed the bank robbers' trail across the Iowa state line and into Daviess County, Missouri. On June 5, they caught up with the gang at George Lee's farmhouse at Civil Bend, Missouri. The robbers saw the posse's approach and ran from the house to the stables as the posse opened fire and continued firing until they had to reload. The gang members mounted their horses and burst out of the stables, firing their revolvers. One shot killed a posse member's horse. A parting shotgun blast hit Frank James, who dropped a revolver and a blood-splattered coat as his hat flew off his head.[57]

The posse ended its chase and returned to Corydon; however, Pinkerton continued dogging the gang's trail as far as the Missouri River, interviewing people along the way about the gang members. He must have strongly suspected the James boys, as he interviewed their friends and rode to the Samuel farm where he talked with Zerelda, but she gave him no useful information. There was nothing more that could be done, so Pinkerton left Clay County.[58]

The gang rode to General Jo Shelby's farm in Lafayette County, Missouri. Frank was bleeding from the lungs and stayed there for over two months while a Dr. Orear treated him.[59]

The gossip throughout Missouri spread that the James boys, Cole Younger, and Clell Miller were the Corydon bank robbers. Newspapers such as the *Hamilton News* and the *Richmond Examiner* believed Frank and Jesse were involved in both the Gallatin murder and the Corydon robbery.[60]

Jesse again sent a letter, dated June 24, 1871, to John Edwards's *Kansas City Times*. In it, he stated Frank and he did not rob a bank in Iowa or any other bank, there were plenty of people who could back up their alibis, and they were not going to turn themselves in because they knew they would not get fair trials and would be mobbed by Radical Republicans.[61]

The Pinkertons were not done with the case and sent Detective R. W. Westfall to continue investigating the bank robbery. Westfall spent several months around Liberty, Missouri, befriending Clell Miller.[62]

Miller was a friend of the James boys and lived on his father's farm near the Samuel farm. He came from a prosperous, slaveholding family and had ridden with Bloody Bill Anderson. When Bloody Bill was killed, Miller, who had been wounded and captured, was about to be executed. Unionist major Samuel Cox had saved him when he recognized Miller was the son of one of his friends. Miller claimed Bloody Bill had kidnapped him and forced him to ride with the bushwhackers. Cox did not buy the alibi but spared Miller's life, sending him to prison in St. Louis. Miller's father and neighbors claimed Clell was a loyal citizen and he was released from prison at the end of the war.[63]

In January 1872, Miller told Westfall he had been accused of robbing the Corydon bank, but he had provided an alibi back in July. Miller bragged there weren't enough men in Iowa to take him out of Clay County. Westfall obtained a warrant from Corydon for the arrest of Miller. He took the warrant to the Clay County sheriff, requesting he go with him to arrest Miller, but the sheriff declined, fearing he would be murdered. Westfall then planned to trick Miller into leaving his home. Westfall sent Miller a letter saying that he would pay him to help steal back some horses that rightfully belonged to him and told Miller to meet him in Cameron, Missouri. Falling for Westfall's trick, Miller arrived in Cameron. Westfall got Miller drunk and, with the help of a constable, arrested him on March 7, 1872. He then took Miller to

Iowa. Clell's father posted $5,000 bail and brought him back to Clay County.[64]

Clell Miller's trial would begin on Monday, October 22, 1872, and would last five days. Reputable residents of Wayne County would testify that Miller was one of the robbers. Miller's family would testify he was with them when the robbery occurred. Westfall's character would be attacked—he was a gambler, had a bad reputation, and could not be trusted. The jury would find Clell Miller not guilty.[65]

In the meantime, on April 29, 1872, five well-dressed strangers wearing dark frock coats and mounted on good-looking horses with expensive saddles rode into Columbia, Kentucky. Claiming to be cattle buyers, the strangers, two of whom were brothers, had been in and around town for a week. Three of the men rode to the alley alongside the Deposit Bank where they tied their horses. Two of them entered the bank while the third remained at the door. The two other men rode a short distance to the public square where they had a good view of the bank.[66]

Inside the bank, cashier R.A.C. Martin was talking with businessman William Hudson, circuit court clerk James Page, and state representative James Garnett. "Good evening," one of the strangers said as his right hand pulled out a revolver from under his left arm. Martin shouted, "Bank robbers!" and the robber fired, hitting Martin in the chest. The three customers scrambled out the windows and door as the robber fired at them.[67]

The two mounted men at the square began shooting their revolvers in the air and shouting for everyone to get off the streets and, "Lowry's gang! Lowry's gang!"[68] One citizen fired back twice, then ran.[69]

Inside the bank, the robbers scooped up $1,500 and dragged the still-conscious Martin into the bank vault. W. W. Morris was in the drugstore across the alley and could overhear the robbers demanding Martin open the locked safe. He refused and soon died.[70]

The robbers took what they could and quickly left the bank. The gang raced north out of town toward Bardstown, Kentucky, where the James boys' old friends Bud and Donny Pence lived in Nelson County. The Pences had fought alongside the James boys in Bloody Bill's bushwhacker band. They were suspects in the Liberty, Missouri, bank robbery and Bud was a suspect in the Richmond, Missouri, robbery.[71]

A large posse followed the robbers, but the gang eluded their pursuit. Several men were arrested in connection with the robbery, but they were all found innocent and soon released.[72]

Louisville detective Delos "Yankee" Bligh, who had investigated the Russellville, Kentucky, bank robbery, believed the descriptions of the robbers matched Cole Younger as one of the mounted men in the square and the James boys as two of the men in the bank. No one was ever arrested for the murder of Martin or for the bank robbery.[73]

Late Thursday afternoon, September 26, 1872, the Kansas City Industrial Exposition was in full swing, attended by sixty thousand people that day and guarded by a large special police force. Each person paid a fifty-cent entrance fee. As a crowd of people were leaving through the Twelfth Street gate, three men wearing checkered bandanas around their necks and pulled up to under their eyes rode through the mass of people to the gate. One dismounted, snatched the cashbox from the ticket booth and pocketed the cash. The others pulled their revolvers and warned people not to interfere. Ben Wallace, the ticket seller, ran out of the booth and grabbed the thief. One of the mounted robbers shot at Wallace, missing him, but hitting a little girl in the leg. The three thieves raced east, disappearing into the nearby woods with a total haul of $978. Their loot would have been more if they had been thirty minutes earlier when the fair's treasurer had collected $12,000 from the booth.[74]

John Edwards's *Kansas City Times* glorified the crime, calling it "The Most Desperate and Daring Robbery of the Age." The newspaper denounced the crime but praised the robbers' audacity to pull off a robbery in broad daylight in front of a crowd of people and escape law enforcement.[75]

On September 29, 1872, Edwards published his editorial, entitled "The Chivalry of Crime." Edwards expanded on his reporting of the exposition robbery and previous bank robberies. Again, he denounced the robberies. However, he praised those who committed the crimes because they did not do it in secret—in lonely places in the night, such as a highwayman, or anonymously in a large crowd, such as a pickpocket, but committed the crime in broad daylight.[76]

Edwards wrote, "But there are things done for money and for revenge of which the daring of the act is the picture and the crime the frame that it be set in. Crime of which daring is simply an ingredient has no palliation on earth or forgiveness anywhere. But a feat of stupendous nerve and fearlessness that makes one's hair rise to think of it, with a condiment of crime to season it, becomes chivalric; poetic; superb."[77]

Edwards continued that they were modern-day bandits who were so bold they would have stolen from legendary bandits from the past; they would have been considered worthy to sit at King Arthur's Round Table. Edwards did not identify Jesse and Frank or any others, but he did say, "But there are now men in Jackson, Cass, and Clay—a few are left—who learned to dare when there was no such word as quarter in the dictionary of the Border." Edwards went on to say, "With them booty is but the second thought, the wild drama of the adventure is the first."[78]

On October 5, 1872, the fair robbers wrote a letter and Edwards published it in the *Kansas City Times*. The robbers identified themselves as Jack Shepherd [Sheppard], Dick Turpin, and Claude Duval, who were all romanticized seventeenth- and eighteenth-century English bandits. The robbers apologized for wounding the little girl and offered to pay for her treatment if her parents would publish their address in the paper along with the amount of the medical bills. They also apologized to Ben Wallace, the ticket taker. The shooter had only meant to scare him so that he would let go of his friend, not kill him. They were offended that they were called "thieves." The writer said that they killed only in self-defense, but then stated if anyone refused to open a safe or vault when they, the bandits, were robbing it, they would be killed; if they cooperated they would not be harmed. President Ulysses S. Grant and his friends were thieves stealing from the poor and giving to the rich. The writer said he and his friends were "bold robbers" such as Alexander the Great, Julius Caesar, Napoleon, and William Wallace. "We rob from the rich and give to the poor." At the end of the letter, the writer spoke of the upcoming presidential election, "I will close by hoping that Horace Greeley will defeat Grant, and then I can make an honest living, and then I will not have to rob, as taxes will not be so heavy."[79]

People suspected Jesse James was the robber and author of the letter. Jim Chiles, a former bushwhacker, said he had seen Cole and John Younger with Jesse outside Kansas City on the day of the robbery. On October 20, the *Times* published a letter from Jesse denying he was involved in the exposition robbery and could provide an alibi. He said Chiles needed to retract his statement. Chiles soon published a retraction in the *Times* and wrote, "I am engaged in attending to my own business."[80]

There is no concrete proof that Jesse and the Younger brothers robbed the exposition and no concrete proof that Jesse wrote the "bold robbers" letter, but no one else was ever accused of the crime, and Jesse was always quick to write to the newspapers.

By publishing Jesse James's letters and his own editorials of glorification, John Edwards molded the James Younger Gang into a band of "bold robbers" who stole from the rich and gave to the poor—modern-day Robin Hoods—and the public became enthralled with their exploits.

In November 1872, Jesse was staying with General Jo Shelby in Lafayette County, Missouri. Joe Miller, Shelby's fifteen-year-old black hired hand, was in town when he got into a fight with a white boy named Catron who shot at Miller three times. Miller raced back to the Shelby residence. Intent on lynching Miller, Catron and a mob came after him. Jesse rode to the bridge between the town and Shelby's place, where he confronted the mob and told them if they harmed Miller "there would be enough business around there to amuse the county undertaker for several days."[81]

Months passed by without any significant outlaw activity, then on Monday morning, May 27, 1873, four men rode into Ste. Genevieve, Missouri, about sixty miles south of St. Louis. Two men held the horses while the other two walked through the busy street and up the steps into the Ste. Genevieve Savings Association. Inside the building, one man held the muzzles of two revolvers to cashier O. D. Harris's head, demanding, "Open the safe, damn you, or I'll blow your brains out." The other man pointed a revolver at the son of General F. A. Rozier, the bank president, and said if he opened his mouth he would kill him. Rozier raced to the door and jumped down the steps, shouting that the bank was being robbed. The robber shot at him hitting his shoulder. Harris opened the safe, and the robbers quickly gathered $3,600 in cash, a box of $200 in gold coins, and some valuable papers belonging to the sheriff. The two men forced Harris to walk with them two hundred yards to where the other two were waiting with the horses. One of the horses spooked and broke loose. They compelled a German driving a wagon to retrieve the horse. Just before mounting up, the robbers relieved Harris of his gold watch. As they galloped away, they fired their revolvers in the air and shouted, "Hurrah for Hildebrand!"[82]

Outside of town, the robbers asked a man on his way into town to pick up the box they had left in the road and return it to the bank. Twenty minutes after the robbery, a twelve-man posse, armed with shotguns, left in pursuit of the robbers. Three of those men outdistanced the rest of the posse and caught up with the robbers, who drew their revolvers and forced them back. After that, the posse lost the bank robbers.[83]

The robbers made a clean getaway and were never captured. The St. Louis police were called in to investigate the crime. After reviewing the evidence and robbers' mode of operation, they determined the James boys and Younger brothers had robbed the bank, and the newspapers soon began printing that the Jameses and Youngers had done it.[84]

By 1870, the family of the boy named Henry, who would become known as Billy the Kid, began to show up in the historical record.

On October 22, 1870, the federal government began allowing white homesteading on the Osage Indian Trust Land in southeastern Kansas, but whites had been moving into the area long before the official opening. The town of Wichita, located on the Arkansas River and Chisholm Trail, boomed to life in the summer of 1870. Wichita was on the edge of the buffalo range, and the buffalo-hide trade was in full swing. Texas cowboys herded longhorns up the Chisholm Trail through Wichita to reach northern markets. Along with the influx of new homesteaders were forty-year-old Catherine McCarty with her two sons and her twenty-seven-year-old friend Bill Antrim, whom Catherine most likely met in Indianapolis, Indiana.[85]

Bill was industrious; homesteading six miles northeast of Wichita, he plowed five acres and planted crops, constructed a stable and corral, dug a well, and built a house that he moved into that August. Catherine, known as the Widow McCarty, established a laundry that did so well she began buying and selling city lots and filed to homestead a quarter section adjoining Bill's homestead. Bill built her a house on her quarter section, and she and the boys moved into it March 4, 1871. Eleven-year-old Henry and his brother, Joe, had the run of the town while Catherine worked. In later life, Marsh Murdock, who claimed to have known Henry during this period, called him a street gamin or urchin. Wichita was a wild town where Henry would have met soldiers, buffalo hunters, teamsters, cowboys, and Indians, not to mention drunks, gunfighters, and prostitutes.[86]

Catherine developed tuberculosis exacerbated by the laundry business. Like others with the disease, she must have heard moving westward to a drier climate would improve her health, and, besides, Bill had most likely become infatuated with prospecting for precious metals. By October 1872, Catherine and Bill sold their properties and, together with the boys, headed west for Denver, Colorado Territory.[87]

Bill, Catherine, and the boys turned up next in Santa Fe, New Mexico Territory, on March 1, 1873, where Catherine and Bill were married in the First Presbyterian Church. At the time, Catherine was forty-three years old, and Bill was thirty years old. They were both described as Santa Fe residents, but they didn't stay there long, soon traveling 350 miles southwest to the mining town of Silver City, New Mexico.[88]

Silver City had boomed to life in the spring of 1870. The namesake of the town, silver, was the ore that miners were prospecting for and extracting. The town was located south of the Pinos Altos Range of the Mogollon Mountains in the valley of La Cienaga de San Vicente. The climate was considered healthy. It was a great place to build a new town, never mind the Apaches who believed the valley belonged to them. The population expanded, new businesses started up, and the population increased. Soon, Silver City became the county seat for Grant County. Like any mining camp, it had its quiet residential and business sections as well as a rough and tumble saloon and brothel district where anything could happen any time of the day or night. The Antrim family arrived in Silver City in the summer of 1873, ready to make their fortune.[89]

The boy Henry would start to use his stepfather's last name, Antrim.

EXPRESS COMPANIES

Since 1839, when William Hamden began charging people to haul their valuable items in a carpet bag from Boston to New York City, express companies have been in the business of transporting cash and goods throughout the country.[90] Hamden's idea quickly caught on, and as railroad lines expanded, the express companies contracted with them to haul the goods entrusted to them. Two of the major express companies at the time of the James Younger Gang were the Adams Express Company and Wells, Fargo & Company.

Alvin Adams was a produce merchant ruined by the economic Panic of 1837. By 1839, he was carrying letters between Boston and Worcester, Massachusetts. His business expanded to become the Adams Express Company. By the time Frank and Jesse James became interested in robbing trains, the Adams Express Company dominated the eastern rail lines while Wells, Fargo & Company dominated the West. Henry Wells and William Fargo established Wells, Fargo & Company in San Francisco, California, in 1852. The company quickly spread across the West delivering cash, valuables, and just about any item available. In the 1860s, Wells, Fargo was considered the biggest and richest corporation in the West. When the railroads arrived, it contracted with them to haul goods, increasing its services and profits.[91]

Express items were loaded into a train's baggage car. In the car, the express company placed a safe where cash, coins, and the most valuable items were stored. An armed express company employee, called a messenger, accompanied the express items to guard them. He was responsible for recording, tracking, and delivering the items.[92] It was a tedious, lonely job, unless someone like Jesse James paid a visit.

As of 2019, the Adams Express Company lives on as the closed-end Adams Diversified Equity Fund with assets of $1.9 billion and trades on the New York Stock Exchange.[93] Likewise, Wells, Fargo & Company lives on as Wells Fargo, an international financial services company with $1.9 trillion in assets, and trades on the New York Stock Exchange.[94]

CHAPTER 4

TRAINS ARE WHERE THE MONEY'S AT

On the evening of July 21, 1873, a new chapter in crime opened for the James Younger Gang with their first robbery of a railroad train. The Chicago, Rock Island and Pacific Railroad regularly transported gold, silver, and currency shipments east through Iowa, every Monday night. The gang learned that the railroad would be transporting a valuable gold and silver shipment the evening of July 21. Their plan was to stop and rob the train of its shipment.

The gang selected a section of railroad in an isolated area approximately seventy miles east of Council Bluffs and three miles west of Adair, Iowa. The track at the selected location made a sharp curve that would force the engineer to slow the train. Just east of the curve, the gang selected a section of track on the north side to remove. Each rail was thirty-three feet in length and weighed about 660 pounds. They used a wrench to unscrew the nuts from the bolts holding the abutting rails together, then they hammered out the bolts. Next, they used a crowbar or crowfoot to pry out the spikes holding down the rail but left it in place. They threaded a rope through the holes in the rail, tied it off, and ran the length of the rope back to a hiding position.[1]

Around 8:30 p.m., the five o'clock express from Omaha approached the gang's position. The steam engine and coal tender were followed by a baggage car, then the express car and six passenger cars. In one of the last cars rode twenty-eight Chinese students with two guardians on their way to New England colleges. The gang expected to find the gold shipment in the express car.[2]

As the train reached its slowest speed, the gang yanked the rope, dislodging the loose rail. Seeing the rail being jerked out of line, Jack Rafferty, the engineer, quickly threw the train into reverse and set the air brakes into emergency. The train continued its forward motion at a slower rate of speed as the gang began shooting at the engine. The engine and tender ran off the rails and fell on their sides. The baggage car jackknifed off the track also, falling on its side. The express car followed by the smoking car derailed, remaining upright. Fortunately, the passenger cars remained on the track.[3]

Rafferty's neck was snapped in the train wreck. When the engine came to rest on its side, his lifeless body lay on top of fireman Dennis Foley. Foley quickly opened the boiler's relief valve, preventing an explosion, then dragged Rafferty's body out of the cab.[4]

In the confusion, none of the passengers or crew knew how many robbers were out there, but they counted at least six. Wearing Ku Klux Klan masks, the gang members went to work, each with his assigned duties. Two stayed outside, walking along each side of the passenger cars, shouting at passengers to keep their heads inside and shooting their revolvers in the air. Two other robbers entered the passenger cars to watch the passengers. With a revolver in each hand, one of those robbers began to quote from the letter that had been sent to the *Kansas City Times* after the exposition robbery. He told his reluctant audience they were bold robbers, out to rob the rich for the poor. The last two robbers entered the express car where they expected to find the loot.[5]

Inside the express car, assistant superintendent H. F. Royce, register clerk O. P. Killingsworth, and express messenger John Burgess had been tossed together in a pile. As one of the robbers entered the car, he removed his mask, revealing sandy hair, full beard, and blue eyes. It was Jesse James. Aiming a revolver at Burgess's head, he demanded, "If you don't open the safe or give me the key, I'll blow your brains out." Burgess gave him the key and Jesse opened the safe finding a total of $2,337. The gang expected more—lots more.[6]

Jesse demanded that they tell him where the rest of the money was. Killingsworth pointed to sacks containing three and a half tons of gold and silver bars. Jesse had expected gold and silver coins. The bars were too heavy to transport on horseback, and there was no way they could be exchanged for cash without the authorities knowing from where they came.[7]

The gang did not rob any of the passengers or employees. They gathered at the engine, and seeing Rafferty's body, Jesse expressed sorrow over his death. He said they did not intend to harm anyone. The gang mounted their horses and rode off to the southwest. The robbery had taken no more than ten minutes.[8]

The gang rode south toward Missouri. The evening after the robbery, five riders stopped at the farmhouse of Mr. and Mrs. Stuckeye in Ringgold County, Iowa, adjoining the Missouri state line. The Stuckeyes knew nothing of the train robbery and invited the strangers in for supper. They had a pleasant conversation discussing agriculture, politics, and religion. The Stuckeyes later provided descriptions of the riders. Four of those descriptions matched Frank and Jesse, Cole Younger, and Clell Miller.[9]

The Rock Island Railroad offered a $5,000 reward and Iowa governor Cyrus Carpenter added a $500 reward for each captured robber. Posses rode throughout southwestern Iowa. Special trains from Council Bluffs brought in additional posse members. The posses tracked the five riders to the Nodaway River, as they headed into Missouri and lost the riders' trail. Public opinion, the

newspapers, as well as the St. Louis police believed it was the work of the James Younger Gang. Many people now considered Jesse to be the leader of the gang.[10]

In August 1873, the James Younger Gang's literary friend John Edwards moved to St. Louis, Missouri, where he wrote for the *Saint Louis Dispatch*. On November 22, the newspaper published a supplement written by Edwards, titled "A Terrible Quintette" in which he gave biographies of outlaws Frank and Jesse James, Cole and John Younger, and Arthur McCoy. Edwards said his writing was based on interviews with McCoy, Frank, Jesse, and friends of the Youngers. In it, he romanticized and justified the lives and actions of the robbers. He wrote why they had been driven to fight for the Confederacy as bushwhackers and he wrote alibis for every robbery they were accused of committing. In Edwards's view, these men were victims of Northern aggression.[11]

On September 18, 1873, the great New York City financier Jay Cooke's company failed and declared bankruptcy causing a domino effect, with thousands of businesses going bankrupt. A grasshopper plague wiped out crops in the midwestern states and the banks foreclosed on farmers who couldn't repay their loans, evicting the farmers and their families from their homes. Tens of thousands of men were unemployed. The railroads had no compassion, colluding to keep freight prices high for farm goods. This depression, one of the country's worst, was called the Panic of 1873. Many people came to think of the James Younger Gang as modern-day Robin Hoods, stealing from the rich—the callous banks and railroads—to give to the poor.[12]

The gang members lay low for months after the Rock Island train robbery. Then on December 29, 1873, the *Saint Louis Dispatch* published a letter dated December 20 from Jesse James. Jesse claimed he and Frank were innocent of all the crimes they were accused of and they had alibis to prove they were not at the scenes of the crimes. Jesse said they would turn themselves in if Missouri governor Silas Woodson would guarantee their fair trial and protection from "mob violence or from a requisition from the Governor of Iowa, which is the same thing." Jesse wrote they would be willing to stand trial in any Missouri town except Gallatin. The letter was from Deer Lodge, Montana Territory.[13]

There is no record of Frank and Jesse anywhere else. The James boys and other members of the gang could have ridden the Union Pacific Railroad to Corinne, Utah, and then traveled by horseback to Deer Lodge, a journey taking about two weeks. During and after the Civil War, thousands of Confederate sympathizers lived in the Montana goldfields and it was rumored many bushwhackers had relocated there. It would have been a prime place for Frank and Jesse to lay low for a while.[14]

Charles S. Warren, known as "General," was the deputy sheriff and then sheriff of Deer Lodge County, Montana Territory, from 1869 to 1875. Years later, Warren said Cole Younger, Frank, and Jesse lived in Deer Lodge County for several months in 1873 and 1874. Lawyer and former Confederate Thomas Napton introduced Sheriff Warren to Jesse and Cole. They asked him for immunity. Warren told them as long as they abided by the laws of Deer Lodge County and Montana Territory, he would not interfere with them. He met them on the road many times and never had any problem with them.[15]

The James boys' cousin and Zee's oldest brother, Robert W. Mimms, had been living in the Deer Lodge area of Montana since 1866 and had served in the Montana legislature twice. Years later, after Jesse's death, the *Fort Benton River Press* published a story about Frank and Jesse in its April 26, 1882, edition, stating, "The James boys were well known by many people in Montana at the time, and it is said that at least twelve members of Quantrill's gang were living in Deer Lodge while they were in the Territory." There is also a story among the old ranch families of the Highwood Mountains that Frank James taught school there in 1873 and 1874.[16]

On January 8, 1874, bandits robbed the Monroe-to-Shreveport stagecoach in Bienville Parish, Louisiana. Then roughly two hundred miles to the north, on January 15, 1874, five robbers stopped and robbed a stagecoach between Malvern and Hot Springs, Arkansas. Many speculated the same gang committed the two robberies. Cole Younger was accused of being the leader, and by default people associated Frank and Jesse with the gang. The robbers returned money and watches to anyone who could prove he was a Confederate veteran, but they said, "Northern men had driven them to outlawry, and they intended to make them pay for it." There was a clue to the involvement of the James boys and Younger brothers that would be revealed a couple weeks later. Of course, they denied involvement in this and other crimes they were accused of, but then there may have been a few they were accused of that they did not commit.[17]

Two weeks after the Hot Springs stagecoach robbery and three hundred miles to the northeast at Gads Hill, Missouri, train robbers struck on January 31, 1874. This would be the first peacetime train robbery in Missouri.[18]

Located roughly one hundred miles south of St. Louis, Gads Hill was named after British author Charles Dickens's estate, which in turn was named after a site in England where highwaymen frequented to rob travelers. Frank James's favorite playwright, William Shakespeare, wrote about robbing pilgrims with rich offerings and traders with fat purses at "Gad's Hill" and where Prince Hal and Poins robbed the robbers in *The First Part of King Henry The Fourth*, act 1, scene 2. With a population of fifteen people, Missouri's Gads Hill, consisting of several buildings and structures including an abandoned sawmill, a railroad freight platform, and adjacent siding off the main rail line, was a whistle-stop on the St. Louis, Iron Mountain and Southern Railway.[19]

Around 3:00 p.m., Cole Younger and one of his brothers, Arthur McCoy, and the James boys trotted their horses into Gads Hill. They rounded up all fifteen residents and led them to a spot near the train platform where the gang built a bonfire to warm their captives. While waiting for the train, the gang relieved the town merchant named McMillan of his rifle and around $800 in cash and found a red signal flag used to warn trains of danger.[20]

The *Little Rock Express*, heading south out of St. Louis, was scheduled to arrive at 4:06 p.m. The engine pulled its tender, a combination baggage and mail car, a smoker car, a ladies' car, and two Pullman sleeper cars. The train carried twelve men, five women, and eight children as passengers.[21]

The train was late. The people of Gads Hill and gang members warmed themselves by the fire. Finally, at 5:15 p.m. they heard the train whistle. As the train approached, the gang members took their positions. One of them held the red warning flag and began to wave it to get the engineer to slow down the train. One of the gang threw the track switch, diverting the train from the main track to the siding by the loading platform.[22]

Seeing the warning flag ahead, the engineer slowed the train and brought it to a stop at the loading platform. As soon as the train passed, one of the gang threw the switch back the opposite way, trapping the train on the siding.[23]

Thinking the track might be torn up ahead, conductor C. A. Alford jumped off the train to see why the red flag had been waved. A man wearing a white mask covering his whole head, with holes for his eyes and nose, grabbed Alford by the collar and stuck the muzzle of a pistol in his face, shouting, "Stand still or I'll blow the top of your damned head off." The masked man then yelled to the train, "If a shot is fired, I'll kill the conductor."[24]

Alford joined the Gads Hill prisoners guarded by one gang member, as two other robbers walked along the train on each side of the tracks to prevent anyone from leaving the train. When one passenger stuck his head out a window, one of the robbers pointed a shotgun at him, stating, "Take your heads in, and not move out of the car!" Two other gang members escorted the engineer and fireman to the collection of prisoners and then walked back to the baggage and mail car.[25]

Entering the car, the two masked gang members were confronted by the Adams Express messenger, William N. Wilson, the mail agent, and the baggage master. Wilson pointed his revolver at one robber, but the other robber leveled a shotgun at Wilson's chest and said, "Give me your pistol you son of a bitch." Wilson handed over his revolver and then the key to the safe. Inside the safe, the robbers found $1,080. They then went through the mail, finding possibly more than $4,000. They rifled conductor Alford's valise, taking a pistol and tobacco. When they were finished, one of the bandits opened the Adams Express registration book and wrote in it, "Robbed at Gads Hill." Then he joked that he had done the same once before. When the robbers were finished with the baggage mail car, they forced the three men outside to join the other prisoners.[26]

The two bandits then entered the smoking car, brandishing their revolvers in some men's faces and poking their revolver muzzles into the sides of others. They had the men show them their hands, and if they were rough workingman hands, they did not rob those men. They took cash and only one gold watch. They were having a good time, laughing and joking. The one bandit quoted lines from Shakespeare while the other exchanged hats with one of the passengers.[27]

The robbers asked if anyone was a Pinkerton detective. They selected one man who they said looked like a Pinkerton. They told their captive audience they believed each Pinkerton detective had a distinctive mark on his body identifying him as such. Marching the man back to a Pullman car, they ordered him to strip. Not finding any marks on his body, they allowed him to dress and rejoin the others.[28]

Instead of robbing the Reverend T. A. Hagbritt, they asked him to pray for them.[29]

Entering the ladies' car, the two gang members robbed a few of the women. They took $400 from Mrs. Scott traveling from Pennsylvania with her son to Hot Springs. They left her one dime. They stole three handkerchiefs from another woman but did not take her gold watch.[30]

In the Pullman cars, they robbed two dollars from porter James Johnson and forty dollars from the train boy who sold reading material to the passengers.[31]

As the robbers were leaving the train, they left a note with one of the passengers and said they wanted it sent as a telegram to the *Saint Louis Dispatch* because, "[We want] this affair reported correctly and not be misrepresented, as we were by [newspaper reporter] Stilson Hutchins, about the Malvern Hill affair."[32]

With that statement there is a clear link between the gang who robbed the stagecoach between Hot Springs and Malvern and the gang who robbed the train at Gads Hill. Another clue is the robber's choice of words. The stagecoach was robbed about five and a half miles east of Hot Springs, closer to that town than Malvern, which was about fifteen miles farther down the road.

Why did he use "Malvern Hill" instead of "Hot Springs?" Malvern, Arkansas, was named after Malvern Hill, Henrico County, Virginia, where a significant Civil War battle was fought July 1, 1862. Malvern Hill, Virginia, was named after a famous spring in England's Malvern Hills near William Shakespeare's home.[33] The statement points to Shakespeare enthusiast Frank James.

The telegram for the *Saint Louis Dispatch* read:

> *The most daring train robbery on record. The southbound train on the Iron Mountain Railroad was robbed here this evening by five heavily armed men, and robbed of . . . dollars. The robbers arrived at the station a few minutes before the arrival of the train, and arrested the Agent, put him under guard, and then threw the train on the switch. The robbers are all large men, none of them under six feet tall. They were all masked, and started in a southerly direction after they had robbed the train, all mounted on fine blooded horses. There is a hell of excitement in this part of the country.*
>
> *(signed) Ira A. Merrill*[34]

The gang members robbed conductor Alford of fifty dollars and his watch, but baggage master Louis Constant spoke up, "For God's sake, don't take his watch. It was presented to him." They relented and returned the watch to Alford.[35]

The robbery took forty minutes and over $6,000 in cash and valuables.[36] As the gang prepared to leave, they shook hands with the engineer. One of them told him to always stop for a red flag. Alford asked if the train could leave, and the robbers said yes. He sent a man to shut off the south switch and he shut off the north switch, freeing the train from the siding. The robbers mounted their horses and raced away into the forest to the west.[37]

The train got up steam and sped seven miles south to Piedmont, Missouri, where Alford informed the sheriff and sent the robbers' telegram to the *Saint Louis Dispatch*. The sheriff formed a twenty-five-man posse, and rode off after the gang the following morning, but the robbers were long gone.[38]

The James Younger Gang pushed sixty miles west to the Current River where they stayed with a widow the next night, resting and cleaning their weapons. The gang rode through southern Missouri, avoiding roads. When meeting others, they were always polite and paid for everything they needed. They spent one night with their benefactor, General Jo Shelby. A large posse followed the gang, but their trail disappeared in St. Clair and Jackson Counties. Missouri governor Silas Woodson offered a reward of $2,000 for each robber, dead or alive.[39]

John Edwards was now working for the *Saint Louis Dispatch* where the robbers' telegram was sent. Earlier he had met and become friends with the James boys. He wrote an editorial about the robbery, saying as he had before that it was wrong for the robbers to steal but at the same time softening the crime as he said government and corporate criminals were the real villains. While Edwards was visiting Jefferson City, Missouri, on February 10, 1874, the *Dispatch* printed his editorial along with a feature story written by city editor Walter B. Stevens who specifically named the James boys for this crime and others from the past. When Edwards read Stevens's story, he fired off a telegram to Stevens stating, "Put nothing more in about Gads Hill. The report of yesterday was remarkable for two things, utter stupidity and total untruth."[40]

With the robbery of the Adams Express Company's safe on the Rock Island train at Gads Hill, William B. Dinsmore, the express company's president, had had enough. He went to Allan Pinkerton, founder of Pinkerton's National Detective Agency, explained that he wanted these robberies stopped, and hired Pinkertons to track down the train robbers. The Iron Mountain Railroad and the US Post Office joined in hiring the Pinkertons.[41]

Pinkerton sent his detectives to discover the whereabouts of the robbers. They learned the gang had dispersed. The Younger brothers were at Monegaw Springs in St. Clair County, Missouri, and the James boys were home at the Samuel farm in Clay County. Pinkerton then sent his detectives to those two counties to gather more evidence on the suspects.[42]

Pinkerton assigned Joseph W. Whicher to gather information on the James boys. Originally from Des Moines, Iowa, twenty-six-year-old Whicher had a reputation for nerve and discretion.[43]

On March 10, 1874, he arrived in Liberty, Missouri, disguised as a farm laborer. He registered at the Arthur House hotel under his own name. He then went to the courthouse and asked the recorder of deeds for the sheriff. He met with Sheriff George E. Patton, identifying himself as a Pinkerton agent. He told Patton he was there to gather information on the James boys and planned to pass himself off as a farmhand at the Samuel farm. Whicher looked at his own hands and said they might not pass as laborer's hands. Patton said he had served with Frank James early in the war and he had not seen Jesse since 1869. Whicher questioned Patton on the location and size of the Samuel farm and if he knew if the James boys were home. Patton didn't think they were home but warned Whicher to stay away from the Samuel farm.[44]

Whicher next went to the Commercial Bank of Liberty, where he met with bank president D. J. Adkins to deposit excess cash. Whicher told Adkins he was a Pinkerton detective and planned to pass himself off as a laborer asking for work at the Samuel farm. Adkins took him to a back room and returned with former sheriff O. P. Moss who warned Whicher to stay away from the Samuel farm, saying, "The old woman would kill you if the boys don't."[45]

Undeterred, Whicher caught a northbound train, reaching Kearney before dusk. He sent a telegraph report to Pinkerton headquarters and walked the next couple of miles to the Samuel farmhouse.[46]

At 3 a.m. the next morning, four riders waited at Blue Mills Ferry on the north side of the Missouri River as the ferry crossed over from the Jackson County bank. One of the riders shouted to ferryman Broxey to be "damned quick." He said he was Clay

County Deputy Sheriff Jim Baxter. They had captured a horse thief and were on their way to capture another. One of the riders' hands were bound behind his back, his ankles were tied together under the horse's belly, and a gag was in his mouth—it was Joseph W. Whicher. Based on the ferryman's later description, one of the men was Jesse James. William Pinkerton believed one of the two others was Clell Miller. Deputy Sheriff John S. Thomason said the other men's descriptions matched Arthur McCoy and Bloody Bill Anderson's brother Jim.[47]

Whicher's body, punctured by three bullets to the head, neck, and shoulder, was found later that morning four miles east of Independence along the road where Robert Pinkerton had ended his chase of the James boys after the Corydon, Iowa, bank robbery. A note was pinned to the body: "This to all detectives." Whicher's body had a tattoo on the wrist, "J.W.W.," most likely the same type of tattoo the James and Younger Gang had looked for at the Gads Hill train robbery. He also had a pistol on him that would not normally be carried by a farmhand.[48]

After Whicher's murder, Jesse was in a rage, racing his horse through the streets of Kearney threatening citizens to stop talking about the James boys committing robberies. He returned to the farm, packed his weapons and gear, and left just before Sheriff Patton arrived with a five-man posse to arrest him.[49]

Pinkerton had two detectives in St. Clair County gathering information on the Younger brothers—Cole, Jim, John, and Bob—who were living about Monegaw Springs. It was suspected that most, if not all, the brothers had been involved in the Gads Hill robbery. John was also wanted in Texas for murder. In January 1871, he had killed Dallas County Acting Sheriff Charles H. Nichols, who had arrested him for shooting too close to the head of an old man during a drinking spree.[50]

On March 17, 1874, the two Pinkerton detectives, Louis L. Lull and John Boyle, posing as cattle buyers, along with their local guide and part-time Deputy Sheriff Edwin B. Daniels, approached the Theodorick Snuffer farm where Jim and John Younger happened to be eating supper. They asked Snuffer directions to the widow Simms's place, but after being told, they rode in the opposite direction. John noted that they were well-armed for cattle buyers. Maybe they were detectives. The Younger brothers rode after the so-called cattle buyers.[51]

Jim and John galloped up to the three men. Boyle, ahead of the others, fled, as John fired one barrel of his double-barreled shotgun, blowing the hat off Boyle's head. John held the shotgun on Lull and Daniels, ordering them to unbuckle their gun belts and drop their holstered guns to the ground. Jim dismounted and retrieved the gun belts. Lull's gun was a British Tranter revolver. The Youngers, not believing a cattle buyer would own such a gun, asked if the two men were detectives. Lull and Daniels denied it. Lull reached behind his back and suddenly pulled out a concealed Smith and Wesson No. 2 revolver, shooting John through the neck. John fired the shotgun's remaining loaded barrel, blasting Lull's right arm. Jim shot Lull in the side and Daniels in the throat, killing him. Lull's horse panicked and raced away carrying Lull with it until the horse ran under a low-hanging branch that knocked Lull out of the saddle.[52]

Jim cradled his dead brother in his arms and then took all his papers, money, and firearms. G. W. McDonald, a black farmhand, witnessed the entire incident. Jim gave McDonald a Remington revolver and asked him to tell Snuffer's people what had happened. Jim mounted his horse and rode away. McDonald saw Lull stagger out of the woods and cared for him until Lull could be moved to the nearest town, Roscoe. Lull gave his testimony at a coroner's inquest and died three days after the gunfight.[53]

On March 19, 1874, Pinkerton detective L. E. Angell was in St. Louis, returning with Whicher's body. Angell gave interviews to the St. Louis newspapers. In part he said, "The people there [Clay County] are of the kind that admire men who ride through town flourishing revolvers, and the James boys have established a sort of terrorism throughout the county, but they have a great many friends. They have established the reputation of robbing the rich to give to the poor, and when they have money they fling it around generously."[54]

Not only did people in Clay County support the James Younger Gang, but many former Confederates nationwide were thrilled by their exploits. They saw the gang as a symbol of their lost cause. They saw them as continuing the good fight against Northern aggression.

Democratic governor Silas Woodson had had enough with the James Younger Gang. He had already offered the extraordinarily large reward of $2,000 for each Gads Hill robber's body. He now asked the Missouri legislature for emergency legislation and funding to establish a police force to catch the James Younger Gang. The legislature quickly passed legislation establishing a police force with funding for up to twenty-five men. Woodson began to immediately hire police officers.[55]

Jesse continued to court his cousin Zee, and on April 24, 1874, they were married in the home of Zee's sister in Kearney by their Uncle William James. Jesse and Zee soon left on an extended honeymoon to Sherman, Texas, staying with Jesse's sister Susie who had married the former bushwhacker Allen Palmer. Of course, Jesse's literary friend John Edwards had to write about the joyous occasion in the *Saint Louis Dispatch* with the front-page headline "CAPTURED" followed by "The Celebrated Jesse W. James Taken at Last. His Captor a Woman, Young, Accomplished, and Beautiful."[56]

What about Frank? He was an avid horse-racing fan, and while at a racetrack in the Kansas City area, he met schoolteacher Annie Ralston from Independence, Missouri. Annie was also a horse-racing fan and they hit it off. Frank visited Annie's parents' home around six times, but they never guessed that the couple were meeting secretly behind their backs. In June 1874, Annie told her parents she was going to visit family and friends in Kansas

City and Omaha. Instead, she eloped with Frank, and they were married in Omaha, honeymooned there, and then joined Jesse and Zee at Susie's home in Texas. Later, Annie's family learned to their dismay that she had married the outlaw Frank James.[57]

The James boys returned to Missouri where they continued their banditry. At 6:00 p.m. on Sunday, August 30, 1874, Jesse and Frank, along with one of the Younger brothers, stopped the stage heading south from the railroad to the Missouri River ferry that crossed to Lexington. They believed that a Parson Jennings was on board with $5,000 after selling a large herd of hogs in St. Louis.[58]

Frank, on horseback, blocked the stagecoach's advance while Jesse and the Younger brother rode up on each side of the passenger compartment. Pointing their revolvers at the passengers, one of them said, "Damn it, he isn't here." Jennings was not on board.[59]

They decided to rob the driver and seven male passengers, ordering them out of the stage and to line up with their hands in the air. As several people walked by, they were ordered to join the lineup. The robbery could be seen from Lexington across the river, and hundreds gathered to watch.[60]

One of the female pedestrians, Mattie Hamlett, had known the James boys and Younger brothers; her husband had ridden with them during the war. She recognized the masked robbers but got their names mixed up calling the Younger brother "Will" and mixing Frank's name with Jesse's. The Younger brother said to her with a laugh, "Well, you are the same saucy girl you always were." Jesse shook hands with her, not correcting her mistake. She scolded them for stooping to rob individuals instead of bigger targets and tried with a little success to intercede for the passengers. The robbers' biggest haul was from a black man, William Brown, from whom they took fifty-two dollars and his revolver.[61]

It seemed everyone, the robbers and the robbed, were enjoying the event. Professor J. L. Allen was forced to trade his coat and vest for a worn linen duster. The *Lexington Caucasian* reported, "[Allen] was exceedingly glad, as he had to be robbed, that it was done by first class artists, by men of national reputation."[62]

As the robbers rode away, Jesse shouted, "Good-bye Miss Mattie, you'll never see us again!"[63]

After the newspapers reported Mattie recognized the robbers as the James boys and a Younger brother, Zerelda Samuel sent her a letter demanding a retraction, and Zerelda soon arrived in Lexington to set the record straight in the newspapers, establishing alibis for her sons. After receiving Zerelda's letter, Mattie wrote back, "After mature reflection on the subject, I am prepared to doubt the accuracy of my recognition sufficiently to warrant me in refusing to make formal affidavit to the fact." Zerelda forwarded a copy of Mattie's letter to the *Kansas City Times*, and it was reprinted in the *New York Times*. The *St. Louis Republican* received an anonymous letter mocking the press for the fictitious Will Younger and stating that at the time of the robbery, Jesse was in Mexico and Frank was in bed suffering from an old wound.[64]

The robbery was an embarrassment to Governor Woodson who was out campaigning for reelection. Lieutenant Governor Charles Johnson contacted the St. Louis police, which at that time was under the authority of the State of Missouri, requesting assistance in apprehending the James boys. St. Louis police board vice president C. C. Rainwater sent Officer Flourney Yancey to Johnson, arriving in Jefferson City on September 3, 1874. Rainwater believed Yancey was the right man for the job of tracking and arresting the James boys. Rainwater wrote to Johnson that Yancey was an excellent officer, brave and determined, and he was a former soldier and scout during the war.[65]

Yancey traveled to Lexington where he interviewed the robbery victims and others, gathering all the information he could. He followed the James boys' and Younger brother's trail through Lafayette County. Yancey learned that on September 6 the gang had attempted to rob the Lexington brass band that was traveling at the time, but the band members not only carried their musical instruments but also firearms. Outgunned, the robbers allowed the band to proceed on.[66]

Yancey followed the gang's trail as it led back north across the Missouri River. As he followed the trail westward, Yancey learned that the Younger brother was Jim.[67]

The James boys and Jim Younger headed toward the Samuel farm, but Clay County was not safe. Clay County Sheriff George Patton was relentless as he chased after them. Frank left for Jackson County, and Jesse and Jim rode east toward Ray County. They learned from the brother of an old bushwhacker friend that Officer Yancey was on their trail.[68]

On September 21, along the Clay and Ray County line, Jesse and Jim spotted a rider following them about three hundred yards back. They found a spot farther down the road where they hid, waiting for the rider to approach.[69]

The rider was Yancey. His pistol was holstered on his belt as he cantered his horse. When he was about forty yards away from Jesse and Jim, Jesse shouted, "Halt!" then he and Jim began firing their revolvers. Yancey drew his revolver and shot Jesse, knocking him to the ground. Jim and Yancey continued to fire at each other as Jesse remounted and began firing again. Yancey's skittish horse couldn't take it and wildly bolted from the scene. Yancey was unable to control the frightened animal and that was the end of the brief fight.[70]

During this time period, many Missourians had become disgusted with their state and local governments over the counties' issuance of bonds to help promote and build private railroads. Not only did citizens' taxes increase to pay off the bonds, but the railroads were increasing their rates to ship farmers' produce. Many thought the railroads and politicians were bigger robbers than the James Younger Gang. The voters removed many in office, including Governor Silas Woodson, who had placed a bounty on the James and Younger Gang's heads, and Sheriff George Patton, who had pursued the James boys.[71]

In late November, Lycurgus Jones, the editor of the *Pleasant Hill Review* and also brother-in-law to the Younger brothers, published a letter from Cole Younger. In the letter, Cole denounced Jesse James, stating that if Jesse had not written a letter denying that Cole, John, and he were involved in the Kansas City fair robbery, that he, Cole, would not be wanted by the law now. Cole continued that his brothers and he had not been in any of the robberies they were accused of and that he had been in Jackson and St. Clair Counties, Missouri, and in Carroll Parish, Louisiana, when all the robberies had taken place. He asked the governor to investigate his claims and offer a reward for him if the governor did not believe him.[72]

On December 7, 1874, four men who had been telling people for several days that they were Kentucky cattle buyers rode up to the Tishimingo Savings Bank in Corinth, Mississippi. One man waited outside with the horses while the other three entered the bank and pulled revolvers on a black customer and Alonzo H. Taylor, who was the cashier, president, and bank owner. When Taylor refused to open the safe, one of the robbers slashed him across the forehead with his bowie knife. He then complied with their demands and they left with approximately $10,000 in cash and valuables. The sheriff formed a posse and gave chase, but when the gang shot a posse member's horse, the posse hung back and finally lost the robbers' trail near Glen, Mississippi, to the southeast. The culprits were never caught. The newspapers speculated it was the work of the James Younger Gang, and the gang leader's description fit that of Cole Younger.[73]

The next day, on the afternoon of December 8, five men wearing masks and scarves covering their faces rode up to the Kansas Pacific Railroad depot at Muncie, Kansas, a small village west of Kansas City. Three of the riders pulled their revolvers on the workers in the yard and ordered them to pile railroad ties on the tracks. The other two riders dismounted and entered the combination general store and post office where they captured everyone inside. When the workers in the yard were finished with their task, they were directed to enter the store and joined the other captives guarded by one of the robbers. As the eastbound express train was making its approach, the robbers forced storeowner John Purtee to flag it down. The train was coming to a stop when the robbers fired shots in the air and ran up to the engine. They ordered the engineer and fireman to uncouple the express car from the tender, but realizing their mistake, the robbers had them couple the express car again to the tender and uncouple the passenger cars from the express car. They then ordered the engineer to drive the engine forward, pulling the express car to the blockage on the track.[74]

As in previous robberies, one gang member guarded all the captives in the store while two robbers stationed themselves along the tracks on each side of the passenger cars to make sure no one attempted to leave. The remaining two robbers entered the express car and got the drop on Wells, Fargo & Company express messenger Frank Webster, ordering him to open the safe. They took a total of $30,000 in cash and valuables, but they did not rob any of the passengers or workers. They stopped a man riding by and forced him to exchange his horse for one of theirs that was exhausted.[75]

As the robbers rode away, they waved to the train crew, and one of them shouted, "Good-bye boys, no hard feelings. We have taken nothing from you." The robbers eluded all posses, including a company of soldiers from Fort Leavenworth, Kansas. Their camp, where they had divided the loot, was later discovered, but they were long gone.[76]

Rewards were placed for the capture of the robbers. The governor of Kansas set $2,500 for each robber. The Kansas Pacific Railroad added a reward of $5,000, and Wells, Fargo offered a reward of $1,000 per robber and $5,000 for the return of the stolen cash and valuables. Missouri governor Woodson, who still had a few weeks left in office, fully cooperated with the state of Kansas in the search for the robbers.[77]

The newspapers reported that a man who knew Jesse James had spotted him riding his bay horse, accompanied by one of the Younger brothers, in Kansas City on December 2, 1874. Then on December 10, Kansas City police officer Collopy arrested William "Bud" McDaniel for public drunkenness. McDaniel, a known friend of the James boys, had on him over $1,000 and jewelry taken from the Wells, Fargo safe. McDaniel was tight-lipped, refusing to say who his accomplices were. Later in June 1874, he would be shot and killed after escaping from jail.[78]

There is no way the same gang could have been involved in two separate robberies, given the fact that one took place the day following the first and the distance between the crimes was over 550 miles. Maybe the James Younger Gang split up during this time to commit both crimes, or maybe they were totally different gangs and the James boys and Younger brothers were innocent of these crimes.

Allan Pinkerton had not forgotten the James boys. After the deaths of his detectives, he was on a vendetta. He wrote to George Bangs, head of his New York office, "I know that the James and Youngers are desperate men, and that when we meet it must be the death of one or both of us. My blood was spilt and they must pay. There is no use talking, they must die."[79]

Henry Antrim's family arrived in Silver City, New Mexico Territory, in the summer of 1873 and set up home in a log cabin near the intersection of Main Street and Broadway. Bill Antrim earned money in a variety of ways, as a butcher, carpenter, and gambler, while always on the lookout for his own silver strike. Catherine earned money by continuing to wash laundry, selling baked goods, and taking in boarders. One of those boarders was Marshall Ashmun Upson, known as "Ash." He stayed with the Antrims for about three months. Years later, he would become friends with Pat Garrett and in 1882 help him write his biography of Billy the Kid.[80]

Henry and brother Joseph were ordinary boys like any others at the time. Henry was small and scrawny while Joseph was bigger. The brothers quickly made friends with the other children, Anglos and Hispanos, running wild through the streets with them. Owen Scott, editor of the town's newspaper, *Mining Life*, named the children the "Village Arabs" and championed the cause to start a school for them.[81]

Catherine was full of life and fun loving. She attended the weekly dances, and it was said "[She] could dance the Highland Fling as well as the best of the dancers." She always provided cookies for Henry's friends when they came to visit, greeting them with smiles and jokes. But Catherine's tuberculosis did not improve; it only got worse. She became so ill, she was bedridden for four months until her death on September 16, 1874.[82]

Bill was good to the boys but didn't pay much attention to them. They left their cabin, lodging with Richard Hudson and his wife, then with Richard Knight's family, and later with the Truesdell family. Bill's prospecting for silver kept him away from the boys for long periods of time. Henry worked in a butcher shop, and when school opened, he attended. He was quiet, enjoying reading every free moment he could get, but he could be fun and full of mischief, too. Music and dancing were his passions. He and his friends put together and performed a minstrel show to raise money for their school. He worked hard at the jobs he was given, and the other children liked him. He was like any other boy in Silver City.[83]

PINKERTON'S NATIONAL DETECTIVE AGENCY

On February 23, 1861, President-elect Abraham Lincoln was on his way to Washington, DC, to take the oath of office as president of the United States. The country was in turmoil. Seven Southern states had seceded from the Union, and more were teetering on the brink. Holding a constitutional convention, the seven states appointed Jefferson Davis as provisional president of the Confederate States of America. To reach Washington, Lincoln had to travel by train through Baltimore, Maryland, a slave-holding state. Baltimore's population leaned heavily toward the Confederacy.

Samuel Felton, president of the Philadelphia, Wilmington, and Baltimore Railroad, had contracted with Allan Pinkerton, founder and head of Pinkerton's National Detective Agency, to uncover and thwart any attacks on the railroad. While working to protect railroad interests, Pinkerton and his operatives in Baltimore uncovered a plot to assassinate Lincoln as he passed through the city.[84]

Lincoln was skeptical of the plot until an independent source revealed corroborating evidence. He reluctantly agreed to Pinkerton's plan to covertly travel through Baltimore to Washington. Lincoln disguised himself in an old coat and a soft hat. At the Philadelphia train station, Kate Warne, a Pinkerton operative, pretended to be his niece helping her invalid uncle onto the train and into a private berth. Pinkerton and Lincoln's close friend Ward Hill Lamon accompanied them. They reached Washington without being discovered and without incident.[85]

When the train that had originally been scheduled to carry Lincoln arrived at the Baltimore station, a crowd of ten thousand people was on hand and gave three cheers for the Confederacy, three cheers for Jeff Davis, and three groans for Lincoln.[86] Some believed Pinkerton exaggerated the assassination plots. Whether the assassins would have made their attempt will never be known, but Lincoln went on to be president for the next four years.

Allan Pinkerton was born in Glasgow, Scotland, in 1819. Leaving Scotland for Canada in 1842, he and his wife settled in Chicago, Illinois. He worked as a barrel maker, but when he discovered and helped apprehend counterfeiters, he entered law enforcement and established his own detective agency. He worked for the US Postal Service to uncover mail fraud and counterfeiting. He began contracting with railroads to prevent and detect crime. The Adams Express Company and other express companies hired Pinkerton to investigate fraud and theft. He was successful at detecting the criminals and acquiring enough evidence to convict many of them. He assisted runaway slaves through the Underground Railroad and provided spy services to the federal government during the Civil War.[87]

In his pursuit of criminals, Pinkerton believed "Intelligent minds must be trained to battle criminals with their own weapons, and these two questions of speedy detection of crime and swift punishment of criminals will be found quite as essential to a preservation of law and society as lofty arguments or high moral dissertations on the right or wrong of the expediencies necessary to bring wrong-doers to immediate and certain justice."[88]

In 1866, the Reno Brothers Gang stopped a train and robbed the Adams Express Company of the money and valuables entrusted to it. The company hired the Pinkertons to track down the gang and recover the stolen loot. Over the next two years, the Pinkertons found gang member after gang member, most of whom were taken from the authorities by unknown vigilantes and hanged. Pinkerton denied his agents had anything to do with the hangings.[89]

On December 10, 1875, about eleven months after the Pinkertons' attack on Jesse James's family home, there was an attack on another residence, only this one was in Wiggins Patch in the Pennsylvania coalfields. The Molly Maguires, a secret Irish Catholic mine workers society, was battling against the mine owners and bosses. There was violence and bloodshed on both sides.[90]

Back in 1873, Pinkerton had sent agent James McParlan to infiltrate the Molly Maguires. Pinkerton had other men, such as senior agent and police captain Robert Linden, working with the coal and railroad companies. Pinkerton wrote to George Bangs, one of his office managers, "If Linden can get up a vigilance committee that can be relied upon, do so. When M.M.'s [Molly Maguires] meet, then surround and deal summarily with them. Get off quickly. All should be masked."[91]

It was learned Charles McAllister and James and Charles O'Donnell, three suspected murderers of a foreman and an innocent witness, were at the O'Donnells' mother's boarding house. On the night of December 10, 1875, thirty masked men stormed into the house. Chaos erupted. They threatened the boarders, pistol-whipped Mrs. O'Donnell, and shot and killed McAllister's pregnant wife, Ellen. The vigilantes dragged McAllister and Charles O'Donnell into the street, shooting O'Donnell fifteen times and wounding McAllister, who was able to escape. The masked vigilantes were never identified, but many residents believed Pinkerton agent Robert Linden had trained them. Robert Linden was the leader of the Pinkertons' raid on Frank and Jesse James's mother's farm.[92]

Hated by some and loved by others, the name Pinkerton became synonymous with investigative work. The Pinkerton's National Detective Agency is with us today as Pinkerton and is a worldwide recognized leader in security and risk management.

CHAPTER 5

PINKERTON RAID ON THE JAMES FARM

After the murder of Pinkerton detective Joseph Whicher, Allan Pinkerton was on a vendetta, vowing the James boys "must die." William Dinsmore, president of the Adams Express Company, had had enough and ended the company's financial support for any further Pinkerton pursuit of the James Younger Gang, but Allan Pinkerton was not done. It was personal, and using $10,000 of his own money, he planned the demise of the James boys.[1]

In the spring of 1874, Pinkerton began making discreet contacts with old Clay County Unionists. One was Samuel Hardwicke, a Liberty attorney, who became Pinkerton's local coordinator in his efforts to capture or kill the James boys. Hardwicke enlisted the aid of another Unionist, Daniel Askew, who owned a 210-acre farm next to the Samuel farm. Pinkerton sent one of his operatives, Jack Ladd, to pose as a farmhand on Askew's farm. From there, Ladd could spy on the Samuel farm and report on the comings and goings of the James boys. Another important Unionist contact was the Kearney postmaster, Anthony Harsel. He assigned one of his deputies to watch for the James boys, and Harsel may have intercepted mail to and from the Samuel farm.[2]

Pinkerton selected Robert Linden, one of his senior detectives, to lead six agents on the Samuel farm raid. He also had permission from General Phil Sheridan to obtain "ammunition" from the US arsenal at Rock Island, Illinois. Pinkerton wrote in a letter to Hardwicke dated December 28, 1874, "Robert has charge of the ammunition in the shape of Greek fire, etc. etc." The Pinkertons would take a special train to within several miles of the Samuel farm, but they did not know the countryside, so Pinkerton asked Hardwicke for guides to take them to the Samuel place and then back to the train.[3]

Pinkerton further wrote in his letter to Hardwicke, "Above all else destroy the house, wipe it from the face of the earth. How the logs will burn. . . . Burn the house down."[4]

At 5:00 p.m., January 25, 1875, Pinkerton learned through his contacts that the James boys were at the Samuel farm.[5] Everything was in order and ready to go. Linden and his men were stationed close by at a Hannibal and St. Joseph Railroad depot where the railroad managers had provided an engine, tender, and caboose for their transport to the Samuel farm. The Pinkertons loaded their weapons, ammunition, and equipment, climbed aboard, and took off. It was 7:30 p.m. as the train approached a remote location outside Kearney. A Pinkerton contact stepped out near the track and flagged down the train. The Pinkertons unloaded their cargo and carried everything into the woods where they waited for four hours. Seven horses were waiting for them by the Haynesville Road.[6]

Their guide led them to the Samuel farmhouse, where they made last-minute preparations for their attack. Most of the men remained mounted as they took up positions surrounding the house. It was about 12:30 a.m. The Pinkertons were ready to capture or kill the James boys.[7]

Inside the house, the occupants were all asleep. There were three rooms to the house: a parlor, a family room, and the kitchen. The Samuel family—Reuben, and Zerelda, along with their children, thirteen-year-old John, ten-year-old Fannie, and eight-year-old Archie—slept in the family room, while the three black servants—fifty-four-year old Charlotte, eighteen-year-old Ambrose, and six-year-old Perry—slept in the kitchen. Charlotte bolted the door between the family room and the kitchen as was their custom. If Frank and Jesse had been there that night, they were long gone.[8]

Several Pinkertons dismounted and approached the kitchen on the northwest side of the house. They pried loose some of the outer weatherboard that covered the log structure, inserted tubes containing combustible material, and lit the tubes. Next, they lit large cotton balls soaked with combustible liquid and were going to throw them through the windows when they discovered the windows were shuttered tight. They opened one of the shuttered windows, raised the window sash, and tossed in a large flaming cotton ball. The Pinkertons had awakened Ambrose. He heard men talking and then saw light outside. As he stood up, he was struck by the ball, which discharged an oily substance when it hit the floor.[9]

A heavy crash followed by the servants' shouts and cries woke Reuben and Zerelda. Since the door was bolted on the kitchen side, Reuben could not enter. He ran outside to get to the kitchen from its outside door when he saw weatherboards on fire. He began tearing flaming boards off the house while shouting repeatedly "murder" to alert the neighbors. Zerelda, followed by her children, ran into the kitchen. The fireball lit up the inside of the room. After removing the burning boards, Reuben ran in. Using long sticks, Reuben and Zerelda rolled the fiery ball to the kitchen's large fireplace hearth where a banked fire smoldered within the fireplace. As they were extinguishing the fireball, a second fireball flew through the window and landed in the middle of the floor, creating a brilliant light. Zerelda tried to move the ball by kicking it, but this one was different from the first. It was metal covered by burning cloth and too heavy for Zerelda to move. Reuben grabbed

a shovel and was pushing the burning iron sphere up onto the fireplace hearth while Zerelda grabbed a burning quilt and threw it out the door.[10]

As Reuben pushed the sphere onto the hearth, it exploded. Iron shrapnel blasted throughout the kitchen. The room went black. Reuben heard shouted hurrahs outside the house, and groans from Archie and Zerelda. The Pinkertons fired four or five shots. One of them shouted, "Hurry up, boys, for we'll have to come back again just to keep up appearances." Hearing the attackers leave, Reuben ran to the door, screaming for help.[11]

The blast was heard up to three miles away.[12] It was later determined the seven-and-a-half-inch diameter metal sphere was composed of two halves possibly joined together with a steel band. A fuse hole with a wick in contact with flammable liquid inside the sphere would continue to feed the outside fire. One half of the sphere was made of wrought iron, which remained intact. The other half was made of cast iron, which blew apart.[13]

Everyone was injured. A small iron fragment hit the side of Reuben's head. Another chunk hit Ambrose in the head, knocking him out the door. A large piece hit Zerelda's right arm above the wrist, breaking the bone and mangling the arm. Archie received the worst wound. A shard of iron sliced through his bowels on his left side. Reuben and Ambrose carried Archie outside and then attended to Zerelda. Archie died shortly after the blast. His last words were, "Tell my moma I'm better." Doctors would not be able to save Zerelda's mangled arm and would have to amputate it above the elbow.[14]

Daniel Askew was one of the first neighbors on the scene to assist. When there was enough daylight, neighbors followed the attackers' tracks in the snow leading to and ending at the railroad tracks. Blood was spotted in the snow as well as a loaded revolver near the barn. The revolver had the initials "P.G.G." etched into the barrel. Many speculated the initials stood for "Pinkerton's Grand Guard" or "Pinkerton's Government Guard." Askew's Pinkerton farmhand, Jack Ladd, disappeared, probably riding away with the other Pinkertons on their special train. The attack not only made statewide news, but the national newspapers carried the story. The papers and the public rightly believed it had been the Pinkertons that had attacked the Samuel farm, but the Pinkertons were not talking—publicly.[15]

Frank and Jesse's advocate John Edwards led the public outrage over the attack, writing in the *Saint Louis Dispatch*, "If . . . Chicago detectives or any other detectives surrounded and set fire to the house . . . [and] threw a hand grenade through the window and into the midst of a family of helpless and innocent children, the citizens of Clay county owe it to their self-protection and manhood to rise up and hunt the midnight cowards and assassins to their death."[16]

On January 30, 1875, Missouri State Representative Stilson Hutchins, owner of the *Saint Louis Dispatch*, introduced a resolution in the House that the governor investigate the attack on the Samuel farm. In his address, Hutchins declared, "This state has been invaded without authority of law." The resolution passed both Houses. Governor Charles Hardin sent Adjutant General George Caleb Bingham to Clay County to investigate the attack. He reported to the General Assembly that men from another state had attacked the Samuel farm and once they could be identified, they would be brought back to stand trial.[17]

In March the Clay County grand jury indicted eight men, five of them unknown, in the murder of Archie Samuel. The three known men were Allan Pinkerton, Jack Ladd, and Robert J. King, which might have been an alias for Pinkerton detective Robert J. Linden. Besides Reuben and Zerelda Samuel, other witnesses included their neighbors, Daniel and Adeline Askew, and Samuel Hardwicke, who claimed he only acted as Pinkerton's attorney. Governor Hardin never sent a request to the governor of Illinois to extradite Allan Pinkerton to Missouri, and the case withered away.[18]

John Edwards went to work again. Now he was writing in the Missouri newspapers that the governor should grant the James boys and Younger brothers amnesty. Edwards worked with Representative Jefferson Jones to introduce a resolution to the Missouri legislature on March 17, 1875, requesting the governor pardon the James boys and Younger brothers for wartime offenses and guarantee them fair trials for crimes committed since the war. The resolution called them "too brave to be mean, too generous to be revengeful, too gallant and honorable to betray a friend or break a promise." It went on to state, "Most, if not all the offenses with which they have been charged have been committed by others." The resolution needed a two-thirds majority in the House to pass. On March 20, it came close to passing but failed.[19]

On March 26, three Wells, Fargo agents arrived in Carrolton, Missouri, to capture James Younger Gang member Clell Miller for his alleged participation in the Muncie, Kansas, train robbery. Sheriff John Clinkscales went with them to Sharpe Whitsett's farm where Miller was supposed to be. He was there. Clinkscales went into the house to talk Miller into surrendering, but Miller had other plans. He took the sheriff hostage, mounted a horse, and as he made his escape, shouted to the Wells, Fargo agents, "Goodbye gentlemen" and laughed as they fired a few parting shots in his direction.[20]

Clay County residents continued to talk about Hardwicke and Askew's probable participation in the attack on the Samuel farm. The *Kansas City Times* interviewed Frank and Jesse's sister Susie, who stated the family suspected Hardwicke and Askew's involvement. It wasn't long after the attack that Hardwicke moved from his farm into Liberty. Some said he believed he was safer in town.[21]

On Monday, April 12, 1875, around 8:00 p.m., Daniel Askew left his house to fetch a bucket of water. Someone stopped Askew and talked quietly with him for five to ten minutes. His wife, Adeline, heard three shots. She went to the front door and called for him, but there was no answer. She ordered the children to hide as she threw all of Allan Pinkerton's letters into the fire. Then she went out and found Daniel who had been shot three times in the head.[22]

Later that night, a rider called neighbor Henry Sears to his door. Hidden in the darkness, the rider said, "We have killed Dan Askew tonight, and if anyone wishes to know who did it say the detectives did it. Tell his friends to go and bury the damned son of a bitch tomorrow. Will you do it?"[23]

Who killed Dan Askew? Some speculated the Pinkertons killed Askew to keep him quiet. Most people believed Jesse shot him. Clell Miller and Frank might have been with him. The morning after the killing, three riders were spotted near the Samuel farm. Two of them rode to Richmond, and the third rode to the Blue Mills ferry. The lone rider was recognized by his fine mare—he was Jesse James.[24]

After Askew's death, Samuel Hardwicke fled to St. Paul, Minnesota. Pinkerton detective Robert Linden was transferred to

Pennsylvania to take care of labor problems in the coalfields. And Allan Pinkerton? He was finished. He gave up his pursuit of the James boys and Younger brothers.[25]

After his mother's death, Henry Antrim continued to live in Silver City, New Mexico, with the Truesdell family during the winter and spring of 1875. Stepfather Bill Antrim had little to do with Henry and his brother, Joe. Henry continued to attend school. He was studious and infatuated with his teacher Mary Richards. After school and between chores, Henry would read anything he could get his hands on, including dime novels and the *Police Gazette*.[26]

After school and when not doing chores or working in the Truesdell's hotel, Henry continued to run wild with the gang of town kids nicknamed the Street Arabs. Many of them were Hispanos, and he quickly learned to speak Spanish.[27]

Henry began to steal. There is no record when he started to do this, but he was caught sometime after March stealing several pounds of butter from rancher Abel Webb and selling it to a merchant. Sheriff Harvey Whitehill admonished young Henry that stealing was wrong. Henry promised not to do it again, Whitehill released him, and that should have been the end of it.[28]

CHAPTER 6

PLENTY OF WAYS TO GET INTO TROUBLE

Early in 1875, Jesse and Zee, who was pregnant, moved to Edgefield, Tennessee, across the Cumberland River from Nashville. Jesse had family nearby. His Uncle George Hite and his family lived on a farm forty miles to the north, near Adairville, Kentucky. Frank had also moved to Tennessee.[1]

Jesse used the alias John Davis Howard, and Zee used the alias Josie. They told the neighbors and acquaintances that "John" was a wheat speculator, and the neighbors noticed he was gone for extensive periods of time.[2]

According to his cousin George Hite, Jesse spent four months in Chicago, Illinois, stalking Allan Pinkerton. He wanted to confront Pinkerton and then kill him, so Pinkerton would die knowing who did it and why. He had plenty of chances to shoot Pinkerton from afar, but he wanted the confrontation. He finally gave up and left Chicago, but would often say, "I know God will someday deliver Allan Pinkerton into my hands."[3]

On May 13, at 7:30 p.m., four well-dressed men riding fine horses dismounted at a combination store and post office in Henry County, Missouri, twelve miles north of Clinton. Believing the store owner had thousands of dollars in gold, they were disappointed to find there was hardly any money there at all. The robbers thought one of the store's customers, a Yankee teacher, looked like a detective. They only relented badgering him when he produced his teaching certificate. Mrs. D. A. Lambert and Miss Bessie Sharp, who were in the store at the time, said, "We suppose them to be the Younger or James Boys from the way they proceeded." Two days earlier, two Younger brothers had been spotted in the area.[4]

Jesse continued to write letters that the newspapers published. As always, he stated his innocence and wrote he could not surrender because he had been lied about so much that public opinion was against him.[5]

On July 11, 1875, the *Nashville Republican Banner* published a letter from Jesse addressed from Raytown in Jackson County, Missouri. Jesse stated that recent sightings of the James boys and Younger brothers in Kentucky were untrue and that he was living in Missouri. He again denied involvement in all the robberies of which he was accused. He wrote about the Pinkerton attack on the Samuel home, "Nine Chicago assassins and Sherman bummers led by Billy Pinkerton Jr. crept up to my mothers [sic] house and hurled a misle [sic] of war (a 32 pound shell) in a room among a family of innocent women and children."[6]

Then on July 28, William Pinkerton wrote to the *Republican Banner*. Pinkerton said it wasn't worthwhile responding to "a murderer and thief, like Jesse James," but he wanted to set the public record straight: "On the very day he says I led the party who stormed his mother's house I was in Chicago attending the session of the Criminal Court as a witness."[7]

Jesse followed up with two letters mailed from Missouri to the *Republican Banner,* both published on August 8. In both letters he denounced the Pinkertons, calling William's letter "a pack of falsehoods." In the second letter, Jesse wrote, "[William Pinkerton] better never dare show his Scottish face again in western Mo. again and let me know he is here, or he will meet the fate of his comrades, Capt. Lull & Wicher [sic] . . . Pinkerton, I hope and pray that our Heavenly father may deliver you into my hands."[8]

A baby boy was born to Zee and Jesse on August 31, 1875. They secretly named him Jesse Edwards James. They gave him his middle name, Edwards, in honor of their literary friend John Edwards and all he had done for them. They never referred to their boy Jesse by his real name but called him Tim.[9]

On September 3, four men rode into Huntington, West Virginia. A Methodist convention was taking place, and it was presumed they were in town to participate. They stayed with Isaac Crump who believed they were pious men as they spent Sunday reading the Bible.[10]

Huntington was a railroad town established in 1871 by railroad tycoon Collins P. Huntington and settled by Yankees from New York and New England. The Bank of Huntington was considered "one of the most substantial banking concerns in the Ohio Valley." News had it that an Adams Express shipment of $100,000 was to arrive at the bank on September 3 or 4.[11]

On Monday, September 6 at 2 p.m., the four pious men Tom Webb, Tom McDaniel, Cole Younger, and Frank James went into action. They tied their horses near a blacksmith's shop, and one man stayed with the horses. The three men entered a grocery store across the street from the Bank of Huntington. There they bought a grain sack, and one man stayed in the store while Webb and Younger crossed the street and entered the bank.[12]

Pulling their revolvers, they forced the cashier, Robert Oney, to remove the cash from the safe. They learned Oney had $7.50 deposited in the bank and gave him that money out of their haul of $15,500 in cash and certificates. They asked Oney where the Adams Express money was held. He told them it had come and gone, being shipped on to Cincinnati, Ohio. They did not believe him until he showed them the express receipt.[13]

As the robbery was taking place, a black employee named Jim entered, and they took him hostage. The robbers were joined by their accomplice from the grocery store as they marched Oney and Jim to the blacksmith shop. The four men mounted their horses and raced west out of town as Oney yelled the bank had been robbed.[14]

A posse was soon on the robbers' trail. For the next couple of weeks, an extensive manhunt followed and, on occasion, came close to capturing the robbers. On September 15, William and James Dillon, who lived near Pine Hill, Kentucky, opened fire on four men who approached their house in the middle of the night. One was wounded and left behind by his comrades. Robert Oney, the Huntington Bank cashier, was brought in and identified the wounded man as one of the bank robbers. The man gave several aliases, but it was finally determined he was Tom McDaniel, a friend of the James boys' who had ridden with Cole Younger during the war and whose brother William had been captured after the Muncie, Kansas, train robbery. McDaniel died from his wounds several days after being shot. Before McDaniel's identity was determined, some newspapers claimed he was Cole Younger and others identified him as Jesse James. Tom Webb's horse threw a shoe, and he was captured on September 27, with $4,000, some of which was bloodstained. Neither McDaniel nor Webb identified their accomplices.[15]

Louisville detective Delos "Yankee" Bligh, who had been involved in tracking the robbers after the 1868 Russellville, Kentucky, bank robbery, was leading the investigation tracking down the Huntington Bank robbers.[16] On September 25, 1875, the *Nashville Daily American* published another Jesse James letter. This one was from St. Louis and dated September 21. In the letter, Jesse blasted Bligh as "the incompetent detective of Louisville" and stated the James boys and Younger brothers' innocence of the bank robbery. Jesse wrote, "Every bold robbery in the world is laid on us. . . . In a few days it will be seen how the James and Youngers have been lied on by such men as Pinkerton and Bligh. . . . I think the public will justify me in denouncing Bligh, and I now do, as an unnecessary liar, a scoundrel and a poltroon."[17]

The James boys must have conferred and decided that it would be wise to leave Tennessee. Missouri and Kentucky were too hot for them. They needed to go somewhere where they could meld in with a large population. In November 1875, the brothers and their families moved to Baltimore, Maryland. John Howard, Jesse's alias, is listed as a laborer in the 1876 *Baltimore City Directory*, and in later life Frank talked about living in Baltimore.[18]

Years later, Zee said Jesse attended the Centennial Exposition in Philadelphia, Pennsylvania, for a week. The exposition, considered the first World's Fair in the United States, commemorated the hundred-year anniversary of the signing of the Declaration of Independence. Lasting from May 10 to November 10, 1876, it was visited by ten million people. The exposition featured the latest in modern machinery, including sewing machines, typewriters, and the telephone.[19]

Zee said Jesse would come and go, but she and little Jesse lived in Baltimore for a year. Sometime after visiting the Centennial Exposition, Frank and Jesse returned to Missouri to make more money.[20]

The James Younger Gang, Frank and Jesse and Cole and Bob, teamed up again. They included Bill Chadwell, also known as Bill Stiles, Charlie Pitts, Clell Miller, and new recruit Hobbs Kerry. Their target was the Missouri Pacific Railroad's Express Number 4, which would be carrying Adams Express Company and the United States Express Company shipments.[21]

On July 6, 1876, the gang approached the railroad bridge over the Lamine River near Otterville in Cooper County, Missouri. Capturing the bridge watchman, they made him hammer a large nail into the bridge's west side and hung the white all's-clear lantern to shine where the engineer could clearly see it. Then taking him with them, they walked eastward along the tracks for three-fourths of a mile until they reached where the railroad ran through a deep cut in a limestone bluff called Rocky Cut. The gang found a pile of railroad ties that they hauled onto the track to block the train. They loosened a rail just in case the engine tried to plow through the ties.[22]

Around 10:30 p.m., Express Number 4, traveling from Kansas City to St. Louis and consisting of the engine, its tender, two baggage cars, three coaches, and two sleepers, approached and passed over the bridge where the white all's-clear lantern shone. The gang forced the watchman to wave the red warning lantern while standing in the middle of the track twenty feet behind the pile of railroad ties.[23]

The engineer saw the red warning lantern and threw the air-break lever to reverse the engine. It came to a stop just as it hit the tie pile. Gang members shot their revolvers and whooped. Two of them stood guard over the train above the cut as Kerry and Chadwell piled railroad ties behind the train so it could not back up, and two other gang members entered the locomotive's cab, covered the engineer and fireman, and escorted them out of the cab.[24]

When the firing started, the messenger for United States Express Company, John Bushnell, rushed to the rear sleeper car and gave the safe's key to the brakeman who hid it in his shoe. Bushnell sat in one of the cars, hoping to blend in with the passengers.[25]

The passengers were panicking. Some women were crying; a few fainted. If anyone stuck his head out a window, the gang members on the bluff would point their revolvers and shout, "Pull in your head you son of a bitch!" Many were finding hiding places for their valuables while others tried to hide themselves under seats. A minister from New York sang a hymn, testified to his faith, and asked that if he was killed to forward his remains to his family.[26]

Twenty-two-year-old Louis Bales, a black man who sold newspapers and other items on the train, walked out on a car's platform with a passenger. Bales fired a small-caliber pistol at a gang member on the bluff. It made a small popping sound and didn't hit anyone. The robbers laughed as one said, "Hear that little son of a bitch bark!" Then a gang member shot, hitting the coach between Bales and the other man. They jumped back inside.[27]

The side door of the baggage car was open to let in the cool night air. Three gang members wearing bandanas covering their faces below their eyes entered the car through the side door. One of the men had blinking blue eyes. It was Jesse. They spotted Pete Conklin, the baggage master, pointed their revolvers at him, and demanded the keys to the two safes. Conklin said he did not have them. They searched him, and then Jesse shoved his revolver in Conklin's chest, demanding Conklin take him to the man who had the keys. Conklin, Jesse, and another gang member walked through the cars of frightened passengers until Conklin found Bushnell. Jesse demanded he go with him and unlock the safes. Bushnell said he didn't have the key. Pointing his revolver in Bushnell's face, Jesse said, "You want to find it damned quick, or I will kill you." Bushnell took Jesse back to the brakeman, and Jesse said to him, "Give us the keys, my Christian friend, and be damned quick about it." The brakeman took off his shoe and gave Jesse the key.[28]

As they returned through the cars to the baggage car, the boot of a passenger hiding under his seat stuck out in the aisle and tripped Jesse. He turned and looked down at the man who apologized profusely. Jesse laughed and continued on to the baggage car.[29]

Two gang members had escorted the engineer and fireman into the baggage car. The gang members opened the United States Express Company safe and filled a wheat sack with its contents. There was no key for the Adams Express Company safe. Bob Younger went to the tender, returned with a coal pick, and took several whacks at the safe with no effect. Cole took the pick and after striking it multiple times, created a hole large enough that Jesse, who had smaller hands, was able to reach in and remove its contents.[30]

They looked about the baggage car, pilfering anything else of value. Opening Louis Bales's chest, they found all kinds of sweets including cakes and pies. Cole took large bites out of a pie, smearing the contents all over his face.[31]

Rummaging through the second baggage car, the robbers found nothing of value. Jesse turned to the train crew and asked if there were any detectives on board. They answered no. He said that was a good thing because "It would be good-bye for the detectives."[32]

One of the gang members wanted a watch and suggested robbing the passengers. Jesse said no, they had been there too long and needed to get away. The robbery had taken over an hour. He told the train crew they were free to go, and they needed to remove the railroad ties from the track. As the gang members mounted their horses, one of them fired a shot in the air and Jesse shouted, "Tell Allan Pinkerton and all his detectives to look for us in hell!"[33]

The train stopped at the next station, Tipton, where the conductor sent a telegraph message to the Missouri Pacific headquarters in St. Louis, and also to Sedalia and Kansas City, informing the railroad of the robbery of more than $17,000.[34]

Posses were soon on the trail of the James Younger Gang, but the trail grew cold. Newspapers had a field day with the robbery and many seemed to be on the side of the "bold banditti," calling them "dashing knights of the road." The *Boonville Daily Advertiser* stated, "No one was hurt, and no one loses anything save the express company."[35]

The gang had divided the money. Hobbs Kerry's share was $1,200. He was not careful, traveling and spending his money wild and free. James McDonough, St. Louis chief of police, was heading the investigation into the robbery and learned of Kerry's actions. McDonough sent officers who arrested Kerry on July 31 and took him to Boonville in Cooper County where he soon broke, confessing his part in the robbery and naming the other gang members: Jesse James, Frank James, Cole Younger, Bob Younger, Clell Miller, Charlie Pitts, and Bill Chadwell. Kerry revealed the gang had secret grips, signs, passwords, and signals and that they had many friends throughout Missouri who helped them before and after their robberies. By August 4, the newspapers published that Kerry had been captured; by August 8, they were reporting the gang members' names; and on August 12, they published Kerry's full confession.[36]

Jesse sent a letter to the *Kansas City Times,* with the heading "Oak Grove, Kansas, August 14, 1876," in which he blasted Hobbs Kerry as a liar. In fact, he wrote, he had never heard of Kerry, Pitts, or Chadwell until Kerry's arrest. He said eight good men of Jackson County could attest that he was not at the train robbery, and then named two of them. He followed up with a second letter to the *Times.* This letter had the heading "Safe Retreat. Texas, August 18, 1876." In it, Jesse elaborated on Kerry's lies. He said the robbery was committed by one of the posse leaders, the former Unionist militia officer Bacon Montgomery, who was also responsible for Archie Clement's death. He ended by continuing his war of words, bad-mouthing the Pinkertons.[37]

Meanwhile the James Younger Gang was planning where it would strike next.

In July of 1875, fifteen-year-old Henry Antrim had to leave the Truesdell home due to domestic problems and moved to Sarah Brown's boarding house. School was out for the summer in Silver City, New Mexico. Along with working odd jobs, Henry learned to play cards and gamble.[38]

He made friends with George Shaefer, another young man living at the boarding house. Shaefer always wore a sombrero and was nicknamed Sombrero Jack. Sombrero Jack liked Henry. He also liked to get drunk, and he also liked to steal.[39]

On Saturday, September 4, 1875, Sombrero Jack went on a drinking spree. Later that night, he broke into Charlie Sun and Sam Chung's laundry, stealing two revolvers, blankets, and customers' clothing worth up to $200. He hid his loot in a pit in the nearby town of Georgetown.[40]

Sombrero Jack told Henry if he went to Georgetown and recovered the items, he would give him a share. Henry agreed, recovered the goods, hid his share in a trunk in his room, and began to wear some of the stolen clothing.[41]

Sarah Brown was cleaning Henry's room when she looked in his chest and found items stolen from the Chinese laundry. She told Sheriff Harvey Whitehill, who tracked down Henry and arrested him Thursday morning, September 23. Learning of Henry's arrest, Sombrero Jack decided it was a good time to leave Silver City with the rest of the loot.[42]

Henry went before Justice of the Peace Isaac Givens. Since Henry was an accomplice to the crime, he was charged with larceny and would have to wait in the county jail until the next session of the grand jury. Both Whitehill and Givens believed a little time in jail would set Henry straight.[43]

After two days in jail, Henry was tired of being cooped up. He told Whitehill that the jailer was rough with him and wouldn't let him out of his cell to exercise. Whitehill told the jailer to allow Henry into the jail's corridor to exercise for a short time each morning. September 25, Henry was left alone in the corridor. After half an hour, Whitehill returned to the jail and unlocked the door. Henry was not there. He had entered the fireplace, pulled himself up through the chimney onto the roof, and made his escape.[44]

Henry was covered with soot from head to toe and had no money. He did not want to go back to jail, and in his mind, he needed to get out of town. People helped him get cleaned up and gave him the means to leave, but who helped him is the question. Wayne Whitehill, the sheriff's son and Henry's friend, said another friend, Manuel Taylor, gave Henry an old shotgun. Chauncey Truesdell said his mother washed Henry's clothes, let him stay the night, gave him lunch and some money, and put him on the stagecoach heading west. Sarah Brown said she put Henry on the stage. The Knight family said he walked fifteen miles to their ranch and stayed with them. His teacher Mary Richards said she was staying at the Knight ranch at the time and they tried to reason with Henry to return to Silver City and give himself up since the crime was not major and the punishment would not be severe. Henry agreed to turn himself in, and they gave him a horse to ride into town, but after leaving the ranch he rode away from town.[45]

Henry made his way west to Arizona. He may have gone to Clifton which was 103 miles from Silver City and the end of the line for the stagecoach. His stepfather, Bill Antrim, may have been working there in the mines. There are two stories as to their meeting. One story is that Bill gave Henry all the money he had. In the other story, when Bill learned of the trouble Henry had gotten himself into, he told Henry, "If that's the kind of boy you are, get out." In response, Henry stole Bill's revolver and some clothes. In either case, Henry left Clifton and never saw Bill Antrim again.[46]

Gambling, stealing, and picking up any job he could find, Henry drifted through Arizona. Some of his friends said he worked cattle for Texas cattleman Pete Slaughter at his PS Ranch on Arizona's Black River. Henry was hanging around Camp Goodwin near the San Carlos Apache Reservation when on March 19, 1876, he decided to leave. Not having a horse of his own, he stole Private Charles Smith's horse before leaving.[47]

In April 1876, he arrived at Camp Grant looking for work. Camp Grant was a military post in the Sulphur Springs Valley near the Pinaleño Mountains.[48]

William Whelan, foreman for Henry Hooker's Sierra Bonita Ranch in the valley, hired Henry to work cattle, but soon fired him, considering Henry a lightweight. That summer, Henry worked on other ranches in the valley and gambled at McDowell's Store, a collection of businesses catering to off-duty soldiers, ranch hands, and miners three miles southwest of Camp Grant. It was in the Sulphur Springs Valley that Henry became known as Kid Antrim.[49]

CHAPTER 7

THE NORTHFIELD RAID

After the Rocky Cut train robbery and Hobbs Kerry's revelation of the James Younger Gang members' identities, Missouri had become too dangerous for them to continue their robberies there. They needed to go someplace new, someplace unexpected. What better than head north and take from the Yankees? They could travel straight north to Minnesota. The state was prosperous, there were lots of banks, and for the James boys, they might even be able to catch Samuel Hardwicke.

Liberty attorney Samuel Hardwicke had been Allan Pinkerton's local coordinator for his attack on the Samuel farmhouse that killed little Archie and mangled the arm of Frank and Jesse's mother. After the murder of Samuel farm neighbor and Pinkerton collaborator Dan Askew, Hardwicke had taken his family and fled to St. Paul, Minnesota, in May 1876. Jesse believed Hardwicke was one of those responsible for Archie's death. He reportedly had sent a letter to his stepfather, Reuben Samuel, stating that the same grand jury that had indicted Allan Pinkerton should have also indicted Hardwicke.[1]

Hardwicke had made a bonehead move. He wrote a letter to the editor that was printed in the July 21, 1876, edition of the *Liberty Tribune*. The newspaper printed Hardwicke's home address, 43 St. Paul Street, St. Paul, Minnesota. It was possible that Frank and Jesse now knew where he lived, and the potential was there to do to him what had been done to his cohort Dan Askew.[2]

An equally important reason, and one that would appeal more to the rest of the gang, was the potential to rob a pair of Yankees hated by the South. If they could score a hit on those two, it would further the James Younger Gang's image as heroes of the late Confederacy.

The gang learned that one of the two men, the hated and rich Yankee Republican Adelbert Ames, was living in Northfield, Minnesota, a small farming and college community thirty-five miles south of St. Paul. They decided if they could, they would rob Ames of his money.

Adelbert Ames had moved to Northfield, Minnesota, in May 1876. His father and brother were prominent citizens in town, owning the flour mill and a fourth of the First National Bank. Ames, a New Englander, had graduated from West Point in May 1861. A Civil War hero, he received the Congressional Medal of Honor, and rose to the rank of general. After the war, he moved to Mississippi to participate in Reconstruction. In 1870, Radical Republicans and blacks elected him to represent Mississippi in the US Senate and then as governor of Mississippi in 1873. During the 1875 election, the Democrats intimidated Republicans and blacks. Riots broke out. People were injured and murdered, and many voters were barred from the polls throughout Mississippi.[3]

After the election, the Democrat-controlled legislature began impeachment proceedings against Ames on trumped-up charges. At the suggestion of his lawyers and wife, Blanche, Ames resigned, but not before the charges were leaked to the newspapers. Ames did not live in Missouri and did not harm any Missourians, but Missouri newspapers used him as a symbol of Northern tyranny and corruption.[4]

Ames joined with his father and brother to manage the Northfield flour mill while Blanche, the beautiful, influential daughter of infamous General Benjamin Butler, remained in New England. In

1870, Ames and Blanche had been married at Butler's mansion in Lowell, Massachusetts, where Butler staged a three-day celebration with enough dignitaries present to resemble "a chapter out of the Arabian Nights."[5]

The James Younger Gang's second target was Ames's father-in-law, New England lawyer and politician General Benjamin Butler. Butler had led Union troops into New Orleans, May 1, 1862, after its surrender. Southerners gave Butler the nickname "Beast Butler" after he issued General Order No. 28 that stated any woman who insulted a Union officer would "be treated as a woman of the town plying her avocation"—in other words, a prostitute. Butler's order horrified Southerners. Then on June 7, 1862, Butler had William Mumford hanged for tearing down an American flag.[6]

Many New Orleans residents believed Butler stole private property, nicknaming him "Spoons." Along with Butler, his staff, and his brother Andrew made money selling confiscated cotton and other goods. After hearing evidence of Butler's mismanagement of New Orleans, President Abraham Lincoln placed General Nathaniel Banks in command over Butler. Resenting the snub, Butler resigned.[7]

In 1866, Butler was elected to Congress as a Radical Republican who helped lead the charge to impeach President Andrew Johnson and punish the South. By 1876, Butler had a wide variety of investments and had accumulated a vast amount of wealth.[8]

The James Younger Gang knew members of the Ames family were major investors in Northfield's First National Bank, and, best of all, they could punish not only Ames, but also Spoons Butler. Cole Younger would later state, "We had been informed that ex-Governor Ames of Mississippi and General Benjamin Butler of Massachusetts had deposited $75,000 in the National Bank."[9]

By heading to Minnesota, the James Younger Gang had the potential to kill two birds with one stone, and so they made their audacious plans to strike deep in Yankee territory. One of the first steps was to determine who would go. Obviously, the gang would include those who had taken part in the Rocky Cut robbery, excluding the incarcerated Hobbs Kerry: Frank and Jesse James, Bob and Cole Younger, Clell Miller, Charlie Pitts, and Bill Chadwell. Brother Jim Younger had returned from California and joined the gang for the Minnesota raid.[10]

Clell Miller was a Clay County resident and longtime gang member. Charlie Pitts, whose real name was Samuel Wells, lived near and was good friends with the Younger family in Jackson County. Charlie, who had been a bushwhacker during the war, married afterwards and moved to Kansas where he had at least two extramarital affairs. A jilted lover disclosed to detectives and newspapers that Charlie was a James Younger Gang member. Bill Chadwell had been born in 1853, in Greene County, Illinois. After his father died, his family moved to Kansas. Chadwell was good friends with Charlie Pitts and became a James Younger Gang member.[11]

The gang gathered in St. Joseph, Missouri, boarding the train to Sioux City, Iowa, where they transferred to another train that carried them to Minneapolis, Minnesota.[12] On August 23, 1876, some of the gang checked in at the Nicollet House in downtown Minneapolis, and others stayed at the Merchants Hotel in St. Paul.[13]

The gang members used aliases and told people a variety of stories as to why they were in Minnesota: They were farmers, they were cattle dealers, or they were on their way to the Black Hills gold camps in Dakota Territory. They wore boots with spurs and long dusters over their clothing to conceal they were heavily armed. They usually tried not to flash around their revolvers. They enjoyed themselves for several days and nights, drinking, gambling, and visiting brothels.[14]

One night, Jesse and two gang members visited Mollie Ellsworth's bordello. Jesse walked into Mollie's room and asked if she wasn't Kitty Traverse who had operated a bordello in St. Louis.

Mollie recognized Jesse whom she had known for years. She asked him what he was doing in Minneapolis. He said, "Nothing. I am going out into the country for a few days and will be back soon; then you and I will go to the Centennial." Molly saw Jesse had several guns and asked what he was going to do with them. He answered that he needed them for "a man that he knew uptown."[15]

The man Jesse talked about would have been Sam Hardwicke, who now lived in St. Paul. Jesse would have known Hardwicke's home address from his letter to the editor, and it would be easy enough to locate his business address. He may have stalked Hardwicke as he had Allan Pinkerton; Jesse may have wanted to confront Hardwicke and then kill him, so Hardwicke would know who was killing him and why. Jesse was cautious. He would have wanted to kill Hardwicke where no one would see the deed and Jesse could make a clean getaway. Even though it did not come to be, Jesse most likely believed someday he would have his opportunity for revenge just as he believed someday he would have his revenge on Allan Pinkerton.[16]

Over the next several days, gang members separated into small groups to prepare for their bank robbery. They bought maps and traveled through the countryside to familiarize themselves with the terrain and to find the best escape routes. They visited towns to determine how many banks were in each of them and, if possible, find out how much money was in each bank. They bought the finest horses they could find and worked with them. They bought good saddles and tack. As always, they would need the best horses to outrun any posses that might try to follow them.[17]

Even though they had their sights set on robbing the Northfield bank, they would not want to pass up a bank with more cash. They investigated the bank at Northfield and those in other towns. They settled on robbing one of the three banks in Mankato, the First National Bank, after learning it had $120,000.[18]

Monday, September 4, was set for the day of the robbery, but red flags appeared. Charles Robinson, who was from Missouri and out on the street, spotted Jesse and greeted him, "Hallo, Jesse, what are you doing up here?" Jesse looked at him and said, "Hell, man, I don't know you," as he trotted his horse away. As the gang members approached the bank, people had congregated in front of it. One man was talking to another as he pointed at the approaching riders. The gang members worried they might have been found out, turned their horses around, and walked away. An hour later they tried again, but the same group of people were there and appeared to be watching them. The gang was suspicious it might be a trap, and calling off the bank robbery, they left town.[19]

The gang decided to rob their original target, Northfield's only bank, the First National Bank. After further discussing how they would raid the bank on Thursday, September 7, they separated into two groups. Cole and Jim Younger, Clell Miller, and Charlie Pitts spent the night of September 6 in Millersburg, eleven miles west of Northfield. Frank and Jesse James, Bob Younger, and Bill Chadwell spent the night in Cannon City, ten miles south of Northfield.[20]

Midmorning on Thursday, September 7, 1876, the eight James Younger Gang members converged on Northfield, Minnesota.[21]

"My! How those fellows can ride. Just like Prussian soldiers," William Ebel overheard Ferdinand Burke marvel as he spied a group of strangers ride into Northfield. Later that morning, Ebel saw the same men carousing in a saloon.[22]

The gang members gathered near town west of the Cannon River. They split into small groups, and during the morning, they ranged throughout town, entering shops and conversing with residents portraying themselves as cattle buyers. Some people were suspicious of the strangers, but then there were more people in town than usual, possibly because of the show that the Great Professor Lingard, an Austrian illusionist, would be presenting that evening, preceded by the flight of two hot air balloons. Jesse James, Bob Younger, and Charlie Pitts enjoyed themselves drinking a quart of whiskey of which the other gang members did not know.[23]

A little before 2:00 p.m., Jesse, Bob, and Charlie tied their horses to hitching posts near the First National Bank on Division Street and lounged by some crates. Cole Younger and Clell Miller rode up the street from the south while Frank James, Jim Younger, and Bill Chadwell waited nearby on horseback in Mill Square on the east side of the iron bridge over the Cannon River.[24]

Adelbert Ames, his brother John, accompanied by his daughter Fanny, and the Ames's father, Jesse, had left the First National Bank after a board meeting. As they walked toward their mill, four riders wearing white linen dusters sat on horses near the Cannon River bridge. They overheard one of the riders say in a low voice, "There goes Governor Ames himself." Adelbert said to John, "Those men are from the South, and are here for no good purpose. No one here calls me Governor."[25]

Inside the First National Bank stood a vault housing a safe with a time lock designed to only open at predetermined times. On this day, the vault door was open. The safe's door was closed but unlocked with $15,000 available for transactions. Behind a wooden, L-shaped counter, three bank employees sat working: bookkeeper and acting cashier Joseph Heywood, assistant bookkeeper Frank Wilcox, and teller Alonzo Bunker.[26]

Jesse James, Bob Younger, and Charlie Pitts entered the bank. Alonzo Bunker thought they were customers until he saw revolvers pointed at him.[27]

"Throw up your hands for we intend to rob this bank and if you holler we will blow your God damned brains out," a gang member shouted as the three of them leaped over the counter and forced Wilcox and Bunker to the floor on their knees.[28]

The robbers asked each bank employee if he was the cashier. They all denied that they were. Heywood was sitting in the cashier's chair. A gang member said to him, "I know you're the cashier. Now open the safe damn quick or I'll blow your head off."[29]

Charlie Pitts started to enter the vault. Heywood jumped up and began to close the vault door on him. The other robbers dragged Heywood from the vault door. Shoving their revolvers in his face, one of them warned, "Open that safe, now, or you haven't a minute to live."[30]

"It is a time lock, and cannot be opened now," Heywood replied. The robbers told him he was lying and again ordered him to open the safe.[31]

Pitts shouted, "Damn you! Open that door or we'll cut you from ear to ear!" Grabbing Heywood by the hair, Pitts jerked his head back, and drew his knife across Heywood's throat enough to make it bleed. "Murder! Murder! Murder!" Heywood shouted, tearing away from Pitts. One of the robbers struck Heywood on the head with the butt end of a revolver, knocking him to the floor. Demanding he open the safe, Pitts fired his revolver close to Heywood's head, but he still refused to obey.[32]

At the same time out on the street, Cole Younger and Clell Miller noticed that the gang members who had entered the bank had failed to close the outside door. Miller and Cole dismounted. Cole pretended to tighten his cinch while Miller walked to the door and closed it just as store owner J. S. Allen arrived. Allen had seen the three men in dusters enter the bank and was suspicious. Miller grabbed Allen's collar and shoved a revolver in his face warning, "You son of a bitch, don't you holler." Allen broke away and ran up the street. "Get your guns, boys," he yelled, "They are robbing the bank!" Across the street from Miller, medical student Henry Wheeler stood in front of his father's drugstore. Seeing the struggle in front of the bank and Allen break away from Miller, Wheeler shouted, "Robbery! They are robbing the bank!" Miller shot over Wheeler's head, yelling, "Get back or I'll kill you!"[33]

Wheeler turned and ran into his father's drugstore. He looked for a weapon but found none. Remembering there was a rifle in the Dampier House hotel, he left through the drugstore's back-door, ran up the alley to the third building, and entered the hotel from the back. There, he borrowed a single-shot carbine and ammunition, then bounded up the stairs to a third-floor window overlooking the street.[34]

Cole shot at people as he shouted, "Get in you son of a bitch!" Frank James, Bill Chadwell, and Jim Younger galloped into Division Street, shooting and shouting. Some people were slow to move. They thought all the hoopla must be part of the Great Professor Lingard's show that would be happening that day.[35]

J. S. Allen ran to his store where he dispensed weapons and ammunition to townsmen. Elias Stacy took a shotgun loaded with birdshot and blasted Clell Miller in the face as he was mounting his horse. The blast knocked Miller to the ground. He was dazed but able to remount. Anselm Manning borrowed a rifle from a store display window and took aim at two robbers standing in the street, but he did not have a clear shot as they took cover behind their horses. He took aim and shot Bob Younger's horse.[36]

Positioned at a third-floor window in the Dampier House hotel, Henry Wheeler had a clear view of the gang members in the street below. He loaded his borrowed carbine, aimed at a mounted robber, and shot, just missing Jim Younger. He reloaded, aimed at another mounted robber, and shot, hitting Clell Miller in the chest, knocking him off his horse, and killing him. As Cole Younger ran to Miller's aid, Manning fired, hitting Cole's left hip. Bloodied, Cole mounted his horse and rode to the bank, shouting to his comrades, "Come out of the bank!"[37]

Anselm Manning fired again, hitting Bill Chadwell in the chest, knocking him off his horse, where he died in the street.[38]

Inside the bank, Bob Younger was gathering money from the counter and drawers, missing a drawer that had $2,000 in cash. Alonzo Bunker made a break for it, running through the back room and out the back door as Pitts shot, missing him. Pitts followed out the back, and as Bunker was crossing an empty lot, Pitts fired again, hitting Bunker in the right shoulder, but he kept running.[39]

Nellie Ames was driving her one-horse carriage in town. Her husband, John Ames, was Adelbert's brother and a bank director.

Hearing shots, Nellie drove up Fifth Street to see what the commotion was all about. She saw Alonzo Bunker running with his hand on his shoulder. She called to him, "What's the matter, Mr. Bunker?" As he ran past, he answered, "I'm shot." A man ran up and told Nellie to get out of the carriage or she would be killed. As she got out, another man led her horse and buggy away. She walked toward the intersection of Fifth and Division Streets. Riders shouting and firing revolvers raced toward her. One was Cole Younger who shouted, "Lady, get off the street or you will be killed!" Cole saw Nicolaus Gustavson, a drunken Swede, weaving toward him. Without hesitation, Cole fired his revolver, hitting Gustavson in the head. He wheeled his horse around and raced back toward the bank.[40]

Cole shouted into the bank, "For God's sake come out! They are shooting us all to pieces!"[41]

Bob Younger ran out of the bank. Charlie Pitts was right behind him. Before following them out the door, Jesse turned and shot Heywood in the head, killing him.[42]

Anselm Manning and Bob Younger were engaged in a shoot-out, each trying to get a clear shot at the other. Wheeler aimed again from his high position and fired at Bob, the bullet hitting and breaking Bob's right elbow. Bob switched his revolver to his left hand to continue shooting at Manning. As bullets continued to fly, one smashed into Jim Younger's shoulder. The six remaining gang members mounted their five horses, Bob riding double with Cole, and galloped south on Division Street and out of town.[43]

The gun battle lasted no more than ten minutes, leaving gang members Clell Miller and Bill Chadwell dead in the street. The gang stole $26.60, where they had the potential to leave Northfield with $17,000 in cash.[44]

The gang was riding south on the road to Dundas when they stopped Phillip Empey driving a team of gray horses pulling a wagon. They told Empey they needed one of his horses, but when Empey refused, a gang member struck him on the head with a revolver, knocking him into the ditch. Two men from Northfield, mounted on Miller's and Chadwell's horses, chased after the gang but backed off when one of the gang held up his hand and shouted "Halt!" The gang unhitched Empey's best horse, mounted Bob on it bareback, and continued down the road.[45]

Three miles south of Northfield, the gang stopped at the bridge over the Cannon River at Dundas to examine and wash their wounds. All three Younger brothers were wounded, and Frank had been shot above the right knee.[46]

Meanwhile back in Northfield, John Ames was with the telegraph operator sending messages alerting neighboring towns of the robbery and requesting assistance from the Minneapolis and St. Paul police forces. Since Minnesota did not have a state police force, smaller communities relied on the state's two largest cities for police support. The gang had planned to wreck the telegraph office after the robbery but didn't have time.[47]

The Northfield telegraph operator sent warning messages to Dundas, but the Dundas telegraph operator was out of the office, so no one in town knew that the band of men riding through had just shot up Northfield. Heading west from Dundas toward Millersburg, they stopped at a farmhouse, telling the farmer they were chasing horse thieves and convincing him to loan them a saddle for Bob. At 4:30 p.m., they rode through Millersburg without opposition, but the word was out about the Northfield raid. Posses were forming, and some began converging in the gang's direction.[48]

The gang headed southwestward into Minnesota's Big Woods where they hoped they would be able to elude any posses. The Big Woods, a deciduous forest of oak, maple, basswood, and elm, encompassed up to four thousand square miles of Minnesota and Wisconsin, a hundred miles long and forty miles wide. Many lakes and wetlands were situated throughout its glacial topography.[49]

At 6:00 p.m., a five-man posse arrived in Shieldsville, riding in a wagon from Faribault, ten miles to the southeast. They were thirsty, and leaving their unloaded weapons in the wagon, they entered Hagerty's Saloon for a few beers. The gang rode into town from the northeast and stopped at the water pump and trough in front of Hagerty's to water their horses and themselves and wash their wounds.[50]

An old man walked out of the saloon and asked the gang where they were going. Jesse pointed to Bob, responding, "[We're] going to hang that damn cuss."[51]

One of the posse members walked to the saloon's doorway and, spying the gang, shouted, "Those are the fellows!" He ran to the wagon to get his weapon as the other posse members rushed out of the saloon, but all of them froze when the gang pulled and cocked their revolvers. After they finished at the pump, the outlaws amused themselves by giving the posse a demonstration of their firepower shooting up the wood pump. However, one stray bullet grazed a little girl who had stepped into the saloon's doorway.[52]

The gang galloped southwest down the road disappearing into the woods as the posse scrambled for their guns and loaded them.

They decided not to follow the gang but waited until another posse arrived, swelling their number to fourteen, then they started in pursuit.[53]

Bob was weak from loss of blood, and his draft horse could not keep up the pace of the other horses. The posse was gaining on the gang. They caught up with them in a ravine four miles outside town and exchanged shots at long distance even though no one on either side had rifles. Cole was leading Bob's horse as a spent bullet fired by a posse member struck him on the "crazy bone." Cole's reflex jerked the reins of Bob's horse and his own horse so that the animals panicked. Bob's horse slipped, throwing Bob who hit the ground screaming in pain. As he began to remount the draft horse, the saddle's cinch broke and the horse ran off. Bob mounted behind Cole, and the gang raced further into the Big Woods. The posse, now more cautious, lost track of the gang.[54]

At dusk the gang ran into a farmer, Levi Sager, riding horseback and forced him to lead them southwest. Before proceeding on, a gang member forced Sager to trade mounts, but the horse, unused to spurs, was uncooperative, and after a quarter-mile fight with the animal, the gang member traded back Sager's horse. Reaching a field south of the small town of Kilkenny, the gang turned Sager loose. Later that night, they came to Lord Brown's farmhouse on the Waterville Road where Brown gave them shelter for the night. Rain began to fall. It would last off and on for the next two weeks, swelling streams and rivers, adding to the wetlands, and saturating the ground, turning it into a miserable quagmire.[55]

As days turned into weeks, the rewards for the gang's capture or elimination grew and so did the number of manhunters. Minnesota governor John Pillsbury increased the state's reward from an initial $1,500 for all the outlaws up to $1,000 per man. Northfield's First National Bank's initial reward was $500 for all the robbers. The public was outraged at the small amount. The following week, the bank raised the amount to $3,000. So, if all six robbers were caught or killed, the total take would be $9,000.[56]

As to the manhunt, posses formed the day of the robbery, numbering more than two hundred men. During the next two weeks, the multiple posses and guards at river crossings swelled to more than a thousand men.[57]

On Friday, September 8, after scaring off men guarding a Cannon River ford, the gang crossed to the west and disappeared into the woods. A half hour later they came upon Ludwig Rosnau's farm. They convinced Rosnau they were a sheriff's posse chasing horse thieves and needed two horses and a guide. When Rosnau hesitated, they pulled their revolvers on him, took two horses, saddles, and tack as well as Rosnau's sixteen-year-old son, Wilhelm, to guide them to the Waterville and Cleveland Road that ran northwestward. Wilhelm led them to the road, where they exchanged one of their worn-out horses for his and told him to wait there while they chased after the horse thieves down the road to the west. Wilhelm waited until a man came along, who stopped to talk. The man asked Wilhelm if he had heard about the bank robbery, which he had not. Putting two and two together, Wilhelm realized the men he had guided were not a posse but the bank robbers. Later, Wilhelm told lawmen everything he could about the robbers.[58]

The gang traveled off the road through the woods to avoid detection. They made camp between Indian Lake and Elysian on Friday night. Soaking wet, they dared not make a fire and draw attention to themselves. They had been leading their horses through the woods and made the decision to leave them behind as the posses would be looking for horseback riders. The next morning, using long lead lines, they tied the horses to trees and, taking only what they could carry, wrapped up in their saddle blankets tied up with their bridles, they walked west through the woods.[59]

For the next several days, they walked southwestward through the wet Big Woods toward Mankato, avoiding towns and roads, and trudging around lakes and sloughs. Their boots were made for riding not walking, and their feet became soaking wet and blistered. They lived off the land, scavenging and stealing whatever they could.[60]

The gang found an abandoned farmhouse three miles outside Mankato and stayed there Monday and Tuesday nights to get out of the rain. That Tuesday morning, one of the posses had discovered their abandoned mounts and saddles.[61]

At 6:00 a.m., Wednesday, September 13, the gang kidnapped farmhand Thomas Jefferson Dunning, and forced him to show them the way to Mankato. They asked Dunning if he knew who they were. He answered he had a good idea who they were. The gang called one of their number "Captain," who said that if the cashier had opened the vault, he would not have shot him. Jesse was referred to as "Captain." The gang was uncertain whether Dunning was leading them in the right direction. They worried he might betray them and discussed whether they should let him go, tie him up, or kill him. The James boys favored killing him. The decision was left up to the wounded Bob Younger, who said, "I would rather be shot dead than have that man killed for fear his telling might put a few hundred men after us." The gang let Dunning go after he promised he would not tell anyone. They threatened if he did, they would track him down and kill him.[62]

Dunning returned to the farm. After considering his promise and the gang's threats, he told his employer of his encounter. The employer, in turn, notified the Mankato authorities, and the manhunt around Mankato intensified as over a thousand men searched for the James Younger Gang, becoming the largest manhunt in United States history. As a cold rain fell, the gang hunkered down in dense woods near town, waiting for nightfall.[63]

Near midnight, the gang entered Mankato, population six thousand, from the east following the St. Paul & Sioux City Railroad tracks through town with no opposition. When they came to the railroad bridge over the Blue Earth River, they hoped it was not guarded. They crossed over the bridge with no opposition, but there were hidden guards—two men and a boy. The two men ran away, but the boy ran to find other guards. When the news reached General Edmund Pope, who was coordinating the manhunt efforts, he decided it was too late that night to do anything but would take up the pursuit the next morning.[64]

As the gang followed the railroad tracks west, they raided a watermelon patch and a chicken coop, killing three hens and a small turkey to eat later. Three miles west of the bridge, they left the tracks, walked fifty paces into the woods, and set up camp at the base of a ridge called Pigeon Hill. They started a fire, cleaned and plucked the birds and began roasting them over the fire.[65]

A posse, led by the Winona County sheriff and by Minneapolis detective Mike Hoy, who had been constantly tracking the gang, was following their trail along the tracks when an engineer in a passing train waved and pointed to Pigeon Hill. Hoy and the others raced into the woods, following the gang's trail, hollering to each other. When they reached the camp, the gang was gone, but they left behind their roasting birds, coats, blankets, and bridles.[66]

As the day progressed, hundreds of posse members scoured the area with no sign of the gang who had hurried to the southeast. When they hit the Blue Earth River, they used every ruse to evade the posses—walking in the water, stepping from rock to rock, doubling back on their trail, and leaving footprints in the wrong direction as it continued raining. Bob was weak and needed rest, so they hunkered down in a thicket along the river for the rest of the day.[67]

That night of September 14, the gang discussed their situation. An argument erupted over letting Dunning live. He must have reported his encounter with them to the lawmen on their trail. They should have killed him. Frank and Jesse said Bob was too weak and if they were going to make their escape, they needed to leave him behind. Cole and Jim said they would never leave their brother. Charlie Pitts sided with them, saying he would not leave Bob. The gang made the decision to split up. The Youngers and Pitts gave the James boys their watches and most of their cash, thinking they had a better chance of reaching Missouri and their relatives. They said their good-byes, and the James boys left.[68]

It was after midnight on September 15. Frank and Jesse had stolen a horse and were riding double westward. At a bridge south of Lake Crystal, a group of nine men were assigned to guard the bridge to prevent the outlaws from crossing. The guards hunkered down, trying to sleep during the cold night, but Richard Roberts remained on duty. As the James boys approached, Roberts challenged them, yelling, "Halt! Who are you fellows?" They spurred the horse forward as Roberts fired his gun. Jumping off the horse, they ran into a cornfield as the horse ran back the way they had come. One of the riders lost his hat, and Roberts claimed it.[69]

At 3:00 a.m., the James boys entered a barn owned by a man named Seymour three miles to the south. There, they found Baptist minister Joseph Rockwood holding a rifle guarding his team of iron-gray mares. Rockwood and his team were there to help Seymour with his harvest. One of the brothers pistol-whipped Rockwood and then they took his team, considered the best in Blue Earth County.[70]

Now with two good horses they made time heading west. At 7:00 a.m. they stopped at the Jackson family farmhouse northwest of Madelia where they bought a loaf of bread, a hat, and sacks stuffed with straw that they tied on the horses as improvised saddles. At dusk they stopped at a German farmer's house five miles south of Lamberton, where they spent the night. They lied, saying they had been in a wagon accident and the farmer's wife helped Frank dress his leg wound.[71]

At 7:00 a.m. the next morning, September 16, the James boys told the German family they were headed to Lamberton and rode off in that direction, but when out of sight, they turned, riding south. At 2:00 p.m., they crossed the Des Moines River and bought bread and milk from a farmer named Swan. They remained in the saddle while eating and having a pleasant conversation with Swan, asking about the countryside and distances to railroads.[72]

The brothers continued riding southwest, eluding all posses tailing them and attempting to block their route. They rode through the night, and on Sunday morning, September 17, at 7:30 a.m., they arrived at the farm of Charles and Sarah Rolf on the west bank of Rock Creek, eleven miles northeast of Luverne, Minnesota. Charles was not home, but Sarah invited them in for breakfast anyway. Inside the house, Sarah said they could take off their rubber coats, but they would not. She asked if they were ill. The brothers lied, saying they had been in a wagon wreck. When they finished breakfast, they paid for the meal, reaching under their coats for the money. They were so stiff they needed to climb on fence rails to mount their horses.[73]

Later that morning, Charles was back home, and a brother-in-law came to visit telling them of the Northfield robbery and the manhunt for the outlaws. Realizing their visitors must have been two of the robbers, Charles rode to Luverne to inform the sheriff and saw the two in the distance slowly riding to the southwest.[74]

Rock County Sheriff Ezra Rice formed a posse and chased after the James boys. They came within rifle shot but lost their nerve and only trailed the outlaws until night, when they gave up the chase.[75]

The James boys crossed the border into Dakota Territory, continuing west until they reached Swedish farmer Andrew Nelson's place several miles south of the palisades cliffs along Split Rock Creek. After talking with Nelson, they intimidated him into going inside his sod house while the brothers entered his barn and exchanged the played-out, iron-gray mares for Nelson's team of blacks. Nelson's teenage son came out of the house and asked them not to take the blacks, but they told him they had need of them as there were at least four men following them.[76]

The James boys soon discovered one horse was blind in one eye and the other horse was totally blind. Twelve miles farther on, they stole two gray geldings, leaving the blacks behind. They rode through the town of Sioux Falls during the middle of the night, and at 3:00 a.m., they stopped a stagecoach traveling southwestward to Yankton, asking the driver directions.[77]

On September 18, they must have hidden out during most of the day. That evening, they stayed with Ole Rongstad, a Norwegian immigrant living seven miles northeast of Canton, Dakota Territory, telling him they were laborers.[78]

As the brothers headed south on the morning of September 19, they met two men driving two teams of horses. They stopped the men and forced them to exchange their best horses for the ones the James boys were riding.[79]

As they crossed the Big Sioux River into Iowa, a mixed posse of Minnesotans and Dakotans chased after them. Three men outdistanced the others. When they got too close, the James boys shot at them. When the posse members realized none of them were armed, they quickly retreated as Frank and Jesse galloped off to the southeast. The posse rode to Beloit, Iowa, where they recruited twenty-five more men, but soon after they started following Frank and Jesse, a thunderstorm hit, wiping out the outlaws' trail.[80]

The James boys made good time heading south toward Sioux City, Iowa, along the Missouri River. By the afternoon of September 20, they were about ten miles northeast of Sioux City when a lone rider approached them. They drew their revolvers as the man asked if they were locals and introduced himself as Dr. Sidney Mosher from Sioux City. He told them he was on his way to Rudolph and Phoebe Mann's farm. Mrs. Mann was very ill, and he wasn't certain if he was headed in the right direction.[81]

At first the brothers didn't believe him. They thought he was a detective out to capture them and forced him to accompany them. They stopped at a few farmhouses along the way and asked people if they had heard of Dr. Mosher, which they had. After searching Mosher's clothes and finding only a lancet and a pocket medicine case, they finally determined he was telling the truth. They then admitted to him that they were part of the gang that robbed the Northfield bank.[82]

At one farmhouse, the robbers obtained bread, butter, and cake, and offered Mosher first pick of the food. At another farmhouse, they borrowed a saddle, claiming Dr. Mosher had need of it, but Frank used it to replace his sack of straw saddle.[83]

One robber told Mosher to tell the Sioux City bankers that when they come to rob their banks "They would do well to give up the vault keys peaceably, and thus avoid making martyrs of themselves." The other said they were not out to rob farmers and the poor but they were taking from men who robbed the poor.[84]

By 8:00 p.m. that night, they were well away from Sioux City. The robbers told Mosher to dismount; they were taking his horse. They made him exchange clothes with Frank. When Frank removed his pants, Mosher saw his leg wound for the first time. Pointing to a light in the distance, Jesse told him it was the Mann farm, where he had been heading. He told Mosher to run and not look back.[85]

Upon reaching the farmhouse, Mosher discovered it was owned by a family of Germans and not the Manns. The family put him up for the night, and the next morning, the farmer drove him in his wagon to Sioux City. Reaching town about noon, Mosher reported what had happened. The news created quite the sensation.[86]

That same day, September 21, 1876, the Younger brothers and Charlie Pitts were in trouble. Cold, wet, and miserable, they had continued to walk westward toward Madelia, Minnesota, but being unhorsed they could not make as much headway as the James boys.

Around 7:00 a.m., Jim Younger and Charlie Pitts walked along the road that ran by the Sorbel farm on the north shore of Lake Linden. Ole Sorbel and his seventeen-year-old son, Oscar, were milking their cows in the middle of the road as it was one of the few dry spots around. Jim and Charlie spoke pleasantly with Ole as they walked by, running their hands along the cows' sides as they passed. Oscar told Ole that those must be two of the robbers. Ole disagreed, saying they were nice fellows.[87]

Oscar was still convinced Jim and Charlie were two of the robbers and watched the direction they were heading. After finishing his chores, he followed and found where their trail led off into the woods. After warning neighbors about the suspected robbers, he returned home where his mother, Guri, told him that two more men, one with an arm in a sling, had walked up to the house and she had given them bread and butter to eat. Oscar was sure these were the Northfield robbers and, with his father giving his reluctant permission, Oscar jumped on one of their draft horses and rode eight miles to Madelia to report his sightings. Watonwan County Sheriff James Glispin and three men rode toward Lake Linden as more men gathered and began following them.[88]

After leaving the Sorbel farm, Cole and Bob Younger joined Jim and Charlie. They walked west of Lake Linden and began heading to the southwest. Bob was hurting and had to rest, telling the others to go on without him, but they refused to leave him. After resting they continued their slow journey.[89]

At about 11:00 a.m., they reached Lake Hanska's outlet where Sheriff Glispin and his three men caught up with them. Glispin ordered them to halt, but the outlaws ran out into a slough where the horses could not go. Glispin and his men fired their revolvers with no effect. They had to ride quite a ways to find solid ground for their horses to continue pursuit. The posse caught up with the gang at the north fork of the Watonwan River. Glispin ordered the gang to surrender, but they refused and approached the river to find a crossing. When the posse fired at them, the gang shot back before disappearing into the brush along the river.[90]

The gang crossed the swollen river to its south bank. Near a farmhouse, they saw a prairie-chicken-hunting party made up of Horace Thompson, president of the First National Bank of St. Paul, his son, four women, and two children. Thinking Thompson's weapons might be rifles and not the shotguns that they were, the gang turned away from them and headed back toward the river and into a five-acre thicket of willows.[91]

By now Sheriff Glispin's posse had grown to more than forty men. He stationed men around the thicket and on the opposite bank of the river, trapping the gang. Glispin asked Civil War veteran Captain William Murphy to lead a group to flush out the gang. Murphy called for volunteers. Six stepped forward, including Glispin. The seven men advanced in line into the willows, some of which reached five feet in height.[92]

Charlie Pitts said to Cole that they were surrounded and probably should surrender. Cole responded, "If you want to go out and surrender, go on. This is where Cole Younger dies." Charlie replied, "All right. I can die just as game as you can. Let's get it done."[93]

The line of volunteers got within fifteen feet of the outlaws. Spotting Glispin, Charlie jumped up, aiming his revolver. Glispin now had a rifle and aimed at Charlie. They both fired together. Charlie, hit in the chest, fell forward dead. Glispin was unhurt. The Youngers stood firing into the volunteers, who were firing back. A bullet slammed into Murphy's stomach, but he was unhurt. His briar pipe had taken the impact of the bullet.[94]

A bullet hit Jim Younger's right thigh and then another smashed through his left jaw, imbedding itself in the roof of his mouth, and he fell unconscious. A shotgun blast hit Cole in the back and the back of his head. He collapsed when a bullet struck him in the head and lodged behind his right eye. Bob was the last man standing, firing with his left, uninjured hand. He was hit in the right lung but fired until his revolver was empty.[95]

Murphy shouted ceasefire and demanded the outlaws surrender. Bob answered, "Do not shoot any more, as the boys are riddled." Sheriff Glispin ordered Bob to walk toward Murphy and surrender his gun. He was doing so when a posse member from across the river shot, hitting him under his arm, causing a flesh wound. Murphy and Glispin yelled again to cease fire.[96]

It was over. Charlie Pitts was dead, and the Younger brothers were shot up, but would survive in captivity.

Back in Sioux City, Iowa, telegrams were sent out alerting surrounding towns after Dr. Mosher had reported his encounter with the Northfield robbers. Two posses picked up the James boys' trail where they had released Mosher and followed it east toward Sac City, Iowa. There were many alleged encounters and sightings of the James boys all over the map. One of the last James boys encounters was with a little girl near Ida Springs, Iowa. She was eating a raw potato, and when she offered them some, they laughed and joked with her. The Iowa posses gave up their chase on the night of September 23. There were plenty of sightings of and encounters with the James brothers, but most of them turned out to be false. The James boys just disappeared as they had in the past.[97]

Joseph Heywood sacrificed his life protecting Northfield's First National Bank's money. The bank established a fund for Heywood's family. Adelbert Ames, who was a major bank investor, contributed $400, lamenting to his wife, Blanche, in a letter dated September 22, 1876, "This would buy the much-coveted stem-winding watch—and—well, I have forgotten what the other thing is I stand so much in need of."[98]

CHAPTER 8
THE KID SPILLS BLOOD

Kid Antrim spent the summer of 1876 working cattle and any other job he could get in Arizona's Sulphur Springs Valley, supplemented by winnings from the gambling tables in the settlement of McDowell's Store. In November, Miles Wood, the justice of the peace, gave the Kid a job as cook at his Hotel de Luna near McDowell's Store. Wood soon fired the Kid. He wasn't much of a cook, and Wood discovered the Kid was running with a gang of rustlers who made McDowell's Store their headquarters.[1]

Seventeen-year-old Kid Antrim fell under the influence of twenty-seven-year old John Mackie, a member of a gang of horse thieves operating between the Salt River and Tucson. Mackie had emigrated from Scotland to the United States, and at the age of fourteen, he joined the Union army as a drummer boy. After the Civil War, most of his life was spent in the army. Mackie was one hard hombre. On Sunday, September 19, 1875, he had been in Milton McDowell's saloon playing cards with T. R. Knox. They disputed over the game, and Mackie fired his pistol at Knox—the bullet entered Knox's throat, exiting his shoulder. Knox survived, and Mackie was thrown into Camp Grant's guardhouse until his October hearing in Tucson. Even though Knox was unarmed, two witnesses said Mackie shot in self-defense and he was released. On January 4, 1876, he was discharged from the Sixth Cavalry at Camp Grant as a private and joined the local gang of horse thieves. Now Mackie recruited Kid Antrim into the gang, showing him the finer points of stealing horses, saddles, blankets, and tack while avoiding detection and capture.[2]

Soldiers would ride into McDowell's Store and tie their horses to hitching rails while visiting the saloons to quench their thirst or the dancehalls for female companionship. While the soldiers were occupied, Mackie and the Kid would steal army saddles and blankets off army mounts and sometimes the horses themselves.[3]

Camp Grant's doctor and a lieutenant thought they could imbibe and protect their horses at the same time. They each tied one end of a long picket rope to his horse. Each carried the other end of the rope with him through the saloon door and held on while standing at the bar with a drink in one hand and the rope in the other. Mackie talked with the officers distracting them while the Kid cut the picket ropes and made off with the horses.[4]

The commander of Camp Grant, Major Charles Compton, was upset with this latest horse theft, declaring McDowell's Store off-limits. He sent Captain Gilbert Smith to Justice of the Peace Miles Wood, swearing out a complaint against Mackie and Antrim. Wood, in turn, sent his constable to arrest the thieves. Three times, the constable, an old man, attempted to find them but never could. Wood suspected the constable didn't want to find them.[5]

Soldiers from Camp Grant continued to visit McDowell's Store even though Major Compton had declared it off-limits. On November 17, First Sergeant Louis Hartman tied his horse outside a McDowell's Store brothel and went inside. When he was done with his visit, he stepped outside to discover his horse, saddle, blanket, and tack stolen.[6]

Returning to Camp Grant, Hartman reported the theft to Compton who ordered Hartman to recover his stolen horse. Five days later, Hartman rode out with four enlisted men, including Private Charles Smith from whom Kid Antrim had earlier stolen a horse.[7]

Hartman may have spent those five days investigating who had taken the horse. It must have been obvious that it was either Mackie, the Kid, or both. Hartman most likely also learned where the thief was heading with the horse.

Hartman's posse rode up the Aravaipa Valley toward the new mining boomtown of Globe, Arizona. On November 25, after riding a hundred miles, the posse caught up with Kid Antrim riding the army horse near McMillen's Camp, an illegal mining town on the San Carlos Apache Reservation. Pulling their revolvers on the Kid, they took the horse. They had no arrest warrant for him, so the posse left him there afoot as they returned to Camp Grant.[8]

Kid Antrim made his way to Globe, rejoining John Mackie and the other horse thieves where they continued to ply their trade. On the night of February 10, at Cottonwood Springs, a popular rest stop, Mackie and the Kid stole three army horses belonging to Company F from Camp Thomas. The soldiers must have recognized Kid Antrim as one of the thieves.[9]

On February 16, Camp Thomas and Camp Grant officers went to Justice of the Peace Miles Wood at his Hotel de Luna, where they presented Sergeant Hartman's horse-theft complaint against Kid Antrim. Wood used that to issue an arrest warrant for "Henry Antrim alias Kid" for horse theft.[10]

Knowing the Kid was in the Globe area, Wood sent a copy of the warrant and hand-drawn wanted posters to a Globe constable. The constable arrested the Kid, but he was able to escape. The constable arrested him again the next day and started to take him to Wood. At Cedar Springs, the Kid escaped again.[11]

Mackie and Kid Antrim brought back five stolen horses to Camp Thomas, most likely hoping that by returning the horses, the army would drop its charges. Mackie and the Kid returned to McDowell's Store, thinking everything was back to normal. Walking into the Hotel de Luna, they sat down at a table and ordered breakfast. Wood saw them come in, and when their food was prepared, he took it out to them on a large platter. Placing the platter on their table and shoving it toward them, he pulled out a six-gun. Wood ordered them to put up their hands and walk straight out the door.[12]

Caleb Martin, Wood's cook, got his gun, and together they marched Mackie and the Kid over two miles to Camp Grant where the two horse thieves were locked in the guardhouse, and Wood and Martin returned to the hotel. The Kid was bound and determined to escape—he had done it before. He was let out of the guardhouse to use the privy. Somehow, he had obtained a handful of salt. As he was being escorted to the privy, he threw the salt in his guard's eyes and ran toward Bonito Creek, but soldiers ran him down and threw him back into the guardhouse.[13]

When Wood learned of the Kid's attempted escape, he had blacksmith Francis "Windy" Cahill rivet shackles on the Kid's ankles. Wood and his wife returned to Camp Grant that evening for a reception being held by Major Compton. While a dance was in progress in Compton's quarters, the Kid was planning his next escape.[14]

Toward the top of the guardhouse wall was an open ventilator. Mackie helped the Kid get up to the small opening where the Kid was able to wiggle his small body through and drop outside into the darkness to the ground below. He hobbled over two miles through the night to George Atkin's cantina at McDowell's Store where Tom Varley, the bartender, broke open the shackles for him.[15]

The Kid left for Camp Thomas where H. F. "Sorghum" Smith gave him a job helping around his hay camp. The Kid must have worked there for quite a while, as he asked Smith for forty dollars of his pay, which he used to buy a six-shooter, belt, scabbard, and cartridges at the Camp Thomas post trader's store. He also had enough to purchase store-bought pants and shoes.[16]

It was Friday night, August 17, 1877, and patrons in George Atkin's cantina at McDowell's Store were enjoying themselves when in walked Kid Antrim. The Kid must have thought he was safe enough from the law and with the butt of his six-shooter protruding from the waist of his pants, he must have thought no one would want to tangle with him. Texas cowhand Gus Gildea said the Kid looked like a "country jake" with his store-bought pants and shoes instead of boots. The Kid sat down to a poker game. At some point, he got into an argument with Windy Cahill, the stout blacksmith who had placed the shackles on his ankles.[17]

Thirty-two-year-old Windy Cahill was a loudmouth bully. Being small and skinny, the Kid had always been one of Cahill's favorite targets. Gildea said Cahill would throw the Kid to the floor, ruffle his hair, slap his face, and humiliate him in front of others—but not tonight.[18]

Cahill called the Kid a pimp. The Kid said Cahill was a son of a bitch. Cahill grabbed the Kid in a bear hug and wrestled him out the door. The crowd followed the combatants outside, shouting as they formed a ring around them. Cahill slammed the Kid to the ground, but the Kid got back up and the two continued to fight. Cahill threw the Kid on the ground two more times. Using his knees to pin the Kid's arms to the ground, Cahill sat on top of him, slapping his face.

"You are hurting me. Let me up!" the Kid said.

"I want to hurt you. That's why I got you down," Cahill said.

The Kid's right hand reached the butt of his six-gun, pulled it out of his pants, and pushed the muzzle against Cahill's stomach. Cahill reached for the revolver as the Kid cocked the hammer then pulled the trigger.[19]

There was a deafening roar. Cahill slumped to the side. The Kid pulled himself away from underneath Cahill and ran. Gambler Joseph Murphey's racing pony, Cashew, was tied nearby. The Kid jumped on Cashew and galloped away into the night. No one chased after him.[20]

Cahill was alive. They put him in a wagon and drove him to Camp Grant where assistant surgeon Fred Ainsworth examined him. There was too much damage to internal organs and Windy

Cahill died the next day. Miles Wood held a coroner's inquest. The jury's verdict was that the death of Francis Cahill was "criminal and unjustifiable, and that Henry Antrim alias Kid is guilty thereof."[21]

Kid Antrim did not wait around to find out if Cahill lived or died but lit out for New Mexico where he thought he might have a chance to elude Arizona authorities. He rode to Richard Knight's ranch and stagecoach station southwest of Silver City in the foothills of the Burro Mountains. From there, he sent Cashew back to Joseph Murphey. After a two-week stay at Knight's ranch, the Kid left, concerned that Arizona posses might be hunting for him.[22]

Heading straight east, the Kid arrived at Apache Tejo southeast of Silver City. There, he joined a band of horse thieves called the Boys under the leadership of Jesse Evans.[23]

Jesse Evans, originally from Missouri, had worked cattle in Texas then traveled to New Mexico where he worked for cattleman John Chisum. Leaving Chisum's employment, he rustled

cattle and stole horses, becoming the leader of the Boys, a gang that ranged throughout New Mexico and beyond.[24]

Back on New Year's Eve 1875, Evans and some of the Boys had been at a dance at a Las Cruces, New Mexico, saloon. A fight erupted between them and soldiers of the Eighth Cavalry. The Boys brutally beat a private who would die several days later. In the melee, the soldiers severely injured John Kinney, who the Boys worked for and who was a major player in New Mexico's rustler network. The Boys left the saloon, and the soldiers stood at the bar celebrating their victory, but the Boys returned with their guns, shooting into the crowd killing a Mexican and a private while injuring three additional privates. No one attempted to arrest the Boys.[25]

Later that month, Quinino Fletcher had been bragging he had killed a friend of Evans named Mansfield in Chihuahua, Mexico. At 10:30 p.m., on the night of January 19, 1875, Fletcher stepped out of a Las Cruces saloon into the main street. Three men confronted him, firing six bullets into his head and body. There was no doubt in anyone's mind that Evans was one of the killers. The townspeople were so afraid of Evans that Fletcher's body lay in the middle of the street until the following day.[26]

On September 18, 1877, Evans and the Boys stole horses from Lincoln County rancher John Tunstall, his foreman, Dick Brewer, and attorney Alexander McSween and drove the herd westward to sell. While the Boys were in the Apache Tejo area, they recruited Kid Antrim to become a gang member. On October 1, 1877, they stole several horses from the L. F. Pass Coal Camp, sixteen miles southwest of Silver City. The horses' owners pursued the thieves until losing their tracks on the road to Apache Tejo. The next day, C. A. Carpenter, a Silver City resident, spotted Kid Antrim riding with the Boys and their stolen horses.[27]

They rode eastward, picking up more horses along the way. Seven miles east of abandoned Fort Cummings, nine of them, well-armed with revolvers and Winchesters, held up a westbound stagecoach. When the driver told them he was not carrying any money, they let him proceed on but not before they made him share a drink of whiskey with them. They stopped at way stations, eating, drinking, and not paying their bills. Passing through La Mesilla, the Kid stole a horse belonging to the daughter of Sheriff Mariano Barela. On October 8, the Boys arrived at one of their hangouts, Shedd's Ranch, on the eastern slope of the Organ Mountains.[28]

Somewhere along the way, the Kid became separated from the Boys. The most likely of several stories as to how he entered Lincoln County, New Mexico, is that he arrived on foot at the Seven River store in the Pecos Valley, claiming Apaches had stolen his horse in the Guadalupe Mountains. Since the Kid was wanted for Windy Cahill's murder, he needed to change his identity. The Kid told people his name was William H. Bonney or Billy.[29]

CHAPTER 9

SAFE HARBORS

After eluding all posses chasing them after the Northfield, Minnesota, bank robbery, Frank and Jesse James vanished into Missouri. St. Louis Chief of Police James McDonough was assigned to track down the James boys. He assured Missouri Governor Charles Hardin on September 29, 1876, that his men would capture the James boys if they should enter the state from the northwest.[1]

McDonough received a tip on October 12 that one of the James boys was receiving medical treatment at Dr. William Noland's house, five miles outside of Independence in Jackson County, Missouri. McDonough's men surrounded the doctor's house and captured a man with a leg wound whom they believed was Frank James; but he wasn't. It took until October 18 to convince law enforcement that the man was John Goodwin of Cheneyville, Louisiana.[2]

On November 22, an informer told Clay County Sheriff John Groom that the James boys were on their way to the Samuel farm. Groom and his four-man posse arrived at the farm after dark. They spotted Frank, who saw them at the same time. Frank fired a warning shot into the air as Groom and a posse member shot at him and missed. Frank fired back at them as he and Jesse mounted their horses and raced away. One of the brothers shouted, "Come on you cowardly sons of bitches."[3]

During the next few days, Groom and his posse attempted to catch the brothers, but they were always one step ahead of the posse and finally vanished. For the next month there were a couple of Frank and Jesse sightings, but they amounted to nothing. The James boys disappeared from public view.[4]

Frank and Jesse were good at covering their trail for the next few years. Jesse may have spent time with their old protector General Jo Shelby in Lafayette County, Missouri. Some believe the James boys went to Texas and owned a cattle ranch on the Pecos River. One man claimed he saw them in Texas and then later in Leadville, Colorado, committing stagecoach robberies, but there was no evidence.[5]

In March 1878, the James boys' good friend John Edwards published his book *Noted Guerrillas, or the Warfare of the Border*, in which he told the story of the war in Missouri from the bushwhacker viewpoint. Thousands of copies were sold, and it became very popular, especially in Missouri. Edwards gave the James boys and Younger brothers prominent roles in the book, stressing they were forced to go to war because of Yankee aggression. Edwards explained that the James boys and Younger brothers had wanted to return to normal lives after the war but couldn't due to Yankee persecution. Edwards wrote regarding the James boys' and Younger brothers' desire to return to normal lives, "No men ever went to work with a heartier good will to keep good faith with society and make themselves amenable to the law. No men ever sacrificed more for peace, and for the bare privilege of going back again into the obscurity of civil life and becoming again a part of the enterprising economy of the commonwealth. They were not permitted so to do, try as they would, and as hard, and as patiently."[6]

The August 6, 1878, issue of the *Saint Louis Republican* reported Jesse James had spent several months in Callaway County, Missouri, using the alias James Franklin. He had wounds that Dr. Martin Yates treated. Franklin lived at the homes of Washington Kidwell and Allen Womack. He gave singing lessons and taught religion. The story is told that Franklin and Dr. Yates entered the Whaley Hotel in Fulton, Missouri. They sat at a table and ate with Pinkerton detectives who were searching for Jesse James. After they finished eating, Franklin disappeared.[7]

John Edwards, now editor of the *Sedalia Democrat*, blasted the *Republican*'s story. He wrote that the James boys had not "touched Missouri soil for one year," and would not be committing any more robberies.[8]

Frank and Jesse went back to using their aliases, blending into new communities. Jesse was again John Davis Howard and would go by Dave. Zee was now Mary and their young son, Jesse, was Tim. Jesse moved his family to Humphreys County, Tennessee, most likely in August 1877. He rented a cabin and farmland near Big Bottom, southwest of Waverly, where his profession was gentleman farmer and grain speculator. Frank used the alias Ben J. Woodson and Annie was known as Fannie. In August 1877, they arrived in Nashville, Tennessee, where Frank said he was a farmer from Indiana. They rented a cabin and farm near Whites Creek where Frank put in ten hours a day working the fields.[9]

Zee was pregnant and gave birth to premature twin boys in February 1878. Jesse named them after the two doctors who cared for them, Gould and Montgomery, but the twins died several days later. Annie was also pregnant and gave birth to a boy on February 6, 1878. They named him Robert Franklin James.[10]

The Howards were hospitable to their Big Bottom neighbors. Zee was an excellent cook, and they were always inviting people over for dinner. Jesse was known to be kind to children and respectful to the women.[11] It was a peaceful time for the Howards and Woodsons. They had found "the obscurity of civil life."

When Kid Antrim arrived on foot at the Seven Rivers store in New Mexico's Pecos Valley in October 1878 he was using the alias William H. Bonney and would go by the nicknames Kid and Billy.

There has been lots of research as to how he came up with his alias, but it all remains speculation.[12]

Physically, the Kid was lean and wiry, standing five feet, seven inches tall and weighing about 135 pounds. He had blue eyes, brown wavy hair, and a light beard. His two upper front teeth slightly protruded. The Kid kept himself clean and wore a Mexican sombrero. Friendly and charismatic, he enjoyed a good joke. He was considered intelligent and could read and write. He didn't smoke and seldom drank. He gambled and enjoyed dancing with the women. He spoke Spanish fluently and readily made friends with Hispanos, who called him *Billito* and *el Chivato*. The Kid constantly practiced with his firearms. This was who the Kid was when he arrived at the Seven Rivers store. He quickly learned that by entering Lincoln County, he was entering a volatile situation.[13]

New Mexico's Lincoln County was massive, totaling thirty thousand square miles, equaling the area of South Carolina. Its topography rose from rangeland bisected by rivers to snow-packed mountains. Established in 1869, the county was located in the southeast corner of New Mexico Territory. In the late 1870s, it was sparsely populated with Mescalero Apaches on their reservation, Hispano farmers, soldiers and former soldiers, small-time Anglo farmers and ranchers, and Texas cattlemen and cowhands. The county seat was Lincoln, a small Hispano town located on the west-to-east-running Bonito River. Nine miles to the west, also on the Bonito River, stood Fort Stanton to guard the Apaches.[14]

The Pecos River ran from north to south through the Pecos Plain in the eastern part of the county. It was public domain and good country for grazing cattle. In 1867, John Chisum had brought Texas longhorns up the Goodnight-Loving Trail from Texas, and by 1876, had eighty thousand head of cattle. Other cattlemen followed Chisum's example, but Chisum had the largest herds, making them susceptible to rustling. Some of the smaller ranchers accused Chisum of rustling their animals, but he countered that he was there first and their animals must have mixed in with his.[15]

Chisum's ranching outfit was known as the Jinglebob. His men would cut the cattle's ears so that the lower portion of the ear hung straight down in what was called a jinglebob. Even with this distinctive marking, Chisum's herds were still a favorite target for rustlers. By 1878, Chisum's sole market for his cattle was the St. Louis cattle-contracting firm, Hunter, Evans & Co. Chisum had sold thirty thousand head of cattle to Hunter, and it was taking years for his men to round up and deliver the cattle to fulfill his contract.[16]

Several settlements sprang up along the Pecos River. To the south was the rough-and-tumble Seven Rivers. In the middle was Roswell near Chisum's South Spring ranch headquarters, which was four and a half miles to the southeast. To the north was Fort Sumner, an old, abandoned military post bought by Lucien Maxwell, who made it his headquarters and settled twenty-five to thirty Hispano families there. Maxwell had died in 1875, but his son Pete carried on the family ranching and mercantile businesses and investments.[17]

Controlling economic and governmental interests, L. G. Murphy and Company, which later became J. J. Dolan and Company, was the major force to reckon with in Lincoln County. Known as "the House," it was the contractor for supplying beef and other goods to the Mescalero Apaches and to Fort Stanton. Lawrence G. Murphy, an Irishman, and his partner, Emil Fritz, a German, owned the fort store, procuring lucrative government contracts supplying the fort and the Mescalero Apaches with beef, corn, flour, and other provisions. Murphy and Fritz also acted as a bank, loaning the soldiers, officers, and civilians money when they needed it. They bribed and intimidated Indian agents. They sold merchandise to Anglo and Hispano farmers at exorbitant prices and then paid for the farmers' produce at reduced rates.[18]

Murphy and Fritz fought for the Union during the Civil War and afterwards served on the frontier. In 1866, both Murphy and Fritz were honorably discharged at Fort Stanton, Murphy as a major and Fritz as a colonel. Murphy was convivial and a heavy drinker. Fritz was all business. He had tuberculosis and liked to spend his time away from the store as much as possible at his ranch several miles south of Lincoln. In the summer of 1873, Fritz returned to Germany for a visit, becoming ill and dying in June 1874.[19]

In the summer of 1873, James J. Dolan had become a junior partner in the firm. Dolan, an Irishman, arrived in New York City at the age of five, clerked in a dry goods store as a twelve-year-old, and joined the Union army in 1863 at the age of fifteen. He was discharged in 1869 in New Mexico where he was hired as a clerk by L. G. Murphy and Company. Jimmie Dolan was a shrewd negotiator and was good at scheming, scamming, and concocting deals in secret. Jimmie was a heavy drinker, too, and had a mean temper, but Murphy adored him and treated him like a son.[20]

That same summer, Jimmie Dolan became embroiled in a dispute with Captain James Randlett and was arrested for attempted murder. Randlett reported to the War Department, "This firm I know to have been defrauding the government since my arrival at the Post." The letter went on to state that the firm's contract as Indian agents was fraudulent, and they tried to pass on inferior goods to the army. Randlett went on to write, "I consider that L. G. Murphy & Co.'s store is nothing more or less than a den of infamy, and recommend the removal of this firm from this reservation." The army acted on Randlett's recommendation and banned the firm from the fort.[21]

Kicked out of the fort, L. G. Murphy & Company moved its operations to Lincoln, where it already had a small store. Murphy built a large two-story building from which the nickname "the House" originated. On the first floor was the store, as well as offices, a saloon, and gambling hall. The second floor had rooms for employees and a meeting room called "the Lodge Room." The House also had a restaurant, hotel, and the Rio Bonito Brewery in Lincoln.[22]

In 1877, Murphy's doctors diagnosed that he had cancer of the bowels, recommending he drink to kill the pain. Taking their recommendation to heart, he removed himself from active participation in the House and spent his time at his ranch west of Fort Stanton. He would later die in Santa Fe on October 20, 1878.[23]

The House became J. J. Dolan and Company and continued to supply cattle and goods to the fort and reservation, acting as a subcontractor for firms such as William Rosenthal out of Santa Fe. Jimmie Dolan took on new partners. One was another hothead Irishman, John Riley. Johnny ran the House's cattle operation. The other partner was silent: Jacob "Billy" Mathews, a former Confederate soldier from Tennessee who worked as a clerk for the House but presented the ruse that he was a disinterested employee so he could glean information they might not otherwise learn.[24]

In the spring of 1877, Jimmie Dolan shot and killed one of his employees, Hiraldo Jaramillo. He claimed self-defense and the justice of the peace in Lincoln bought it; however, many Lincoln residents thought otherwise. Members of the House bragged that it controlled the sheriff and county government and was in league with those controlling New Mexico territorial government. Many believed the New Mexico territorial government was controlled by the Santa Fe Ring, a small group of businessmen and government officials, including Governor Samuel Axtell, who colluded to financially benefit themselves. One of the major players in the ring was US District Attorney Thomas Catron, who made loans in Lincoln County through the House. Virtually controlling its politics and economy, Catron was considered the dictator of New Mexico. Of course, those who allegedly took part in the ring denied its existence. The so-called Santa Fe Ring was made up of Republicans, while Lincoln County's ring, the House and its cronies, were Democrats. However, when making money was involved, political affiliations were set aside between the Santa Fe Ring and the Lincoln County Ring.[25]

The House had a cattle herd and cow camp on the Pecos River downstream from Seven Rivers. Although the House provided beef to the reservation and the fort, its herd size remained constant. There were those who believed it was replenished by animals stolen from John Chisum. People believed that the rustlers, Jesse Evans and the Boys, were secretly on the House payroll.[26]

John Chisum had been having rustler problems ever since he moved his headquarters to South Springs ranch. Lots of thieving of Jinglebob cattle was taking place in the Seven Rivers area. Chisum's response to the thieving would result in what was called Chisum's War or War on the Pecos.

In early 1877, one of Chisum's informants notified him about suspicious activity taking place around Hugh Beckwith's ranch, several miles north of Seven Rivers. Chisum sent some men to investigate, where they found a thousand cattle ears buried out by Beckwith's corrals. Since Chisum had his animals' ears cut to form the drooping jinglebob, the only way a rustler could sell stolen Jinglebob cattle was to cut off the animals' ears. There was no doubt in Chisum's mind that those ears belonged to Jinglebob cattle. Chisum went to El Paso, Texas, where he found his cattle and got descriptions of the men who had sold them. Chisum's foreman tracked down one of the thieves and shot, killing him.[27]

Chisum believed ranchers in the Seven Rivers area were in cahoots to steal his cattle. When it was reported that he named six small ranchers who he suspected and said they needed killing, those ranchers became his enemies and aligned themselves with the House.[28]

On April 10, 1877, Jimmie Dolan and others were on their way below Seven Rivers to drive cattle up to Lincoln to fulfill a contract. Some of Chisum's men were spotted on the road behind them. When Dolan and the others saw Chisum's men disappear into an arroyo, they turned back, charged the Chisum men, firing a volley of shots at them, then turned and made a run for it. Chisum believed this action proved rustlers from the Seven Rivers area were in league with the House to steal his cattle. He went to the commander of Fort Stanton, Captain George Purrington, and asked him to go after the Seven Rivers ranchers. Purrington said it was a civil matter and to take it up with Lincoln County Sheriff Bill Brady. Forty-seven-year-old Brady, an Irishman, had served in the army with Murphy and Fritz. He was a family man and respected leader in the community. However, he was friends with Murphy and Dolan and heavily in debt to the House. Brady told Chisum, Seven Rivers was currently part of Doña Ana County and he needed to take his problems to the sheriff of that county.[29]

Since Chisum believed no one was going to help him, he decided to take matters into his own hands. On April 20, 1877, Chisum led thirty men on an attack of Beckwith's ranch. The adobe ranch house was built like a fort, and a number of ranchers in the Seven Rivers area had taken refuge there as they were worried Chisum would carry out his earlier threats. Chisum's men surrounded the ranch house and cut off the water-supply ditch to the house, meaning to eventually force out the defenders. A few shots fired from both sides took place during the day with no one hurt. That night two defenders sneaked out and rode to Mesilla, Doña Ana County seat, to get help from the sheriff. When Chisum learned this, he sent a man under a flag of truce, saying the women and children could leave the ranch house and would not be harmed; however, they refused. The fighting continued, but Chisum's men were at positions seven hundred to eight hundred yards out, and their shots had little effect. They refused to move closer for fear of being shot. By April 22, the battle fizzled out, and Chisum's men rode away.[30]

Doña Ana County Deputy Sheriff Andy Boyle led a posse after Chisum and his men, who had returned to the South Spring ranch. Boyle found Chisum in bed at Bob Wyle's cow camp. He had come down with smallpox and could not be moved. Chisum posted bond, and the posse left him there. Chisum's War sputtered but did not die out.[31]

Chisum needed allies to take on the House. One of these was Alexander McSween, known as Mac. McSween was born in 1843 to Scottish parents in Canada. He studied law at Washington University in St. Louis, Missouri, then moved to Kansas, where in 1873 he married Susan Hummer in Atchison. He suffered from asthma so the McSweens were on their way to Silver City, New Mexico, where they thought the climate might be helpful for Alexander, when they met Miguel Otero Sr., who convinced them to try Lincoln, New Mexico, where they arrived in March 1875. Liking what they saw, they decided to stay.[32]

McSween was a good lawyer, and his business boomed so much that he invited a brother-in-law, David Shield, to become his partner. McSween was honest and if he didn't like a case, he would not take it. He handled legal matters for both John Chisum and the House. A member of the Republican Party, he was active in the community, working to improve the school and asking the Presbyterian Church to send missionaries.[33]

McSween learned early what kind of men were running the House. He showed his wife samples of inferior flour they were selling the Indian agent as top quality. On one occasion, when he presented a bill for a hundred-dollar service to Johnny Riley, Riley argued over the price, wanting it reduced. McSween responded, "All right, I'll cut the bill in half, as you wish. I consider it worth $50 to find out the sort of man you are." McSween's disapproval of the House's business practices soon put him at odds with them.[34]

Another John Chisum ally was John Tunstall. Tunstall was born in Hackney, London, England, on March 6, 1853. His family was well-to-do, his father being a partner in a successful mercantile firm. Tunstall first arrived in Canada on business in 1872, and then traveled through the American West in search of a place for long-term investment. After conducting his own research, he settled on cattle ranching in Lincoln County, arriving in the town of Lincoln on November 6, 1876.[35]

One of the first people Tunstall met was Mac McSween, and they soon formed a solid friendship. When the House learned Tunstall was looking for a ranch, Jimmie Dolan offered McSween $5,000 to persuade Tunstall to buy the Lawrence Murphy ranch. Knowing the title to Murphy's ranch was not free and clear, McSween refused the bribe and told Tunstall. The next time the House approached Tunstall about buying Murphy's property, he told them he knew the title was in question and would not be duped by them.[36]

McSween suggested Tunstall look at other land that could be considered free public land. Being a foreigner, Tunstall could not claim public land for himself, but with McSween's help he had proxies—Sam Corbet and Dick Brewer, who would act as Tunstall's ranch foreman—make claims for him. Tunstall's first acquisition was southeast of Lincoln, the former Mathews and Freeman place on the Rio Peñasco, which had good springs. His next acquisition was four thousand acres south of and closer to Lincoln in the valley of the Rio Feliz. For years it had been the Robert and Ellen Casey place. William Wilson had shot and killed Robert Casey in the street in Lincoln in 1875. The Caseys had failed to file a claim on their land, so Tunstall acquired it. Some people believed that by filing on the Casey place, Tunstall and McSween had stolen the land from Ellen Casey.[37]

To stock his land, in May 1877, Tunstall bought at public auction four hundred head of cattle at half their value. The cattle had belonged to Ellen Casey, who was forced to sell them to settle her debts. Tunstall assured the widow Casey if she could come up with the money in a reasonable amount of time, he would sell the cattle back to her at the price he paid with moderate interest.[38]

Tunstall had additional investment plans, including a store and bank. With his mercantile background, he believed he could break the House's economic stranglehold on Lincoln County and turn a good profit. McSween helped him get established and operating for a percentage of the profit and Tunstall planned to make him a partner. In the spring of 1877, J. H. Tunstall and Co. was opening for business in its new building down the street from the House's building.[39]

Jimmie Dolan walked by Tunstall's building as it was being erected and said, "They'll never do much business in that store."[40]

Lawrence Murphy commented to Robert Widenmann, a friend of Tunstall's, "He [Tunstall] is not in very good standing with the people." Widenmann told Tunstall what Murphy had said. Tunstall laughed and said, "I am going ahead with my store. If they make trouble, I'll not hesitate to show up their crookedness and general rottenness. They have oppressed this section long enough. I shall do all I can to lift their yoke from it."[41]

Concentrating on the start-up of his store, Tunstall hired Sam Corbet as store clerk. McSween had introduced Tunstall to John Chisum, and the three of them decided what Lincoln needed was a proper bank, so they formed the Lincoln County Bank. Part of

Tunstall's store was partitioned off for the bank office. Chisum was named president, McSween was vice president, and Tunstall was cashier. The bank opened in August 1877. Things were looking up for Tunstall and his friends.[42]

However, on September 18, 1877, Jesse Evans and the Boys stole horses and mules from Tunstall, McSween, and Dick Brewer. Brewer, who had his own ranch but was also Tunstall's foreman and no friend of the House, gave chase and caught up with the Boys at Shed's Ranch. Having no backup, all he could do was demand the horses and mules back. Evans laughed at him and said no, not after all the hard work it took to get them. Evans admired Brewer's courage and told him he could have his own horses back, but Brewer said he wanted all the horses or nothing and Evans could go to hell. Continuing west, Evans kept all the horses and Brewer went home empty-handed.[43]

When the Kid entered Lincoln County in October 1877, the situation was a powder keg with a short fuse, and it was lit. Somehow the Kid became separated from the Boys, who went straight to Hugh Beckwith's ranch for rest and relaxation.[44]

There are several stories about how and where the Kid arrived in Lincoln County. One of the best ones is that he arrived at the Seven Rivers store, owned by small-time rancher Heiskell Jones. His wife, Barbara, was known as "Ma'am Jones," and together they had nine boys and one girl. Ma'am Jones was a legend in her own time—taking care of neighbors and strangers alike—feeding them, treating their wounds and illnesses, and giving them shelter. When the Kid arrived, Ma'am Jones took him in and cared for him. The Jones family all liked the Kid.[45]

Ma'am Jones remembered the arrival of the Kid. Heiskell was not home. The time was after 3 a.m., "for she could feel the approach of dawn." She heard a noise outside. Could it be Apaches? She got her Winchester and when she looked out through a slit in the wall, she saw movement and ordered whoever was trying to hide to come out. A slender boy stumbled toward the house. She ran out and helped him inside. It was the Kid and he was in bad shape. Ma'am Jones fed him, put him to bed, and nursed him back to health. Later he told her his name was Billy Bonney.[46]

The Kid told Ma'am that he and another rider named Tom O'Keefe were crossing the Guadalupe Mountains when they were attacked by Indians. He became separated from O'Keefe, who raced away with the horses while the Kid hid from the Indians. For three days, he hid by day and traveled by night until he reached Seven Rivers.[47]

The Kid stayed with the Jones family, helping with the chores, playing with the children, and shooting at targets with one of the Jones boys, John. They liked the Kid and gave him a horse so he could get around.[48]

After losing her ranch and four hundred head of cattle to Tunstall, Ellen Casey decided to take her five children and what possessions and cattle she had left and return to Texas. Reaching the Seven Rivers store, they stayed there for about three weeks. Casey's fourteen-year-old daughter, Lily, recorded seeing the Kid in action. She said he constantly practiced with his pistol and rifle. He hung along the side of his horse as it galloped, shooting like an Apache. He prided himself in picking up handkerchiefs and other items from the ground as his horse raced by.[49]

According to Lily, the Kid had ridden downriver to the House cow camp, where he got into trouble with the foreman William "Buck" Morton. Morton gave the Kid "a bawling out" when the Kid took an interest in Morton's girlfriend, considered the Belle of the Pecos Valley. The Kid swore he would get even with Morton.[50]

Jesse Evans and the Boys were still at Hugh Beckwith's ranch. Evans was not happy with the Kid. When they had passed through Mesilla, New Mexico, unknown to Evans, the Kid had stolen a horse belonging to the daughter of Evans' good friend Doña Ana County Sheriff Mariano Barela. According to Lily Casey, the Kid told her mother, Ellen, that Barela had sent word to him through Jesse Evans that his daughter was brokenhearted over the loss of her pet. If the Kid did not return her horse, Barela would come after the Kid and kill him. Through a couple of transactions, Barela's daughter's horse was now in the possession of Ellen Casey. The Kid wanted to trade his horse for it, but Ellen would not do so when she saw the Kid's horse had Chisum's brand on it. She was worried the Kid might have stolen his horse from Chisum.[51]

Evans and the Boys must have believed themselves invincible. The October 13, 1877, issue of the *Mesilla Valley Independent* published a sarcastic article about the Boys' return from their latest horse-stealing raid. The newspaper called them the Banditti and gave Evans the title "Captain." In the same issue, it published a letter to the editor from "Fence Rail" with the heading "Lincoln, N.M. Oct 9th. 1877" describing the Boys' victory party after their successful raid.[52]

The story noted that while the Boys were in camp in the Sacramento Mountains, "About 8 o'clock p.m. Messrs. Riley and Longwell came along in a buggy . . . and on passing, the entire party, numbering seventeen well-armed and mounted men, paraded on the roadside." This had to be House partner Johnny Riley and House employee Jim Longwell.[53]

Fence Rail's letter contained a lengthy resolution from the Boys, stating in part, "Resolved: That the public is our oyster, and that having the power, we claim the right to appropriate any property we may take a fancy to, and that we will exercise that right regardless of consequences."[54]

Tunstall and McSween learned that the Boys were at Hugh Beckwith's ranch at Seven Rivers. They persuaded a reluctant Sheriff Bill Brady to head a posse to go after the Boys. Dick Brewer, who was deputy constable and who would go with Brady, selected fifteen men he could count on for a posse, and Tunstall outfitted them with firearms, ammunition, and supplies. The posse left Lincoln for Beckwith's ranch on Friday, October 12.[55]

The posse reached Beckwith's on October 17. After a brief gun battle, the posse captured four of the Boys: Jesse Evans, Frank

Baker, Tom Hill, and George Davis. They had in their possession one of Tunstall's horses and horses belonging to John Chisum's brother Pitser. Three days later, they were locked in the Lincoln County jail.[56]

The jail was an adobe building overtop a ten-foot-deep pit. The pit's walls were lined with timber, and the ceiling was timber. Prisoners were made to descend through a hatch down a ladder into the pit. They were made to wear leg irons that were attached to the walls, the ladder was pulled up, and then the hatch shut. As they spent their time in the pit, the Boys played cards and boasted their friends would come for them.[57]

What was the Kid doing at that time? There is no record. He most likely took whatever jobs he could find in the Seven Rivers area.

In Lincoln, Tunstall and McSween opposed bail for the Boys. Shackled to the walls of the unsanitary pit, the Boys were brought outside for one hour a day. On Sunday, November 4, Tunstall visited them and did some odd things. He had run into the posse when it was bringing in the Boys, and the Boys reminded Tunstall that he had promised them a bottle of whiskey. They told him they had sold his team of mules to a priest down in Old Mexico. They joked and laughed together. Tunstall sent them that bottle of whiskey he had promised and returned to joke with them again.[58]

About a week after Tunstall's visits, Caterino Romero, who was in jail along with Lucas Gallegos for the murder of Gallegos's nephew, escaped during the one-hour exercise period. Earlier, before his escape, Romero had told the jailer that the Boys were weakening their shackles fastened to the walls and were filing through their leg irons. The jailer then told Sheriff Bill Brady and Mac McSween. McSween informed Tunstall; but Brady took no action.[59]

Instead, Brady, who had been drinking, entered Tunstall's store and said to Tunstall that Dick Brewer and Tunstall only wanted to visit the prisoners, so they could help them escape. McSween was there and heard the exchange between Tunstall and Brady.[60]

Tunstall responded by saying Brady knew the prisoners were cutting through their shackles and he was taking no action. Tunstall continued, "You dare accuse me, who have aided in the arrest of these persons who have threatened my life, with assisting in their escape?"

Brady put his hand on the butt of his pistol as if to draw it, but McSween stepped between them and put his hand on Brady's shoulder and said a peace officer should not violate the law by shooting someone. Brady relented and as he left he said to Tunstall, "I won't shoot you now, you haven't long to run, I ain't always going to be sheriff."[61]

More than twenty of the Boys' friends, including the Kid, rode quietly into Lincoln at 3:00 a.m., November 17, 1877. Seven Rivers rancher Andy Boyle, who as Doña Ana County deputy sheriff back in April had led a posse after John Chisum and his men, now led the Boys rescuers. Ten of them dismounted and entered the unlocked jail door. They pulled their revolvers on the sleeping guard and began to smash the locked hatch with rock-filled sacks. In the pit below, the Boys had worked the iron shackles out of the wooden walls and were busting them from their legs with tools that someone had sneaked to them. Once the hatch was broken open, the ladder was lowered, the prisoners climbed out, and all rode away with no pursuit.[62]

The Boys and their liberators were on their way to Dick Brewer's ranch when they stopped the brothers Juan and Francisco Trujillo. Francisco tried to get away. The Kid chased after him. Francisco stopped, pulled his Winchester, and aimed at the Kid, and the Kid did the same. The standoff ended when the Boys threatened to kill Juan, and Francisco stood down. The Boys "borrowed" Juan's saddle and weapons for Don Lucas Gallegos, who was not one of the Boys but who had also been set free in the jail break.[63]

Brewer was not at his ranch when the Boys and friends arrived. Brewer's ranch hands cooked them breakfast and then the Boys helped themselves to eight of Tunstall's horses. They told the ranch hands they promised not to steal from Tunstall ever again and that they would send the horses back later. Seven of the eight horses were later returned.[64]

The Kid returned with the Boys to Seven Rivers; most of them went to Beckwith's ranch. The Kid probably hung out at Jones's Seven Rivers store.[65]

Someone informed John Tunstall that the Kid had his team of horses. The Kid and the horses were found at Seven Rivers, where he was arrested, taken to Lincoln, and locked in the pit. The evidence against the Kid must have been flimsy. He and Tunstall may have reached an agreement for the Kid to leave the Boys and join with him. Tunstall must have dropped the charges, and the Kid was free again.[66]

After leaving jail, the eighteen-year-old Kid spent time with Missouri cousins Frank and George Coe at their places on the Rio Ruidoso below Lincoln and became good friends with them. Years later, Frank said the Kid first arrived at Charlie and Manuela Bowdre's farm and he brought the Kid over to Frank's place. He also became good friends with Frank's brother-in-law Albert "Ab" Saunders. The Kid was easygoing and had a good sense of humor, making friends with Anglos and Hispanos alike.[67]

Lorencita Miranda said, "[The kid was] always nice to the Spanish people and they all liked him." Guadalupe Baca de Gallegos said the Kid was "always courteous and a real gentleman." Carlotta Baca Brent remembered the Kid being "brave and loyal to his friends." Francisco Gómez said of the Kid that he was "kind and gentlemanlike with me and all the inhabitants of Lincoln."[68]

Reminiscing years later, George Coe said the Kid liked to go hunting with them for bear, deer, and turkeys and then sell the meat at Fort Stanton. The Kid was constantly practicing with his firearms. George remembered the Kid as a good singer and "a mighty nice dancer and what you would call a ladies' man." One of his favorite tunes was "Turkey in the Straw." The Kid was popular and easily made friends "because of his humorous and pleasing personality."[69]

Dick Brewer's ranch was on the Rio Ruidoso, and if the Kid had not already met him, he would have at this time. By early December, Brewer hired the Kid to work for John Tunstall. Not only was the Kid a good worker and rider, but he was handy with firearms, being proficient with his Winchester '73 rifle, but favoring his .41-caliber Colt double-action Thunderer revolver.[70]

During the time the Kid worked for Tunstall, he was respectful to his employer and must have admired him, but they probably never became very close. Tunstall never wrote anything about the Kid to his family, but he did write, "It cost a lot of money, for men expect to be well-paid for going on the war path."[71]

The Kid became friends with Tunstall's hands, many of whom would be his lifelong friends. Life was good. The Kid had found a steady job. He had plenty of Anglo and Hispano friends, male and female. He had found a safe harbor—but it was only temporary.

CHAPTER 10

LINCOLN COUNTY WAR

Tension continued building between the House and its supporters on one side and the Chisum, McSween, and Tunstall alliance on the opposite side throughout December 1877 and into 1878. Tunstall's employees, including Billy Bonney, the Kid, knew there was bad blood between the two factions, but they probably didn't know the details.

The rustler gang called the Boys was still active. There were threats against Mac McSween and others who stood in opposition to the Boys. The *Mesilla Valley Independent* published a letter dated December 3, 1877, signed by "Lincoln" that included a threat from the Boys who had escaped the Lincoln County jail, "We have recently heard from them [the Boys]. They were between Fort Stanton and Major Murphy's cow camp, and were there seen and interviewed. Lucas Gallegos was the spokesman. He told our informant that McSween's, [Juan] Patrón's, and [José] Montaño's death warrants had been signed."[1]

John Tunstall employee Robert Widenmann was appointed a US deputy marshal. Federal arrest warrants for stealing horses from Indians were issued for Jesse Evans and some of the Boys. Learning Evans and other Boys were at Lawrence Murphy's ranch, Widenmann went there to arrest them, but they were long gone, and Murphy denied they were ever there.[2]

The Lincoln County powder keg was set to blow. The lit fuse was a wrangle over a life insurance claim.

When Emil Fritz, Lawrence Murphy's partner, died back in June 1874, he had a $10,000 life insurance policy. His brother and sister, who both lived in New Mexico, were executors of his estate. The insurance company would not pay the estate. In May 1875, the House and the Fritz estate executors had Mac McSween attempt to collect the money. At his own expense, McSween spent two months traveling to St. Louis and then to New York City, meeting with the insurance company that claimed it couldn't pay because it was insolvent. McSween hired a New York financial firm to get the money from the insurance company. Finally, on August 1, 1877, the New York firm notified McSween that it had recovered the money. McSween received $7,148.94 after the firm deducted its expenses.[3]

McSween notified the Fritz estate executors of the recovered money. The House was in financial trouble, and when Jimmie Dolan learned about the recovered insurance policy money, he claimed the entire amount for the House, saying Fritz owed the House that money. McSween refused to turn the money over to the House, believing its claim was invalid and that the money rightfully belonged to the Fritz heirs. He was holding on to it until the Fritz heirs paid his legal fees. There was lots of legal wrangling back and forth.[4]

On December 18, 1877, McSween and his wife, along with John Chisum, left on a business and pleasure trip to St. Louis. The first leg of the trip was by horse and buggy to Las Vegas, New Mexico, and then on to Trinidad, Colorado, where they could board a train. Jimmie Dolan went to see Emilie Fritz Scholand, one of the Fritz estate executors, who was living in Las Cruces, and convinced her that the McSweens were leaving Lincoln County with the insurance money. Dolan had her sign an affidavit stating she believed McSween was fleeing New Mexico with the insurance policy money. He took it to District Attorney William Rynerson, who charged McSween with embezzlement; Judge Warren Bristol in Mesilla consented. Rynerson sent a telegram to Santa Fe Ring boss US District Attorney Thomas Catron, who had McSween and Chisum detained in Las Vegas on December 22. Catron had old charges dug up for Chisum that left him lingering in jail for two months.[5]

After more legal wrangling, two San Miguel County deputy sheriffs escorted McSween back to Lincoln on January 8, 1878. There he remained under house arrest, supervised by San Miguel County Deputy Sheriff Adolph Barrier, as he waited for his hearing before Judge Bristol in Mesilla.[6]

In the meantime, the House was experiencing its own difficulties, and by January 10, 1878, it was bankrupt, mortgaging everything to Santa Fe Ring boss Thomas Catron. Tunstall wrote a letter to the *Mesilla Valley Independent* that was printed in the January 26 edition. In the letter, Tunstall laid out facts accusing Sheriff Bill Brady, Johnny Riley, and Jimmie Dolan as being the real embezzlers in Lincoln County.[7]

McSween's hearings, both criminal and civil, before Judge Bristol began in the judge's Mesilla house on February 2 and ended on February 4. Deputy Sheriff Barrier escorted McSween to Mesilla, and Tunstall and other friends traveled along to provide moral support. Jimmie Dolan was in attendance, along with his employee Jim Longwell. Dolan, upset with Tunstall's letter in the newspaper, tried to pick a fight with Tunstall out in the street, but Tunstall refused to fight.[8]

Judge Bristol granted a continuance for the criminal embezzlement hearing to April when the grand jury would meet in Lincoln. Bristol set McSween's bail at $8,000 and left it to the discretion of District Attorney William Rynerson to accept it or not. McSween was going to pay the amount, but Rynerson would not accept it, meaning that McSween would remain under arrest and turned over to the custody of Sheriff Bill Brady when he returned to Lincoln.[9]

After McSween and friends left the hearing, and unknown to them, Judge Bristol required a surety in the amount of $10,000 for the civil case and issued a writ of attachment on McSween's property, which meant Sheriff Brady could impound $10,000 worth of McSween's property to cover the surety. They all believed McSween and Tunstall were partners, so this could include Tunstall property too. Jimmie Dolan was still in Mesilla and assured the judge he would get the writ of attainment into Sheriff Brady's hands.[10]

Deputy Sheriff Barrier, escorting McSween back to Lincoln, and Tunstall and friends stopped at Shedd's ranch to camp for the night. Jesse Evans and two of the Boys rode up. They asked Tunstall and his escort if they had seen Jimmie Dolan on the trail, and they answered they had not. Dolan and his friends arrived after midnight and went into camp with the Boys. The next morning, Dolan and Evans approached Tunstall. Dolan carried his Winchester carbine and demanded Tunstall fight him. Tunstall declined, and Dolan called him a "damn coward." Deputy Sheriff Barrier stepped between the two men and ended the confrontation. As Dolan walked away, he said, "You won't fight this morning, you damn coward, but I'll get you soon."[11]

Dolan raced back to Lincoln, arriving there on February 8, two days before McSween and Tunstall. Dolan gave the writ to Sheriff Bill Brady who formed a posse and entered McSween's office and home to inventory his property. Believing McSween was Tunstall's partner in Tunstall's store and ranches, Brady began inventorying Tunstall's store goods. Rob Widenmann, who Tunstall had left in charge of the store, protested the sheriff's actions, but Brady ignored him.[12]

Tunstall, McSween, and the others arrived in Lincoln on February 10. Tunstall learned about the sheriff's men inventorying his store property, and the next day, he and Widenmann, wearing pistols, confronted Brady and his men at the store. The Kid and another Tunstall employee, Fred Waite, carrying Winchesters, stood behind them. Brady allowed six horses and two mules belonging to Tunstall to be removed from impoundment but continued to hold the store and its goods. Tunstall had his men take the animals back to his ranch.[13]

Brady was prepared to place McSween in the Lincoln County jail's pit. McSween asked Deputy Sheriff Barrier not to turn him over to Sheriff Brady. Realizing the tense situation, Barrier allowed McSween to return to his house, keeping McSween in his custody.[14]

On February 9, Sheriff Brady had decided to include Tunstall's cattle in the impoundment and planned to send a posse to Tunstall's ranch to round them up. Tunstall's ranch hands learned of Brady's plans and the threat that the posse intended to kill them if necessary. Tunstall's men began preparing to defend themselves.[15]

Brady deputized Billy Mathews, the House silent partner, to lead a posse of four House employees. The posse was joined by four of the Boys—Jesse Evans, Tom Hill, Frank Baker, and Frank Rivers. Back on January 19, Evans had stolen horses south of Silver City and was being chased by a posse when he was shot in the butt, with the bullet exiting his groin. The wound was healed enough that Evans was now able to ride. Evans told Mathews he had loaned the Kid horses and wanted them back, so he and the Boys would be riding along with the posse.[16]

When the posse reached Tunstall's ranch on the Rio Feliz early in the morning on February 13, the ranch hands, including the Kid, were barricaded and waiting for them. Rob Widenmann stood out front, and when the posse was fifty yards away, he told them to halt. Mathews read the writ and said he was there to collect McSween cattle. Widenmann said there were no McSween cattle there. Mathews persisted, and Widenmann said if they had to, they would fight. It was a standoff. Mathews weighed the odds and said he would have to go back to Lincoln for further instructions.[17]

Being hospitable, Tunstall foreman Dick Brewer invited the posse and the Boys in for breakfast, which they accepted.

Widenmann in his role as US deputy marshal wanted the ranch hands to help him arrest Evans, Baker, and Hill, using the federal warrant for their theft of Indian horses on the reservation, but Brewer said no, they were all peaceable ranchers, and he was concerned about retaliation from the House henchmen. Spinning and pointing their guns at Widenmann, Evans and Baker told him if he tried to serve a warrant for their arrest, they would kill him.[18]

Widenmann needed to get further instructions from Tunstall. Along with the Kid and Fred Waite, he rode to Lincoln with the posse, while the Boys, along with the House employee Andrew "Buckshot" Roberts, rode to the Rio Peñasco.[19]

Widenmann reported to Tunstall and McSween what had happened out at the ranch. Widenmann believed Mathews would return with more men to take the livestock. Tunstall was determined to fight and the next morning, February 14, sent Widenmann, Waite, and the Kid back out to the ranch to prepare for a fight.[20]

Widenmann was right—Mathews would be returning to the ranch. Mathews met with Sheriff Brady, and they were determined to impound Tunstall's cattle. Brady told Mathews to find more men for the posse. He did so, even including Jimmie Dolan. A messenger rode down to the House's cow camp on the Pecos River to tell Buck Morton, the cow camp boss, to bring as many Seven Rivers men as he could. They would rendezvous at Paul's Ranch on the Rio Peñasco.[21]

Tunstall spent the next couple of days looking for people to help defend his cattle. The night of February 16, he found Jim Longwell, Brady's chief deputy and House employee, in his store. Tunstall was angry, threatening and cursing Longwell. Later that night, George Washington, a black handyman and former cavalryman, told Tunstall that Dolan was boasting that with the backing of the district attorney, judge, and the Santa Fe Ring, he had a forty-three-man posse that would "settle the difficulties with

Tunstall and McSween once and forever." Tunstall's men would be killed, and the cattle taken.[22]

Tunstall had had enough. He didn't want it to come to bloodshed. He rode out to the ranch and told his men he didn't want any fighting. He would let the posse's attachment of the herd take place.[23]

On February 18, Tunstall sent part-time ranch hand Bill McCloskey to tell Mathews they would allow the attachment to take place. Tunstall and his men left the ranch, leaving the cook, Godfrey Gauss, and another hand behind to attend to the ranch. They drove a herd of nine head of horses that they would take with them to Lincoln. Six had been released by Brady, two belonged to Brewer, and the last belonged to the Kid. Maybe it was the horse Evans said was his. Henry Brown left Tunstall and headed south, passing the posse with no incident.[24]

The posse split into two groups and approached the ranch from two different positions, finding it just as McCloskey had told them—abandoned except for two men.[25]

Mathews learned Tunstall was taking a small horse herd to Lincoln. He was undecided as to what to do. Jimmie Dolan arrived on the scene and took charge. He told Mathews the horses needed to be brought back and if Tunstall and his men resisted that they needed to be arrested and brought back too. Dolan selected the men to go after Tunstall, then Mathews deputized twenty-two-year-old Buck Morton to lead a fourteen-man posse, including Tunstall's part-time employee, McCloskey, to retrieve the horses. The Boys said they were going along to get Evans's horses from the Kid. Morton said, "Hurry up boys, my knife is sharp and I feel like scalping someone," and the posse and Boys took off after Tunstall and his men.[26]

It was toward dusk. Fred Waite had separated from the Tunstall party and was driving a wagon along the main road to Lincoln. Tunstall and the rest of his men had taken a shortcut trail away from the road through the hills to Lincoln. They were climbing through scrub timber-covered hills when they spotted a flock of turkeys. Hoping to shoot a bird or two, Brewer and Widenmann chased after the flock heading up a ridge to the left. Tunstall was ahead on the trail with the horses following single file behind him while the Kid and John Middleton rode five hundred yards to the rear.[27]

The trail topped a ridge and followed the descent on the far side; the Rio Ruidoso was about four miles to the north. Tunstall and the horses continued along the trail. When Middleton and the Kid reached the ridge, they looked behind and saw a group of riders galloping toward them. The Kid encouraged his horse to move as fast as it could upslope to warn Brewer and Widenmann, who were in an open area about two hundred yards above, and Middleton raced after Tunstall to warn him.[28]

Spotting the Kid riding up toward Brewer and Widenmann, the posse members began chasing after and shooting at them. The three were able to reach the top of the higher ridge where they found cover.[29]

Other posse members galloped down the trail after Middleton, who was shouting to Tunstall, "Follow me! For God's sake follow me!"

"What John? What John?" Tunstall responded. Middleton thought Tunstall appeared confused. Not waiting around, Middleton forced his horse to race up the ridge toward the other three Tunstall men.[30]

Tunstall must have finally realized he was in danger. Leaving the horses, he left the trail to try to get away from the pursuers. One hundred yards off the trail, Buck Morton, Jesse Evans, and Tom Hill caught up with him in a stand of scrub oak.[31]

Middleton reached the Kid and the others as shots rang out from below where Tunstall had been chased. "They've killed Tunstall," Middleton guessed.[32]

John Tunstall and his horse were dead. He had a gunshot to the chest and one in the head. His horse was also shot in the head.[33]

HATZELL 2019

Buck Morton told the rest of the posse that Tunstall had been killed while resisting arrest. He claimed that he was reading Tunstall the writ when Tunstall drew his revolver and fired at him. Morton shot and killed Tunstall in self-defense. Tunstall's revolver was examined, and two of the six chambers were empty. They laid him out next to his horse and left his body there. Rounding up the nine horses, the posse headed back to Tunstall's ranch in the dark, not wanting to attack the Tunstall men's position. One of the posse members heard Evans or one of the other Boys say that Tunstall's death was small loss, that he deserved to be killed. Later, Evans would claim that he had not ridden along with the posse.[34]

As time went on, a different story would emerge from posse members other than the one that Tunstall's killers told. In affidavits for Judge Frank Angel, posse members would relate what they knew from talking with the killers and observing the scene of Tunstall's death.[35]

Buck Morton, Jesse Evans, and Tom Hill urged on their horses so that they outdistanced the rest of the posse. Passing the horse herd, they chased after Tunstall, who had left the trail. Realizing three riders were coming up behind him, he stopped and turned toward them. One of them called to Tunstall, telling him to ride to them and he would not be hurt. The three had their rifles out and at the ready. One said quietly to the others, "Not now, let's wait until he gets nearer."[36]

As Tunstall rode closer, Morton brought his rifle up to his shoulder, aimed, and fired. The bullet smashed into Tunstall's chest and exited through his right shoulder blade. Tunstall fell to the ground, face forward. One of the Boys, either Evans or Hill, jumped off his horse, grabbed Tunstall's revolver, and fired a bullet into the back of Tunstall's head. The bullet entered behind Tunstall's right ear and exited above the left eye. The killer turned to Tunstall's horse and shot it in the head.[37]

The rest of the posse rode up to where Tunstall had been killed. Posse member George Kitt saw that Tom Hill had Tunstall's revolver in his hand and passed it on to others who laid it by Tunstall's body. They laid out a blanket on the ground beside Tunstall's horse and put his body on top of the blanket, laying his head on top of his folded jacket. Another blanket was laid overtop, covering his body. His dead horse's head was lifted, and his hat was placed under the horse's head. Twenty-four-year-old John Henry Tunstall's short life had ended in violence.[38]

Responding to Tunstall's earlier call for help, forty to fifty men had gathered at Mac McSween's house. After Morton's posse had left, the Kid and the other Tunstall men rode to Lincoln, arriving there about 10:00 p.m. Riding straight to McSween's house, they reported on Tunstall's death. The news spread quickly and by midnight the crowd of supporters at McSween's house had swelled.[39]

Visibly shaken and drunk, Johnny Riley entered McSween's house. To convince everyone that he was unarmed, he emptied his pockets, including a memorandum book that he placed on a table and failed to take with him when he left. The book contained information on the House's dealings, including its purchase of stolen cattle from the Boys. Tucked in the book were letters from District Attorney William Rynerson showing he was in cahoots with the House and stating McSween would never get a fair hearing. Riley left Lincoln for the safety of Fort Stanton.[40]

Later that night, McSween sent a message to John Newcomb, who lived on the Rio Ruidoso, asking him to find Tunstall's body and bring it to Lincoln.[41]

Sheriff Bill Brady was worried. Most of his supporters were out of town at Tunstall's ranch. He requested Captain George Purrington, commander of Fort Stanton, send an officer and troops to help him in case McSween and his supporters started to make trouble. Purrington reluctantly sent Lieutenant Cyrus Delany with a mounted detachment of the Fifteenth Infantry to guard the House's buildings. However, McSween preferred using legal means instead of violence.[42]

On Tuesday morning, February 19, Rob Widenmann rode to Fort Stanton and, in his capacity as US marshal, asked Purrington for troops to assist him in the capture of Evans, Hill, and Baker.[43]

Mac McSween could expect no help from the sheriff, district attorney, or judge, but he did have another legal avenue to use to go after Tunstall's killers and that was going through the local justice of the peace, John "Green" Wilson, and Lincoln's town constable, Atanacio Martinez.[44]

McSween took the Kid, Dick Brewer, and John Middleton to Wilson's office, where they swore affidavits listing the killers of John Tunstall as Buck Morton, Jesse Evans, and others. The list included Jimmie Dolan and Frank Baker, who were not present at the killing. McSween also swore an affidavit for larceny against Sheriff Brady and his men at Tunstall's store. When the troops Brady requested from Fort Stanton had arrived, they needed hay for their horses, so Brady told his men to give them hay owned by Tunstall. Wilson issued warrants for the arrest of five of the Boys and twelve members of Mathews's posse for Tunstall's murder and for Sheriff Brady and five of his men for larceny. Wilson gave the warrants to Constable Martinez, who organized a posse of eighteen men from McSween's supporters, including the Kid.[45]

John Newcomb brought Tunstall's body into town around 6:00 p.m. and laid it out in McSween's parlor. There, Justice of the Peace Wilson impaneled a six-man coroner's jury. After listening to the witnesses, the jury concluded that John Henry Tunstall was killed by William Morton, Jesse Evans, Thomas Hill, George Hindman, James Dolan, and "others not identified by the witnesses." As the Kid stared at Tunstall's body, he said, "I'll get some of them before I die."[46]

Before dawn on February 20, Deputy US Marshal Rob Widenmann returned to Lincoln with Lieutenant Millard Goodwin and thirty black troops of the Ninth Cavalry. Constable Atanacio Martinez gathered his posse and followed behind Widenmann and the troops as they first searched the House's store, not finding any of the Boys or those on Martinez's arrest warrants. They then walked down the street to search Tunstall's store. First, Widenmann and the troops entered, looking for but not finding the Boys. Then Martinez and his posse entered and got the drop on Jim Longwell and four other House employees who were on the larceny warrant. They were escorted to the jail and placed in the pit. McSween supporters stayed and occupied Tunstall's store. Later that morning, Sheriff Brady arrived in town from his home. He was arrested, too, and along with the others, was taken to Justice of the Peace Wilson who let them all go. Brady had to post a $200 bond and appear at a later date before the district court.[47]

Fort Stanton surgeon Dr. Daniel Appel arrived in Lincoln to assist in the embalming of Tunstall. Presbyterian minister and physician Taylor Ealy, who had arrived in town with his family the day before, assisted Appel. Sheriff Brady paid Appel $100 for a postmortem, which was an extreme amount of money for the time. Appel and Ealy had two differing points of view on the condition of Tunstall's body. Appel wrote that, besides the two bullet wounds, there were "no other bruises on head or body." Ealy stated, in addition to the two bullet wounds, Tunstall's head was badly mutilated. Widenmann wrote he believed Buck Morton "smashed Tunstall's skull with the butt of his gun."[48]

Captain Purrington rode into Lincoln. He talked with Sheriff Brady and McSween to find out what was happening. He believed McSween's men were little more than a mob, and if Brady, Dolan, and Riley were turned over to them, their lives would be in jeopardy.[49]

Purrington left Lieutenant Goodwin and his thirty black troops in Lincoln to keep the peace while not interfering with the civil authorities. Goodwin stationed his troops around the outside of the House's buildings to keep McSween's supporters away. Goodwin was angry with Widenmann and Martinez. He believed they had deceived him and that the use of his troops in their searches and arrests was wrong. They both apologized, with

Martinez adding that the Kid and others threatened to kill him if he did not serve the warrants.[50]

The McSween supporters learned Jimmie Dolan, Billy Mathews, and others on the murder arrest warrants were back in town at the House's store, along with Sheriff Brady. They wanted to go in there after them, but Goodwin would not allow it, considering them a mob. The McSween mob came back to Goodwin with the proposition that if only Constable Martinez and two deputies went into the store to arrest the men, would Goodwin let them pass? Goodwin agreed to allow that, as he had orders not to obstruct a civil officer in the discharge of his duties.[51]

Constable Martinez and his two deputies, Fred Waite and the Kid armed with his Winchester, walked into the House's store and were greeted by Winchesters pointed at them. Brady leveled his gun at the Kid saying, "You little sonofabitch, give me your gun!"

The Kid responded, "Take it, you old sonofabitch!"[52]

Brady had them disarmed, then asked what they wanted. Martinez began to read the arrest warrants, but Brady cut him off, stating those men listed were acting under his authority and Martinez was not going to arrest them. Furthermore, he did not believe Justice of the Peace Wilson could issue arrest warrants. The men in the store then "cursed and abused" Martinez and his deputies.[53]

Brady and some of his men escorted the constable and his two deputies to the jail, forcing them to descend into the pit. After several hours, they released Martinez, refusing to return his weapons. However, they did not release the Kid and Waite.[54]

That night, someone fired a shot, killing one of the cavalrymen's horses. The next morning, Thursday, February 21, Purrington sent an infantry detachment to support the cavalry.[55]

The Kid and Fred Waite languished in the pit as the town mourned and buried John Tunstall. Dick Brewer, Tunstall's foreman, stood at the graveside and was overheard to swear he would not rest until everyone involved in Tunstall's death paid for it with their lives. The funeral services were officiated by the newly arrived Presbyterian minister, Taylor Ealy. After the service, Lincoln citizens gathered together to discuss the plight of their town and how to return it to a semblance of order instead of armed camps. After the meeting, probate judge Florencio Gonzales and three other prominent citizens went to visit Sheriff Brady at the House's store. They asked why he had seized Martinez and his two deputies and still had the deputies in jail. Brady's answer was, "Because I have the power." They said they wanted to end the present difficulties, and two of the men who were store owners in town were willing to put up double the amount of the bond for McSween if Brady would end the McSween and Tunstall attachment. Brady adamantly refused, but he did release the Kid and Waite, minus their weapons. After thirty hours in the pit, the Kid would remember what Brady did to him and he was not willing to forgive.[56]

McSween was still under house arrest and the watchful eye of San Miguel County Deputy Sheriff Adolph Barrier, who believed if he turned McSween over to Sheriff Brady that would be the end of McSween. McSween tried again to post bond for his embezzlement criminal charges, but again District Attorney William Rynerson rejected it. Dolan left for Messila to get Judge Warren Bristol to issue a rearrest warrant, so Sheriff Brady could arrest McSween and put him in the jail's pit. The rumor was floating that once McSween was in the Lincoln County jail Dolan would bring in Jesse Evans "to do his part." McSween made his will, fled Lincoln, and went into hiding along with Deputy Sheriff Barrier.[57]

Even though McSween was gone, those who were outraged by Tunstall's murder and opposed to the House and its cronies continued to work with Justice of the Peace John Wilson. Wilson wrote out a new warrant for the arrest of the alleged murderers of Tunstall, and on March 1, 1878, appointed rancher and Tunstall's foreman, Dick Brewer, as a special constable with the authority to arrest Tunstall's murderers.[58]

The old Martinez posse was regrouped and deputized under Brewer's leadership and gave themselves the name Regulators. The Regulators' numbers would fluctuate over the next five months from ten to sixty, depending on the situation. The core group, which included the Kid, were mostly Anglos, but Hispanos would join them at times.[59]

Justice of the Peace John Wilson empowered the Regulators to arrest the culprits in Tunstall's murder and bring them back to Lincoln. They announced they would not take vigilante actions delivering immediate punishment, but they would bring Tunstall's murderers to Lincoln to be held for trial. They wanted the public to know they were not connected with McSween's issues with the Fritz estate. They developed and took an oath called the "iron clad," swearing they would not bear witness against any other Regulator or divulge to outsiders their activities. The Regulators claimed they were the champions of justice.[60]

The first man on the Regulators' list was Buck Morton, the House's cow camp boss on the Pecos River and posse leader, who had shot Tunstall in the chest. Brewer led the Regulators, including the Kid, over to the Pecos River where, on March 6, they spotted Morton and one of the Boys, Frank Baker, with three other riders on the Rio Peñasco, about six miles from the Pecos.[61]

The five riders took off as the Regulators gave chase. The group of five split, two heading in one direction, and Morton, Baker, and Dick Lloyd racing toward Beckwith's ranch. Ignoring the other two, the Regulators pursued Morton, Baker, and Lloyd, firing what seemed to Morton like over a hundred shots as they rode over a distance of five miles. Lloyd's horse was finished and threw him to the ground. The posse raced past him—they wanted Morton and Baker. Morton and Baker's horses were soon played out, so they took cover in a depression.[62]

Brewer negotiated their surrender, promising they would not be hurt if they laid down their weapons. Although after they did so, Morton wrote in a letter, "There was one man in the party who wanted to kill me after I had surrendered, and was restrained with the greatest difficulty by others of the party." This man could have been the Kid. Morton also wrote, "The constable himself [Dick Brewer] said he was sorry we gave up, as he had not wished to take us alive."[63]

As the Regulators and their captives rode toward Chisum's South Springs ranch, they ran into Bill McCloskey, who joined them. Even though McCloskey had worked part-time for Tunstall, Brewer did not trust him as he was good friends with Morton and was a part of Morton's posse that killed Tunstall. McCloskey believed nothing would happen to Morton and Baker while he was with them.[64]

They spent the night of March 8 at Chisum's ranch. The next morning, they rode into Roswell, where Morton gave a letter to postmaster Ash Upson, who years later would help Pat Garrett write his book *The Authentic Life of Billy the Kid*. Upson asked Buck Morton, who also went by the nickname "Billy," if he was afraid for his life. Morton replied he was not afraid as the posse had pledged Baker and he would be delivered safely to the authorities in Lincoln.[65]

Standing there, McCloskey said, "Billy, if harm comes to you two, they will have to kill me first."[66]

The Regulators heard rumors that Jimmie Dolan had sent men to rescue Morton and Baker. They were also concerned that when they reached Lincoln, Sheriff Brady would turn the prisoners loose. On their return to Lincoln, they left the main road and took a roundabout trail up Blackwater Canyon, hoping to avoid rescuers from the House.[67]

On April 11, 1878, Ash Upson was working in the Roswell post office when Frank McNab, one of the Regulators, walked in.

"Hallo! McNab," Upson said. "I thought you were in Lincoln by this time. Any news?"

"Yes," McNab replied. "Morton killed McCloskey, one of our men, made a break to escape, and we had to kill them."

"Where did Morton get weapons?" Upson asked.

"He snatched McCloskey's pistol out its scabbard, killing him with it, and ran, firing back as he went. We had to kill them, or some of us would have been hurt," McNab said.[68]

The Regulators' official version was similar to what McNab told Upson, but the House believed the Regulators had killed McCloskey because he had vowed to protect Morton and Baker, and that they then forced Morton and Baker to their knees, executing them as they pleaded for their lives. There are several versions as to what happened, however Regulators were the only witnesses.[69]

According to the Regulators, as they were riding single file along the trail, either Morton or Baker pulled McCloskey's pistol from its holster and shot him dead. Morton and Baker tried to get away atop their played-out horses. The posse fired after the prisoners, riddling their bodies with multiple bullet holes.[70]

Another story emerged, which Garrett and Upson recorded in their book. Frank McNab rode up to Bill McCloskey and said, "Your [sic] are the son-of-a-bitch that's got to die before harm can come to those fellows, are you?" and fired his revolver, killing McCloskey. The two unarmed prisoners tried to escape on their slow-moving horses as the Regulators shot at them. The Kid, who had been riding at the front of the group, headed them off and fired a shot at each, killing them both.[71]

However it happened, Brewer claimed it was against his wishes. He found some local Hispanos to bury the bodies, and the Regulators rode on. The Kid and the rest of the Regulators rode to their favorite village, San Patricio, and Brewer rode alone to Lincoln.[72]

Sheriff Bill Brady had sent a letter to US Attorney General Thomas Catron justifying the killing of Tunstall and stating, "Anarchy is the only word which would truthfully describe the situation here." Brady requested federal troops from Fort Stanton to help maintain the peace. Catron passed the letter on to Governor Samuel Axtell, who sent a request for troops to President Rutherford B. Hayes, who granted the request.[73]

Governor Axtell decided to investigate the problem firsthand. Arriving at Fort Stanton on March 8, he stayed the night. The following morning, accompanied by Lawrence Murphy and Jimmie Dolan, he visited Lincoln for three hours. Before he left, he issued and signed a proclamation, stating in part, "John B. Wilson's appointment by the county commissioners as a justice of the peace was illegal and void, and all processes by him were illegal and void, and said Wilson has no authority whatever to act as justice of the peace." The governor went on to revoke Rob Widenmann's appointment as deputy US marshal and proclaimed President Hayes was allowing the use of troops to help Judge Bristol and Sheriff Brady and his deputies enforce the law.[74]

Mac McSween arrived in Lincoln that afternoon right after the governor left. When Brewer arrived in town on March 10, McSween told him about the governor's proclamation. Governor Axtell, who was part of the Santa Fe Ring controlling the House's debt, had officially sided with the House. McSween went on to tell Brewer since the governor considered Wilson's actions illegal, the Regulators could be charged with false arrest and murder and that Jimmie Dolan was taking steps to track down and arrest the Regulators. McSween recommended Brewer stay out of Lincoln until district court convened on April 1. Brewer rode to San Patricio to inform the Kid and other Regulators and then returned to his ranch. The Regulators had gone from lawmen to outlaws.[75]

Through the remainder of March, the Regulators were quiet. The Kid and Fred Waite spent their time around San Patricio. Mac McSween and his wife, Sue, were staying at John Chisum's ranch.[76]

The Boys were still busy. On March 13, 1878, Jesse Evans and Tom Hill raided the camp of John Wagner who was herding a flock of four thousand sheep. Wagner got the best of the Boys, killing Hill and wounding Evans in the wrist. Even though he was in rough shape, Evans was able to make his escape. Needing medical attention and protection from the Regulators, he turned himself in at Fort Stanton where he did receive both. While he was at it, since Morton and Hill were now both dead, Evans blamed the killing of Tunstall on Hill.[77]

Toward the end of the month, Mac McSween met with Regulators, including the Kid. Sheriff Bill Brady was one of the topics of discussion. Brady was a respected member of the community, but McSween saw him in a bad light, no more than a tool for the House to ruin him. The Kid and other Regulators held grudges against Brady, ranging from imprisonment to physical abuse. Whether it was sanctioned by McSween or not, the Regulators plotted to kill Sheriff Bill Brady.[78]

On March 28, 1878, Sheriff Brady, with a detachment of troops commanded by Lieutenant George Washington Smith, visited Chisum's ranch looking for McSween, who must have been away at the time. Sue McSween assured Brady that her husband would show up for court on April 1. Believing what he heard, Brady returned to Lincoln, arriving on March 30. While at Chisum's ranch, Smith had proposed to Sue that if McSween surrendered, he and his soldiers would escort him to Fort Stanton to await the start of district court. After Brady departed, McSween was still convinced Brady would try to arrest him and place him in the Lincoln County jail pit, which he believed would be his death sentence.[79]

The evening of March 31, six Regulators quietly rode into Lincoln and entered the adobe-walled corral at Tunstall's store. The corral was mostly behind the building with an extension along the east side with a wooden gate leading to the street. The gate offered a good view of the street and provided cover. The men waiting in the corral were Frank McNab, John Middleton, Fred Waite, Jim French, Henry Brown, and the Kid.[80]

Someone realized there was an error in the public notice for when court was to be in session. The public notice announced the opening date as April 1 when it actually was to be April 8. Brady prepared a notice to post at the courthouse, correcting the date.[81]

About 9:00 a.m., on April 1, 1878, the wind was blowing and it was sleeting as Sheriff Brady left the House's store with his deputies, Billy Mathews, George Peppin, Jack Long, and House employee George Hindman, who had been with Morton's posse that killed Tunstall. They walked down the street past Tunstall's store to the courthouse where Brady posted the notice.[82]

Brady and his men walked back up the street toward the House's store. When they were in front of Tunstall's corral, the Regulators threw open the gate and began blasting away with their Winchesters. A barrage of bullets slammed into Brady, who crumpled to the street. Mathews, Peppin, and Long raced for cover. A bullet hit Hindman, who fell to the street and started crying for water. Saloon keeper Ike Stockton ran to Hindman and started to help him to safety when another bullet slammed into Hindman, killing him. Former Justice of the Peace Wilson was working in his garden when a stray bullet hit him in the butt.[83]

The Kid and Jim French ran into the street. French covered the Kid as he ran to Brady's body and picked up the Winchester Brady had been carrying—the Winchester Brady had confiscated from the Kid.[84]

Billy Mathews, who had taken cover across the street in the Cisneros house, fired at the Kid—the bullet grazing his thigh then hitting and passing through French's thigh. Dropping the Winchester, the Kid and French ran back to the safety of the corral.[85]

An uneasy peace held Lincoln paralyzed. No one ventured outside. The Regulators took their good old time leaving town. The Kid was good enough to ride, but French needed a doctor. They took him along the backsides of the buildings to McSween's house, where missionary doctor Taylor Ealy cleaned and bandaged his wound.[86]

After the Regulators rode out of town, the deputies fired parting shots at them, and one Regulator, John Middleton, got off his horse and fired back. The people ventured out of their houses and businesses and gathered in the street. The town was abuzz.

Jim French was still in town. The deputies searched for him but could not find him. He was able to sneak out of town later that night. Deputy Sheriff George Peppin sent a request for troops to Fort Stanton. At noon, Captain George Purrington and Lieutenant George Washington Smith, leading a cavalry detachment of twenty-five black troops, rode into town.[87]

That same morning, John Chisum arrived driving a buggy full of people, including the McSweens who had come to town for the court session. Deputy Sheriff Peppin attempted to arrest McSween, who argued the warrant was invalid since Brady was dead. McSween, still believing he would be murdered in the Lincoln County jail, requested that if he had to be taken into custody that they hold him at Fort Stanton until April 8 when district court would be in session. Both Peppin and Lieutenant Smith, who was present during the discussion, agreed to McSween's proposition. When Captain Purrington found out, he was not happy McSween was coming to the fort but allowed it anyway.[88]

For good measure Deputy Sheriff Peppin arrested Rob Widenmann and two black workmen, George Washington and George Robinson, who had been in the corral that morning, and McSween's brother-in-law David Shield, who knew nothing until he heard the shots. They were all sent to Fort Stanton with McSween.[89]

Many believed the Kid was the first to put a bullet in Sheriff Brady, and that Frank McNab, who had a grudge against Hindman, shot him first and then Fred Waite fired the second bullet, killing him. McSween and the Regulators lost lots of support after the assassinations of Brady and Hindman. People now believed the Regulators were no better than the House.[90]

The next day, April 2, Lieutenant Colonel Nelson Dudley of the Ninth Cavalry arrived at Fort Stanton. He was to take over command the following Friday, but Captain Purrington was happy to turn over command to Dudley right away and go on a planned extended leave of absence. Dudley was efficient but unpopular with his fellow officers. He was a heavy drinker and was considered arrogant and vindictive. Back in November 1877, US Attorney General Thomas Catron's law firm had defended him in a court martial but lost.[91]

About 11:00 a.m., Thursday, April 4, 1878, Dick Brewer and fourteen Regulators, including the Kid, rode into Blazer's Mill, located along the Tularosa River on the Mescalero Apache Reservation. They had heard that some of the men on their warrant were on the reservation, and they were hunting for them. Brewer and his men rode up to the large house Frederick Godfroy, the Indian agent, leased from Dr. Joseph Blazer, a dentist. Clara Godfroy was known to cook meals for travelers. Brewer requested a meal for his men, and they were invited into the house.[92]

Clara did not allow firearms in the building, so while the regulators were inside eating, John Middleton waited outside on guard. A man riding a mule entered town and Middleton overheard him say his name was Roberts. Middleton went inside and told Brewer. Andrew "Buckshot" Roberts was one of the names on the warrant for Tunstall's murder.[93]

Allegedly Buckshot got his name because he had been hit by a shotgun blast. Some of the buckshot was still in his right shoulder. With the injury leaving him unable to raise his right arm above his waist, he had learned to shoot from the hip. Roberts occasionally worked for the House and had been on the two posse rides to Tunstall's ranch, but he was not a part of the Morton posse that killed Tunstall.[94]

Roberts had had enough of what was becoming known as the Lincoln County War. He knew the Regulators were after him and had sold his property. He only rode to Blazer's Mill to find out at the post office if his check for his ranch had arrived; if so, he was leaving for Las Cruces immediately.[95]

Frank Coe was friendly with Roberts and told Brewer he would go out alone and try to talk Roberts into surrendering. Coe found Roberts cradling his Winchester while sitting on the porch to Dr. Blazer's office, which happened to be in the same building that the Regulators were having their meal. The two men talked for half an hour. Roberts worried if he surrendered, the Kid would kill him. Earlier that March, Roberts had spotted the Kid and Charlie Bowdre near San Patricio. Roberts had thought they were out to get him, so he shot at them long distance, and they had fired back. No one was hurt in the exchange, but Roberts was sure they knew who he was.[96]

Brewer became impatient and sent Bowdre, Middleton, and George Coe to arrest Roberts. After retrieving their weapons, they walked around the corner of the building to where Roberts and Coe were still talking.[97]

"Throw up your hands!" Bowdre yelled.

"No!" Roberts replied, as he brought his Winchester up to his hip. They both fired at the same time. Bowdre's bullet hit Roberts in the stomach and passed out his back. Roberts's bullet hit the buckle on Bowdre's gun belt, ricocheting and hitting George Coe's right-hand thumb and index finger. The rest of the Regulators came running at the sound of the gunshots. Roberts kept firing as he backed into Blazer's office. Middleton was hit in the chest, the bullet puncturing a lung. Another bullet hit Doc Scurlock's holstered pistol and ricocheted down his leg. Roberts shot at the Kid, grazing his arm.[98]

Roberts was out of ammunition, and he had left his revolver and gun belt on his saddle. The Kid rushed the door and pointed his Winchester at Roberts who jammed the barrel of his gun into the Kid's stomach. The Kid fired, the bullet missing Roberts, and the Kid jumped back.[99]

Roberts found a single-shot, 1873 officer's model .45-70 Springfield rifle and box of cartridges in Blazer's office. He dragged a mattress to the door, barricaded it, and lay prone to continue the fight.[100]

Brewer was furious; he tried to get several people, including Blazer and Godfroy, to go in and get Roberts, which they refused to do. He threatened to burn the building down, but they still wouldn't move. Finally, he decided to take matters into his own hands.[101]

Brewer circled around the house and hid behind a pile of logs about 125 yards from the house. He could see the open door and Roberts inside. He aimed his rifle and fired. The bullet missed Roberts, hitting the wall behind him. Roberts saw a puff of smoke at the log pile from where the shot had been fired. He watched the spot and when he saw Brewer's hat, he aimed and fired. The bullet pierced Brewer's left eye and blew out the back of his skull.[102]

The Regulators stopped shooting and rode away. They had had enough, with one dead and three wounded. They knew it was only a matter of time until Roberts died, and they needed to get their wounded medical attention.[103]

The next day, Roberts died and was buried beside Brewer. Middleton would survive his chest wound as would Scurlock and Coe, whose thumb and index finger had to be amputated.[104]

Learning of Brewer's death, Mac McSween wrote, "Richard M. Brewer was one of nature's noblemen." The Kid told his friend John Meadows, "Yes sir, he [Roberts] licked our crowd to a finish." The public was sympathetic to Buckshot Roberts and admired his heroic stand against overwhelming odds. It was another black mark for the Regulators.[105]

Judge Warren Bristol convened district court in Lincoln on April 8. The judge and the attorneys from Mesilla stayed at Fort Stanton and traveled each day with a military escort between the fort and Lincoln.[106]

The first thing Judge Bristol did was appoint a sheriff to serve the warrants for the murder of Sheriff Brady. He selected John Copeland, a longtime resident of Lincoln County and someone the judge believed would be neutral between the McSween faction and the House. Later in April, the county commissioners agreed with Copeland's appointment, officially making Copeland Lincoln County sheriff for all duties.[107]

On Saturday, April 13, Judge Bristol addressed the grand jury of fifteen citizens, a mix of Anglos and Hispanos, with Dr. Joseph Blazer as foreman. When Bristol addressed the McSween embezzlement case, his remarks were strongly anti-McSween.[108]

On April 18, the grand jury delivered its findings for Tunstall's murder, indicting Jesse Evans, George Davis, Manuel Segovia, and John Long, with Jimmie Dolan and Billy Mathews as accessories. Evans, the only principal who could be found since he was under arrest at Fort Stanton, was able to make his $5,000 bond, and so were Dolan and Mathews, who each made their $2,000 bond.[109]

As to Sheriff Bill Brady's murder, there were no indictments for Rob Widenmann, George Washington, George Robinson, and David Shield, so they were released. However, for Brady's murder, the jury did indict William H. Bonney, John Middleton, Fred Waite, and Henry Brown. Those four were also indicted for the murder of Andrew Roberts at Blazer's Mill as well as Charlie Bowdre, Doc Scurlock, Steve Stephens, John Scroggins, and George Coe. Jimmie Dolan and Johnny Riley were indicted for cattle theft. As to the charge that McSween embezzled $10,000 from the Emil Fritz estate, the grand jury stated, "We fully exonerate him of the charge, and regret that a spirit of persecution has been shown in this matter."[110]

In more bad news for the House, US District Attorney Thomas Catron, who held the mortgage on the House's assets, foreclosed on the mortgage and sent his brother-in-law Edgar Walz to close the store and take charge of the assets.[111]

McSween published an announcement in the newspapers that John Tunstall's father had authorized him to pay a $5,000 reward for the apprehension and conviction of the murderers of his son. The announcement stated there were twenty murderers and McSween would pay a proportionate amount for any of them.[112]

Life was good for the Regulators. Sheriff John Copeland was friends with McSween and the Regulators. Even though he carried with him arrest warrants for the Kid and the others, he did not arrest them and was seen associating and drinking with them. The Regulators were always invited to McSween's house for social gatherings. The Reverend Dr. Taylor Ealy's wife, Mary, had fond memories of playing Sue McSween's piano while the Kid and other fully armed Regulators gathered round to sing. "They were very nice and polite," she said.[113]

The Regulators elected Frank McNab as their new leader, and San Patricio Justice of the Peace Gregorio Trujillo appointed McNab deputy constable.[114]

The deputy sheriffs of the dead sheriff, Bill Brady, believed they still had full authority, and no one told them otherwise. They saw Sheriff John Copeland was not arresting anyone on the warrants for the murders of Brady, Hindman, and Roberts, so Billy Mathews and George Peppin decided to take it upon themselves to do so. They rode out of Lincoln with a few men to Seven Rivers where they found about twenty men to join their posse. One of the posse members happened to be Manuel "Indian" Segovia, who was named in the arrest warrant for the murder of Tunstall.[115]

On April 29, the posse arrived at the Fritz ranch nine miles outside Lincoln, where they ambushed three Regulators, Frank McNab, Frank Coe, and Ab Saunders. The posse shot, killing Saunders's horse; McNab's horse bucked him off, and then they shot Coe's horse. Saunders was shot in the hip and could not move. McNab ran up a small canyon, chased by Indian Segovia who shot and killed the Regulator leader. Coe ran up another small canyon but was trapped and surrendered. The posse told Coe they had thought he was the Kid when they were chasing him.[116]

The posse rode on to Lincoln with their prisoners and that night took positions in timber on the east side of Lincoln and in the House's store. The next morning, they sent a message to Sheriff Copeland that they were in town to help him arrest the Kid and others listed on the murder warrants.[117]

The Regulators took up positions around town. George Coe had heard a rumor that the posse had killed his cousin Frank Coe.

George climbed up on the roof of the Ellis store and, spying a man sitting on a cow skull with his legs crossed, took a pot shot at him. The bullet passed through the legs of "Dutch" Charlie Kruling. That was the opening shot of the battle of Lincoln where both sides fired at each other for four hours. The posse members in the House's store charged the Ellis Store, leaving their prisoner Frank Coe unattended, and he walked away.[118]

Sheriff Copeland sent a message to Fort Stanton requesting assistance to quell the violence. Late that afternoon, Lieutenant George Smith, leading twenty black cavalry troopers, entered town and rode between the feuding sides, ending the shooting. No one other than Kruling was wounded.[119]

Copeland wanted the Peppin and Mathews posse arrested, but the posse members would not allow themselves to be arrested. After negotiations, they surrendered to Lieutenant Smith and his troops, who escorted the still-armed posse members to Fort Stanton. The Regulators, including the Kid, left town for San Patricio.[120]

Sheriff Copeland had San Patricio Justice of the Peace Gregorio Trujillo issue an arrest warrant for eighteen members of Peppin and Mathews's posse for the murder of Frank McNab. By now, Lieutenant Colonel Dudley had formed a dislike for McSween and the Regulators. He had David Easton, the Justice of the Peace in Blazer's Mill, issue a warrant for the arrest of McSween, the Kid, and twenty others for rioting. Sheriff Copeland now had thirty prisoners from both sides on his hands and finally let them all loose by telling them to go home and quit feuding.[121]

With the death of Frank McNab, the Regulators elected a new leader, Doc Scurlock, who Sheriff Copeland appointed as a deputy sheriff. The Kid was included in a new twenty-man posse Scurlock put together with a Hispano contingent under the leadership of Josefita Chavez. Scurlock had learned Jimmie Dolan was at the House cow camp on the Pecos rounding up cattle to fulfill the beef contract for the reservation and that many of the men who were on warrants were down there working on the roundup.[122]

On May 15, Scurlock, leading a twenty-man Regulator posse, invaded the House cow camp, confiscating twenty-five horses and two mules that had been taken from Tunstall and others. They scattered the cattle that had been rounded up and arrested Indian Segovia for the murder of Frank McNab. The Regulators reported that on the ride back to Lincoln, Indian Segovia attempted to escape. The Kid and Josefita Chavez chased after him and shot him dead.[123]

US District Attorney Thomas Catron was furious that the Regulators killed one of his men, took the horses and mules, and scattered the House's herd, since it was now his herd. Dolan went to Santa Fe and, working with Catron and Governor Axtell, they found a legal technicality to remove Copeland as sheriff and appointed loyal George Peppin to replace him. Peppin was also appointed a deputy US marshal.[124]

The British government demanded an investigation into Tunstall's death, and the US Department of Justice sent Judge Frank Angel to investigate the matter. He took depositions from the Kid and others on both sides of the dispute. Angel concluded that Tunstall's conflict with the House directly led to his murder. Angel could not ascertain who actually killed Tunstall, but he narrowed it down to Morton, Hill, and Evans, who were the ones present at the time. There was no evidence United States government officials caused Tunstall's murder. However, irregularities were found with the management of the Mescalero Apache Reservation and Agent Frederick Godfroy was told he would have to resign.[125]

On June 19, Sheriff Peppin rode into Lincoln at the head of a posse made up of Jimmie Dolan and his men, a twenty-seven-man cavalry detachment, and some old friends—horse thief John Kinney and his gang of twelve desperadoes all deputized. Rumors flew that District Attorney William Rynerson had sent Kinney and his men to help, and that Dolan was offering Kinney $500 to kill

McSween, and his gang could then take possession of Tunstall's cattle.[126]

Peppin was armed with a new warrant for the arrest of the Kid and others named in the killing of Buckshot Roberts. Since Roberts was killed on the Mescalero Apache Reservation, considered federal land, the killing was a federal offense, and the warrant was issued by US Marshal John Sherman. McSween and the Regulators learned the posse was on its way to Lincoln and left before it arrived.[127]

Judge Bristol served double duty; not only was he a territorial judge, but he was also a US district court judge, so when the Kid and the other Regulators failed to appear in US district court in Mesilla on June 22, the grand jury indicted them all for Buckshot Roberts's murder. The Kid now had territorial murder charges for Sheriff Bill Brady and federal murder charges for Buckshot Roberts against him.[128]

The Kid and the other Regulators established a camp in the mountains near their old hangout, San Patricio. From time to time, they would visit the town for supplies and to socialize.[129]

On June 27, Sheriff Peppin sent Deputy Sheriff Jack Long and a five-man posse, assisted by Kinney and his twelve men, to San Patricio to arrest Regulators. They spotted George Washington who was acting as the Regulator's cook. Washington attempted to escape, running through a wheat field, but Kinney fired his Winchester, kicking up dirt around Washington's feet. Washington stopped, dropped his rifle, and surrendered. He was forced to reveal what he knew of the Regulators' whereabouts. Long and his men rode up the Ruidoso in search of Regulators while Kinney and his men stayed in town.[130]

Two miles to the west, Long and his men ran into eleven Regulators, including the Kid, McSween, and former Sheriff Copeland. Firing erupted between the two groups. The Regulators shot two of the posse's horses, including Long's, shot out from under him. The sounds of the shots brought Kinney and his men to the rescue. The Regulators retreated up a mountain slope where it would be hard to approach them. The standoff lasted four hours until the Regulators slipped away. Peppin and his posse left, and the Regulators soon returned to San Patricio.[131]

Peppin wasn't done. On July 3, he sent another posse to San Patricio—this one was made up of fifteen Hispanos led by Deputy Sheriff José Chavez y Baca. The Regulators were waiting for them as they rode into the plaza before sunup. The Regulators opened fire, killing one horse and shattering Julian López's arm before the posse retreated from town.[132]

As the Regulators rode out of town down the Rio Hondo, Deputy Sheriff Jack Long followed with a second, larger posse including Jimmie Dolan with John Kinney and his men. Four miles east of town, Doc Scurlock had the Regulators dismount at the top of a ridge and take defensive positions. Firing into the oncoming posse, they killed two horses. Long decided they couldn't overwhelm the Regulators, so they returned to Lincoln, but not before they terrorized and ransacked San Patricio in revenge for the town's support of the Regulators.[133]

It was about this time that news reached Lincoln County that neither the House nor the Regulators could rely on the military for support anymore. On June 18, 1878, President Rutherford B. Hayes signed into law the Posse Comitatus Act, which forbade the army from interfering in civil affairs unless authorized by the president.[134]

The Regulators rode to John Chisum's ranch. Chisum wasn't there, but they were welcomed and were invited to stay for the next day's Fourth of July celebration and dinner. Chisum's sixteen-year-old niece, Sallie Chisum, was there, and the next morning the Kid, along with several other Regulators, rode to Roswell where the Kid bought candy for Sallie from Ash Upson at Captain Lea's store.[135]

On their ride back to the Chisum ranch, they were attacked by a large pro-House posse from Seven Rivers led by Buck Powell and Marion Turner. It was a five-mile running fight back to the ranch. Chisum's ranch had excellent defenses, so all the fighting that day was done with long-distance shots that didn't hurt anyone on either side. The Chisum ranch Fourth of July celebration went ahead as planned. The Seven Rivers posse sent to Lincoln for help, but when reinforcements arrived, the Regulators had slipped away.[136]

Back in June, Rob Widenmann had left Lincoln County never to return. During that same month Texan Tom O'Folliard joined the Regulators and would become the Kid's best friend. O'Folliard was sixteen, two years younger than the Kid, who took a liking to him. The Kid taught O'Folliard how to shoot, and he became the Kid's constant companion.[137]

The Kid practiced his marksmanship from every conceivable angle, mounted and dismounted. He only cared to have enough money to buy more cartridges. Along with becoming a good shot, the Kid was a callous killer when it came to dealing with those belonging to the opposition. Sue McSween did not like him, saying he was "too much like Dolan, did not think it amounted to much to take a man's life." He was considered cool under pressure, intelligent, and a quick thinker. To those not his enemies, he was kind, courteous, and displayed a good sense of humor. The Kid was a good horseman and was always kind to his horses.[138]

Mac McSween was tired of running. He just wanted to return to his home in Lincoln. He might have believed he had won the war after Judge Frank Angel sent word to him that Governor Samuel Axtell, US District Attorney Thomas Catron, and Indian agent Frederick Godfroy were to be removed from office. However, he was taking no chances and returned to Lincoln the night of July 14, 1878, with sixty Regulators.[139]

The Regulators occupied several defensive positions in town. The Kid and twelve others went to McSween's house. Doc Scurlock took twelve men to the Ellis store, Martin Chavez and his men occupied Patrón's and Montaño's stores, while others went to a grain warehouse behind Tunstall's store.[140]

Sheriff Peppin had stationed Deputy Sheriffs Jack Long, Billy Mathews, and several additional men in the *torreón*, a stone tower that had been built to defend against Apaches. At the opposite end of the street, at the Wortley Hotel across from the House's abandoned store, were Jimmie Dolan, recovering from a broken leg, Sheriff George Peppin, and a few others. The Regulators clearly outnumbered them.[141]

Sheriff Peppin sent messages to Marion Turner and Buck Powell's Seven Rivers posse and to John Kinney and his posse searching for the Regulators to come quickly to Lincoln.[142]

On July 15, McSween learned Captain Saturnio Baca, who had a house on property McSween owned, was supplying food and water to Peppin's men in the *torreón*. McSween sent Baca a message ordering him to leave his property in three days as he was assisting "murderers for the purpose of taking my life." Mrs. Baca had just given birth, but McSween insisted since they had aided his enemies, they must leave. The Bacas asked Lieutenant Colonel Dudley for help. With the new Posse Comitatus law in effect, Dudley could not interfere, but he did send the post doctor, Lieutenant Dan Appel, to town to investigate. Appel went to see McSween, who told him Baca was helping his enemies and so they had to go. He also said, "I've returned to my home and they won't drive me away again alive."[143]

Appel attempted to negotiate between the two factions. Deputy Sheriff Jack Long proposed that they would leave the *torreón* if the army occupied it. McSween was leery of the idea, and it fell through. Appel interviewed a few other residents in town who were apprehensive that there would be another fight. Only about twelve families remained in Lincoln—everyone else had fled.[144]

Buck Powell's Seven Rivers posse and John Kinney's posse joined forces outside town. Jesse Evans was back with them. Judge

Bristol had allowed him to be freed on bail while awaiting trial for Tunstall's murder.[145]

The combined posse galloped from the west into town. Dismounting at the Wortley Hotel, they began firing their rifles at the McSween house. Regulators in the McSween house fired back. No one was hit in the exchange. Some Regulators in the Montaño store started to run toward the McSween house. Deputy Sheriff Long in the *torreón* shouted to them to halt. Their answer was to shoot at him, so he and his men opened fire on them.[146]

Jimmie Dolan had Sheriff Peppin order Deputy Sheriff Long to serve warrants and arrest McSween, the Kid, and other Regulators in the McSween house. Long walked toward the house and called out for them to surrender. He was answered by several shots being fired in his direction. He did not fire back but quickly left the street and went to the Wortley Hotel to report his efforts to Peppin.[147]

No one was hurt during all the shooting that first day. Approximately forty men in Sheriff Peppin's posse faced about sixty Regulators, but the Regulators were divided into several different positions. It was almost impossible for the Regulators to go from one building to the other without being shot at, so the posse could concentrate their efforts on the Regulator positions one at a time. Sue McSween, her older sister, Elizabeth Shield, and her five small children were in the McSween house, and Dr. Taylor and Mary Ealy and their two small children, along with schoolteacher Susan Gates, were in the Tunstall store.[148]

On Tuesday, July 16, there was lots of firing back and forth between the two sides, but again no one was hit. Someone on Peppin's posse had an idea—if the army was not authorized to come help them, why not borrow a howitzer from them. Someone wrote a note to Lieutenant Colonel Dudley and Peppin signed it.[149]

Lieutenant Colonel Dudley wrote a response saying his sympathies were with Sheriff Peppin and he would like to help, but he was constrained by law and orders and had to refuse. Black cavalryman Berry Robinson carried the dispatch back to Peppin. As he reached the Wortley Hotel at 6:30 p.m., men on the roof of the McSween housc shot at him. Peppin hoped to use this incident to possibly bring the army into the fight on his side and sent a message to Dudley about the shooting.[150]

Peppin had posted men along the hills behind the Montaño store. The next morning, July 17, it was quiet at the store, and Peppin's men left their position to walk back to the Wortley Hotel. On top of the Montaño store roof was crack shot Fernando Herrera who fired at one of Peppin's men, Charlie Crawford, sending a bullet through his body entering one hip smashing the spinal column and exiting out the other hip. Crawford could not even crawl, and no one was willing to go to his aid.[151]

Later that day, Dr. Appel and other officers from Fort Robinson arrived with a black cavalry escort to investigate the firing upon Berry Robinson. Of course, Sheriff Peppin and his posse said it did happen, and McSween denied the Regulators had shot at Robinson. While the soldiers were in town, they learned about the wounded Crawford, still lying on the hillside in the hot sun. Appel, Captain Thomas Blair, and two enlisted men went to Crawford's aid and were shot at by a Regulator from the Montaño store. That did not deter them, however, and they took Crawford in an ambulance back to the fort, where he later died.[152]

That night, Isaac Ellis's son Ben was feeding a mule outside the store when he was shot in the neck. The wound was serious, and under cover of darkness, two Regulators made their way to Tunstall's store and asked Dr. Ealy to return with them to treat Ben's wound. He agreed to go with them, but as they made their way toward the Ellis store, the posse members in the *torreón* saw them and started shooting. They had to return to Tunstall's store.[153]

The next morning, July 18, Dr. Ealy, holding five-year-old daughter Pearl's hand with Mary alongside him holding baby Ruth, walked into the street past the *torreón* unmolested and went into the Ellis store where they treated Ben's throat wound. He was lucky and would survive.[154]

There wasn't much fighting during the day, but there was a rumor that John Chisum was on his way to Lincoln with men and a cannon to help the Regulators. That afternoon, Jimmie Dolan went to Fort Stanton to personally ask Lieutenant Colonel Dudley to intervene. After Dolan left, Dudley ordered all available artillery to be made ready for use. Dudley then conferred with his officers and they agreed it was a dangerous situation for women and children in the town. If they made a show of force, maybe that would settle down the situation.[155]

On July 19, 1878, Dolan informed the posse they needed to begin surrounding the McSween house and attack it. They determined who would take which strategic position around the house once the army arrived. Dolan must have been sure the army would show. At 7:00 a.m. both sides began firing at each other between the Wortley Hotel and the McSween house.[156]

At 10:30 a.m., Dudley arrived in town with four officers, thirty-five enlisted men—both infantry and black cavalry—a twelve-pounder mountain howitzer, and a Gatling gun with plenty of ammunition. Dudley stopped in front of the Wortley Hotel and informed Peppin and his posse that he and his troops were not there to help them but only to protect women and children, and if any of them fired upon his troops he would retaliate.[157]

Dudley led the troops down the street past the McSween house and then to an open area strategically placed between the Ellis store and McSween's house and across the street from the Montaño store. There the troops began to set up camp. Dudley's first order was to unlimber the mountain howitzer and point it at the Montaño store.[158]

While Dudley's troops were marching down the street, Dolan and Peppin's men were taking positions surrounding the McSween house. Dudley did nothing to stop them.[159]

The Regulators in McSween's house saw Sheriff Peppin on the street escorted by soldiers and feared the army was working with him. Another unnerving sign appeared. Peppin's posse hung out a black flag—the Mexican signal for no quarter.[160]

Dudley informed the Regulators in the Montaño store and the Ellis store, if they fired on his troops he would fire the mountain howitzer at their buildings. The men in the Montaño store left and walked down the street to the Ellis store. Once the Montaño store was abandoned, Dudley had the howitzer swung around to face the Ellis store and the Gatling gun positioned to cover the area behind the store. Shortly thereafter, all the Regulators from both stores, forty men, mounted their horses and rode out of town led by Doc Scurlock and Martin Chavez. Peppin and some of his deputies raced on foot after the departing Regulators. Peppin shouted for them to halt, but they were out of gunshot range and proceeded to disappear into the hills. McSween had lost two-thirds of his men.[161]

Peppin's posse had the McSween house and Tunstall store completely surrounded, and the Regulators could not fire at those posse members located to the east of the house as the soldiers were stationed there. McSween sent a note to Dudley asking why his soldiers were surrounding his house and stating, "Before blowing up my property, I would like to know the reason." McSween also wrote that the constable, Jose Chavez y Chavez, was with him and had warrants for the arrest of Sheriff Peppin and his posse for murder and larceny.[162]

Dudley did not respond directly but had his adjutant, Lieutenant Millard Goodwin, reply that his troops were not surrounding the house and that Lieutenant Colonel Dudley "desires to hold no correspondence with you." The message went on to say if McSween wanted to blow up his own house Dudley had no objection, just don't injure any troops in the process.[163]

McSween, seeing he was in a desperate situation, sent another note to Dudley stating he was willing to surrender to him, but did not want to surrender to a mob. Dudley refused, saying he was only there to protect women and children.[164]

Earlier, Dudley had forced Justice of the Peace John Wilson to issue warrants for the arrest of McSween and other Regulators based on affidavits signed by his officers. Wilson, finding no one willing to execute the warrant, turned it over to Sheriff Peppin, who in turn gave it to Deputy Sheriff Marion Turner from Seven Rivers to deliver.[165]

Turner and four men reached one of the windows at the front of McSween's house, pried open a shutter, and smashed the window. Turner shouted into the house that he had warrants for the arrest of McSween and others in the house.

"We have warrants for you," McSween shouted back.

"Show me your warrants. Where are they?" Turner shouted.

"Our guns are our warrants," Jim French replied for the Regulators.

Turner left and returned to the Wortley Hotel to report to Peppin.[166]

That afternoon, Sue McSween left the house to talk to Lieutenant Colonel Dudley. She passed posse members making preparations to set fire to her house and then ran into Sheriff Peppin and railed at him about attacking her home and preparing to burn it down. He told her the only way to save her house was to have McSween and his men surrender. She found Dudley at the army camp and their discussion quickly became a shouting match. Sue denounced Dudley for siding with Peppin and pleaded with him to save her husband. Dudley refused, saying he could not interfere with a sheriff carrying out his lawful duties. Dudley ordered the guard to remove her from camp. Sue returned to her home where her sister and five children were sheltering. So far, Dudley was refusing to follow through on his self-proclaimed mission to protect women and children.[167]

The McSween house was an adobe structure facing the main street with two wings on each side forming an angular U. The

McSweens lived in the west wing and the Shields in the east wing. At the end of each wing was a wooden summer kitchen.[168]

Deputy Sheriff Jack Long and another man, known only as Dummy since he did not speak, ran to the east wing summer kitchen, opened the door, threw in kindling, dowsed it with coal oil, lit it on fire, and retreated through the gate in the wooden wall between McSween's and Tunstall's store.[169]

As Long and Dummy were racing through the gate, they were joined by Deputy Sheriff Buck Powell. George Coe and two other Regulators located in the Tunstall store saw them and opened fire. Their only cover was a privy. The three of them quickly entered it and slid down into the pit as the Regulators riddled the building with bullets. They were pinned down in the privy pit until nightfall.[170]

The Shields' daughter, Minnie, opened the door to the summer kitchen and saw flames. She called to her mother who was able to extinguish the fire.[171]

Deputy Sheriff Andy Boyle and other posse members went to the summer kitchen at the end of the west wing and were successful in setting that on fire. The men inside the house rushed to put it out but were shot at by Peppin's posse and had to retreat. The fire burned into the house, the flames slowly creeping from room to room. There was no water to douse the flames and no way to stop the fire's advance. The flames reached a keg of gunpowder that exploded, causing the fire to burn even more rapidly.[172]

Firing continued throughout the day as McSween, despondent, sat with his head down. Even though he was one of the youngest Regulators in the house, the Kid took over leadership. He grabbed McSween and shook him, telling him the fire was burning slow enough they could stay in the house until night and then make a break for it down to the river. The Kid turned to Sue McSween and told her it was time for the women and children to leave.[173]

Mary Ealy, who was living in the Tunstall store with her two children, went to Dudley and requested protection. Dudley sent soldiers and a wagon to the store to pick up the women and children. When they saw the soldiers and wagon outside the Tunstall store, the women and children from the McSween house came out and were also granted protection and taken away.[174]

The firing was intense that evening. Some army officers estimated over two thousand rounds were fired. As darkness descended, the flames from the building lit up the immediate area as if it were daylight. The defenders retreated into the last of the building not yet on fire—the summer kitchen that Long and Dummy had tried to set on fire first.[175]

The Regulators' plan was that the Kid and four others would make a break for the Tunstall store hoping to draw the posse's fire while McSween and the rest of the men would try to sneak out the back gate and down to the river.[176]

About 9:00 p.m., the Kid's group started off quietly with the Kid bringing up the rear. To reach Tunstall's store, they had to pass through a gate in the wooden wall between McSween's property and Tunstall's property. As they began passing through the gate, shots were fired at them from Tunstall's store. As Harvey Morris reached the gate, he was shot and killed. The others made it through, but realizing the posse now occupied Tunstall's store, they turned and ran in the direction of the river.[177]

The Kid saw a figure near the wall behind the house and shot at it. It was John Kinney. The Kid's bullet tore off Kinney's mustache grazing his upper lip. Kinney fell to the ground and the Kid thought he had killed him, but Kinney was only startled.[178]

McSween's group had quietly left the house and had reached the gate through the adobe wall at the rear of the property. But blocking their escape route were posse members Andy Boyle, Joe Nash, Bob Beckwith, John Jones, Marion Turner, and Dummy, who had climbed out of the privy pit.[179]

The posse members began shooting at McSween and his men. Some took shelter in a chicken coop, and McSween and the others went behind a woodpile. Someone in McSween's group called out they wanted to surrender. Bob Beckwith replied, "Yes, I can receive your surrender." Dummy walked in first, followed by John Jones, Bob Beckwith, and Joe Nash. As they walked up to McSween and his men, the Regulators hidden in the chicken coop opened fire, killing Beckwith with a shot to the head. Everyone shot at each other as they dove for cover. McSween fell dead with five bullets in him.[180]

Several Regulators made their escape. Boyle and Nash called for the men in the chicken coop to surrender. They refused. Boyle and Nash used a log to punch a hole in the adobe wall and shot into the coop. When the fight was over, Regulators Francisco Zamora and Vicente Romero were found dead. Fifteen-year-old Yginio Salazar lay on the ground unconscious from two bullet wounds. John Kinney walked up and kicked him. He prepared to shoot Salazar when Milo Pierce told him not to waste his bullets on a dead man. Kinney walked away. Later Salazar regained

consciousness and dragged himself to his sister-in-law's house where he was treated and eventually recovered.[181]

The battle was over. The victorious posse partied around McSween's burning house, forcing McSween's employees, George Washington and Sebrian Bates, to play their fiddles while the posse members sang and danced and got drunk, whooping it up and shooting their guns in the air. As for the army, some soldiers came to the celebration, and no one had anything negative to say about what had happened. Other than one man dragging McSween's body away from the flames, no one touched the four Regulators' bodies until the following day.[182]

With Tunstall's store vacated, the mob ransacked everything in it and robbed the bank. The next morning, Tunstall employee Sam Corbet went to Sheriff Peppin asking for help to recover the goods and money looted from the store and bank. Peppin responded he was not responsible for what had been looted.[183]

That night the Kid and the other Regulators who had escaped hid out in the hills. They later rendezvoused with fellow Regulators at Frank Coe's ranch on the Rio Hondo.[184]

The Regulators remained together, although now without Tunstall or McSween they had no purpose other than getting more horses and revenge.[185]

The Kid and the others who escaped the McSween house were on foot. Peppin had confiscated their horses in Lincoln, so they spent the next couple of days stealing horses. Once remounted, they terrorized those who supported Peppin's posse. They threatened they would kill Peppin and others, even including Lieutenant Colonel Dudley, who they believed sided with Peppin. Mescalero Apache Indian agent Frederick Godfroy, who had worked closely with the House, believed the Kid was out to kill him and asked Dudley for an army escort.[186]

On August 5, twenty Regulators including the Kid, half Anglo and half Hispano, rode onto the Mescalero Apache Reservation near Blazer's Mill. Frank Coe later said they were only there to visit Dick Brewer's grave. As the band neared the agency, the Anglos left the road to visit a spring. The Hispanos continued along the road and encountered a band of Apaches who may have been thinking they were after their horse herd. The Apaches opened fire on them.[187]

Hearing the gunfire, Indian agent Godfroy and his clerk, Morris Bernstein, mounted their horses and galloped to the scene of the gunfight. Godfrey said Bernstein reached the scene of the fight before he did, and when Godfroy got there, Bernstein had been shot and killed. Godfroy wheeled his horse around, raced back to the agency, and returned to the scene of the fight with soldiers.[188]

At the springs, the Kid had dismounted and dropped his reins to drink the spring water. When the gunshots sounded, his horse bolted. The soldiers and Indians spotted the Regulators by the springs and raced toward them. The Kid jumped up behind George Coe and they raced away with bullets zipping around them.[189]

The Regulators eluded the soldiers and Apaches and made their way back to the agency corral. Three other Regulators had lost their horses during the fracas and needed new mounts. The Regulators took all the animals in the corral. The Kid roped an Indian pony and rode his new horse bareback to George Coe's ranch.[190]

The Kid was accused of killing Bernstein, and public opinion again turned against the Regulators. Bernstein's body was found with four bullet holes in it. He had been robbed of his guns and everything on him. His pockets were even turned inside out, but anyone who really knew who killed him and why was not talking. Since the Regulators had stolen US government horses, Lieutenant Colonel Dudley sent his cavalry after them, but they were long gone.[191]

On August 13, 1878, the Kid and some of the Regulators arrived with their stolen herd at Chisum's ranch at Bosque Grande on the Pecos River. John Chisum's brothers, Jim and Pitser, were there with a large cattle herd they planned to take north. Sallie Chisum was also with them. She and the Kid had been exchanging letters, and she recorded in her diary a couple entries about candy and an Indian tobacco sack he gave her.[192]

The Kid and the Regulators stayed with the Chisums as they moved the herd upriver to Fort Sumner. The Chisums continued on while the Regulators stayed. There the Kid and his friends enjoyed themselves for a week, throwing parties and dancing with the Hispano girls. They rode upriver to Puerto de Luna and then to Anton Chico, continuing their parties in each town.[193]

The first night in Anton Chico they heard that San Miguel County Sheriff Desiderio Romero, with an eight-member posse, was in Manuel Sanchez's saloon inquiring about the "Lincoln County War party." The Kid gathered the Regulators, walked into the saloon, and told the sheriff they were the Lincoln County War party and if he wanted to take them, now was the time to do it. The sheriff saw he and his men were outgunned and backed down. The Kid bought them a drink before telling them to ride out of town.[194]

Doc Scurlock had dropped out of the Regulators, who now elected the Kid as their new leader. The Coes said they were done and moving on to Colorado. The rest of the Regulators under the Kid's leadership returned to Lincoln County to help Doc Scurlock and Charlie Bowdre move their families away from Lincoln where they now felt insecure after the death of McSween. While they were at it, on September 7, they decided to take along fifteen head of horses belonging to House supporter Charles Fritz. The Regulators escorted the Scurlock and Bowdre families to Fort Sumner where Pete Maxwell gave the two men jobs herding cattle.[195]

The Kid, along with Tom O'Folliard, Henry Brown, Fred Waite, and John Middleton, raided a few more ranches to increase their number of horses to forty and then drove their herd toward the Texas Panhandle where there was always a market for horses. On September 25, they caught up again with the Chisum outfit. It was the last time the Kid and Sallie would ever see each other.[196]

BILLY THE KID'S PHOTO(S)

The photograph of Billy the Kid standing as he holds the barrel of his Winchester is an iconic image of the Old West. An unknown photographer took it in either 1879 or 1880 at Fort Sumner, New Mexico. This is the only known photograph of the Kid that has the documentation to prove it actually is the Kid.

The photograph is called a tintype and to create a tintype image was quite an involved process. When tintypes were finished, the image was the reverse of the person or object being photographed, so even though Billy the Kid was right-handed, many people later wrongly assumed he was left-handed after viewing the tintype and noticing his pistol was on his supposed left hip.[197]

This particular tintype of the Kid was called a Bon Ton. The camera had four lenses so when the photographer took the picture, four separate images of the same subject were created. At the end of the developing process, the plate was divided into four pieces, each a slightly different copy of the same subject. The Kid gave the four photos to four friends.[198]

He gave one to his good friend Dan Dedrick who passed it on to his nephew Frank Upham in 1930. The world knows the Kid by this photo.[199]

According to *True West Magazine* publisher emeritus Robert McCubbin, the Kid gave a second photo to Deluvina, one of Pete Maxwell's female servants and good friend to the Kid. This photo was reported to have been lost in a 1930s fire. He gave a third photo to his sweetheart Paulita Maxwell. No one knows the whereabouts of this photo. The Kid may have given the fourth photo to his friend Celsa Gutierrez who was Sheriff Pat Garrett's sister-in-law. Garrett sent this photo to a Chicago publisher for use in one of the editions of *The Authentic Life of Billy the Kid*. Someone at the publishing house must not have thought much of the photo and tossed it in the trash.[200]

Billy the Kid's tintype remained with the Upham family for years until 2010 when they made the decision to sell it. They contacted auctioneer Brian Lebel, who agreed to sell it at his Old West Show & Auction in Denver, Colorado. On Saturday, June 25, 2011, collector Bill Koch bought the credit-card-sized tintype for $2.3 million.[201]

There are many images people claim are of Billy the Kid, but none of them have solid provenance—there is no documentation to back up the claims.[202]

On October 19, 2015, the National Geographic Channel aired a program claiming a photo had been found that shows Billy the Kid, Sallie Chisum, Paulita Maxwell, Tom O'Folliard, Manuela and Charlie Bowdre, and others playing croquet or located near the game.[203]

In 2010, Randy Guijarro had bought some tintypes at a Fresno, California, flea market for two dollars. He believed one of the individuals in one of the photos was Billy the Kid. When he showed it to Billy the Kid historians, they dismissed it as not being the Kid. Undaunted, Guijarro convinced producer Jeff Aiello and his wife that the photo was authentic and showed Billy the Kid. Eventually the show was produced and sold to National Geographic Channel with actor Kevin Costner as executive producer and narrator.[204]

Proponents believe the photo is the correct time period and location and that the figures in the photo match the Kid and his friends. Kent Gibson, one of the top forensic scientists in the country, believes facial recognition matches Billy the Kid, Charlie Bowdre, Tom O'Folliard, Sallie Chisum, and Paulita Maxwell.[205]

Opponents believe the photo does not show the Kid and friends. There is no provenance for the photo; the location and time of year appear wrong for the characters to have been together. There is no recording of them all getting together for a game of croquet. Some of the characters just don't seem to be correct, based on height, weight, and age. The face of "the Croquet Kid" is blurry.[206]

The only thing that is certain is the debate will continue.

CHAPTER 11
OUTLAWS

From 1878 and into 1880, Frank and Jesse James continued living in Tennessee, hiding their lives of crime, and using the aliases of Ben J. Woodson for Frank and John Davis Howard for Jesse. They continued farming, and Jesse traveled widely as a grain speculator. The brothers would meet from time to time, claiming they were brothers-in-law. Both liked to gamble. Frank was a good poker player, Jesse was not. They were both avid horse racers—owning racehorses and betting at the races.[1]

Jesse had mounting debts. In cases where he believed he had been cheated, he refused to pay the bill. By the spring of 1879, Jesse needed money and began recruiting new gang members, but Frank took no part, being content to continue farming. Jesse's responsibilities increased when on July 17, 1879, Zee bore a daughter they named Mary.[2]

Shortly after Mary's birth, Jesse took a trip on the Atchison, Topeka and Santa Fe Railway, riding the rails to the end of the line, Las Vegas, New Mexico Territory. From July 26 to 29, he visited old Missouri friends Scott Moore and his wife, Minnie, who ran a hotel and bathhouse at hot springs six miles outside of town. Possibly Jesse was looking for a new place to settle to escape creditors, maybe he was looking for easy targets to rob, maybe he visited the hot springs to ease his old wounds, or maybe he was looking for recruits for his new gang. There were stagecoach and train robberies in the Las Vegas area during this time, and people speculated that the James boys were the culprits, but there was no evidence. Some of the robberies were committed by a gang, the Dodge City Gang, based out of Las Vegas, and other crimes by two Texans called the Thompson brothers.[3]

By October 1879, Jesse had formed his new gang. The members were Jesse's cousin Wood Hite, Tucker Bassham, Bill Ryan, Dick Liddil, and Ed Miller, brother to deceased Clell. Jesse's target was the Chicago and Alton Railroad station at Glendale in an area called the Cracker Neck, south of Independence, Missouri. Jesse learned that on the evening of October 8, an eastbound train would be hauling a load of gold and silver bullion from Leadville, Colorado.[4]

The James Gang struck the small, isolated settlement of Glendale at dusk on October 8, 1879. All wore masks except for Jesse and Hite. The gang members split into two groups. One group collected thirteen people at the store and in the houses and herded them to the two-story depot building. The other group entered the depot where they got the drop on the railroad agent, his mother, and a railroad auditor as they smashed the telegraph machine.[5]

The gang forced the agent to take a signal light out to the tracks to stop the next eastbound train. Bill Ryan accompanied the agent to set up the signal light. The agent was curious as to who they were, and Ryan responded, "We are the James gang." Other gang members found large rocks and placed them on the track to block the train if it failed to stop for the light.[6]

At 8:00 p.m., the engineer saw the signal and slowed the train to a stop at the station. Liddil captured the engineer and fireman as two gang members walked the opposite sides of the tracks along the cars to ensure no passengers left or stuck their heads out the windows. The gang had no plans to rob the passengers; instead Jesse and Ed Miller went to the express car. The doors were locked, and they shouted to the messenger inside to open the door. The messenger was United States Express employee William Grimes who was not about to open the door. Miller swung a coal hammer at the front door, busting it open. Grimes had opened the safe, stuffed its contents into a valise, and ran to the car's back door. His plan was to jump out of the car and disappear into the darkness. Jesse rushed in, struck Grimes over the head with his revolver, and grabbed the valise. He discovered there was no gold and silver bullion shipment; it had been transferred to another line in Kansas City, Missouri.[7]

Jesse left a note with the railroad agent which read, "We are the boys who are hard to handle, and will make it hot for the party who tries to take us," and listed nine fictitious names. The James Gang whooped as they galloped south.[8]

Several miles down the road, they broke into an abandoned house where they split the loot, discovering most of it was non-negotiable securities. The actual amount of cash available to them was $6,000, which Jesse divided among them. He advised the gang members not to carry more than fifteen dollars and to be careful how they spent the money. They split up, going their separate ways. Ed Miller and Jesse traveled together, hiding out in the woods for several days. The Jackson County sheriff led a posse in search of the robbers but only came up with what the gang had discarded at the abandoned house. The railroad and express company offered rewards totaling $1,250 per gang member.[9]

On November 4, 1879, Kansas City newspapers reported that one-eyed George Shepherd had shot and killed Jesse James near Galena, Kansas. Shepherd, a former bushwhacker leader, had served time for the 1868 Russellville, Kentucky, bank robbery. Kansas City Marshal James Ligget confirmed Shepherd was on his payroll. Many people believed the tale. When a party went to the scene of the shooting, no body was found, but it was explained that Jesse's friends had recovered his body and buried it. Cole Younger learned the news and believed it, saying Jesse and George had been enemies after George was released from prison. James boys supporter John Edwards wrote about the shooting, "From the days of Judas Iscariot down, all men despise those who follow his example." Robert Pinkerton did not believe the story. Jesse's mother, Zerelda, said it would take a two-eyed man to get Jesse. Frank James knew Jesse was not dead because Jesse was in Nashville at the time. Frank later said, "We laughed a good deal over it but never learned what it all meant."[10]

In early 1880, the James boys' national notoriety skyrocketed again with the publication of J. A. Dacus's book, *The Life and Adventures of Frank and Jesse James and the Younger Brothers*. It was claimed twenty-one thousand copies were sold in the first four months of publication. Another book published at the same time was R. T. Bradley's *The Outlaws of the Border* which contained a reprint of John Edwards's *Noted Guerrillas*.[11]

The James boys continued their horse-racing ventures into 1880. Frank stayed away from outlaw activities while Jesse continued to plot new robberies. James Gang member Tucker Bassham had been arrested with a large amount of cash, and Jesse must have wondered if he would tell what he knew.[12]

Sometime in the late spring or early summer of 1880, Jesse, along with Ed Miller, who had borrowed a horse from former bushwhacker Jim Cummins, rode from Nashville, Tennessee, into Missouri. Near Norborne, Missouri, Miller and Jesse had a falling out. One story said it was over stopping for some tobacco. Another story was that Miller had come into an inheritance from his father's estate and wanted out of the gang. The story continued that Miller shot at Jesse, knocking the hat off his head. Jesse returned fire, killing Miller. Much later, a decomposed body was found in the Norborne area, and Miller was never heard from again. In July, Jesse returned to Tennessee, bringing with him gang members Dick Liddil and Bill Ryan, searching for new targets of opportunity.[13]

Mammoth Cave, Kentucky, was a major tourist attraction, drawing visitors from around the world to marvel at its natural wonders. The cave's owners made quite a bit of money from entrance fees and running a stagecoach line to the cave. Jesse learned that the owners sent money out to heirs of the property owners on a regular basis.[14]

At 5:00 p.m., on September 3, 1880, the stagecoach left the Cave Hotel with eight passengers. Several miles out, near Little Hope Baptist Church, Jesse and his accomplice, Bill Ryan, held up the stagecoach. Unfortunately for them, they found the stagecoach was not hauling any money for the Mammoth Cave heirs. They robbed the passengers anyway, taking cash as well as a valuable gold watch from Judge Rutherford Rowntree, and three rings, one of which held a diamond, from the judge's daughter Lizzie. Jesse presented a quart bottle of whiskey to the victims and made everyone take a drink except for the judge and Lizzie. Eluding a Cave City posse, Jesse and Bill returned home to Nashville, Tennessee, where Jesse presented the diamond ring to Zee.[15]

On October 15, Jesse, along with Bill Ryan and Dick Liddil, held up John Dovey's store at the Dovey Coal Mines near Mercer, Kentucky. They had learned that the mine payroll was arriving that day. Unfortunately for them, the payroll had not arrived yet, and their take was a gold watch and thirteen dollars.[16]

For the remainder of 1880, Jesse continued planning robberies and racing horses. He became suspicious of gang members and friends, moving the family to a Nashville boarding house and then later renting a house outside the city in Edgefield. Believing his old bushwhacker friend Jim Cummins might betray him, Jesse considered killing him, but the gang members would not go along with it. Frank and Jesse argued over Bill Ryan. Frank considered Ryan a drunk and believed he would get them all caught.[17]

A story emerged that was told throughout Missouri, Kentucky, Tennessee, and Arkansas. It varied slightly from locality to locality, but the basic story was this. The James Gang had pulled off a robbery. Riding through the countryside they spotted a small farmhouse and, being hungry, stopped and asked the woman of the house for something to eat, which they would gladly pay for.

She had little food but agreed to feed them. As she was preparing the food, the gang members noticed she was weeping. Jesse asked why she was crying. She said her husband was dead and that she had several children in school. To make matters worse, the mortgage on her house was overdue. She owed $1,400, which she did not have, and the old miser who held the mortgage was to arrive that very day to evict her if she didn't pay. After eating, Jesse gave the widow $1,400 to pay the man and a little extra for her needs. Then he instructed her in writing a receipt and told her to make sure the lender signed it in ink. Jesse asked her to describe the man, the direction he would be arriving from, and the time she expected him. The widow wept tears of joy as the James Gang rode away. They found a place to hide along the road and watched as the lender drove his buggy to the farmhouse. On his return trip, he was whistling "Old Dan Tucker" as the gang surrounded him and relieved him of the $1,400.[18]

It's possible this story is based on the Benton family encounter with the James Gang. The 1880 census for Sumner County, Tennessee, lists Nancy Benton, widow of Richard Benton. The Benton family tradition is that the James Gang stopped at Nancy's home for a meal and left her a large amount of money.[19]

Late in September 1878, the Kid and his Regulator friends Tom O'Folliard, Henry Brown, Fred Waite, and John Middleton drove their herd of forty stolen horses into the Texas Panhandle. The Panhandle was a good market for horses and no one asked questions about where they came from.[20]

About ten miles outside Tascosa, the Panhandle's major settlement, the Kid and his friends met twenty-four-year-old Dr. Henry Hoyt and inquired about the countryside, local ranchers, and the market for horses. Hoyt willingly answered their questions.[21]

Hoyt, a Minnesotan who had studied to be a physician, was exploring the West while practicing medicine. He had been to

Deadwood, Dakota Territory, searching for gold, and was now working as a cowhand in the Texas Panhandle to supplement his medical practice.[22]

Because the Regulators' reputation had preceded them, residents were concerned when the men arrived in Tascosa. Since Tascosa had no law enforcement, a group of local cattlemen met with the Kid and asked him what the Regulators' intentions were. The Kid explained they were in town to sell horses and enjoy themselves, nothing more. The cattlemen and the Kid came to an agreement. The cattlemen would not bother the Regulators as long as they behaved themselves. The Kid replied all they wanted was to be left alone.[23]

The Regulators found a good, steady market for their horses and began enjoying their profits. While his friends smoked and drank, the Kid was content to gamble, enter shooting matches, horse races, and attend the local *bailes,* enjoying the music and dancing with the Hispano girls.[24]

The Kid and Henry Hoyt became good friends. One of the reasons may have been that neither of them drank; however, the other Regulators were not teetotalers. Hoyt saw the Kid in action when John Middleton had too much to drink at Howard and McMaster's store. With his hand on his holstered revolver, a belligerent Middleton was swearing and challenging anyone in the store to fight him. The Kid walked in and told Middleton to get out of there and head back to camp. Middleton challenged the Kid, who rested his hand on his revolver and quietly and firmly replied he would see Middleton out back. Middleton backed down and returned to camp.[25]

Hoyt witnessed the Kid's shooting ability. Behind Howard and McMaster's store was a supply of empty quart beer bottles. A popular pastime was to line up six beer bottles fifty yards out and see who could shoot the most in the shortest amount of time. Hoyt said, "Here Billy was champion. He could pull his gun and demolish the six bottles in just half the time of any one else. . . . He was also a marvelous shot with a Winchester."[26]

Hoyt had won a lady's gold watch in a draw poker game. The Kid liked it very much and wanted to buy it. Hoyt suspected the Kid wanted to give it to a beautiful fifteen-year-old Hispano girl at Fort Sumner. The Kid was smitten with this girl whom Hoyt called "Lolita." Hoyt gave the Kid the watch which greatly pleased him.[27]

In late October 1878, Hoyt was preparing to leave Tascosa for Las Vegas, New Mexico, when the Kid rode into town leading his favorite horse, Dandy Dick. Hoyt had ridden the horse several times and admired him. The Kid gave Dandy Dick to Hoyt as a present and wrote out a bill of sale to him, so no one would question that it was his. The horse was a sorrel with a BB brand on the left hip. When Hoyt asked the Kid where he got Dandy Dick he only answered, "There's a story connected with him." Years later, Hoyt learned the horse had belonged to Sheriff Bill Brady.[28]

After the Regulators sold all their horses, the Kid wanted to go back to New Mexico, but the others, except for Tom O'Folliard, wanted to head east. It was the end of the Regulators. They went their separate ways. The Kid would never see John Middleton, Fred Waite, or Henry Brown again.[29]

The Kid and O'Folliard spent several weeks at Fort Sumner before returning to Lincoln, where the old McSween supporters welcomed him back.[30]

While the Kid had been away from Lincoln, there were developments that would affect his life. A band of rustlers calling themselves Selman's Scouts had gone on a three-week rampage through Lincoln County in September, killing, raping, and robbing anyone and destroying anything in their path. At the same time, several revenge killings had taken place between old Regulator and House factions. Sheriff George Peppin was defeated in the November election by George Kimbrell,[31] but Kimbrell did not take over right away due to an election-qualifying dispute. Lincoln County law enforcement was minimal through the early part of 1879.[32]

However, the biggest change was the removal of the governor. In September 1878, after reviewing Judge Frank Angel's report on the situation in New Mexico Territory, President Rutherford B. Hayes removed Governor Samuel Axtell from office and forced District Attorney Thomas Catron to resign later that fall. On October 1, 1878, President Hayes appointed veteran Union Civil War General Lew Wallace as governor of New Mexico Territory.[33]

Sue McSween was determined to bring Lieutenant Colonel Dudley to justice. She believed he directly caused her husband, Mac McSween's, death. She hired and brought to Lincoln a one-armed lawyer named Huston Chapman to help in her crusade against Dudley. Chapman sent letters to Governor Wallace denouncing Dudley, stating Dudley was a liar, drunkard, and "criminally responsible for the killing of McSween." Dudley retaliated with affidavits from eight citizens and three of his officers stating that Sue McSween was "a lewd, licentious, immoral, scandalous, dishonest, and ruthless woman."[34]

Right after appointing Wallace as governor, President Hayes issued a proclamation that Lincoln County insurgents were prohibiting the proper execution of the law and warned it must stop and all involved must disperse and return to their homes by October 13, 1878. With the president's proclamation of an insurrection in Lincoln County, he allowed the civil authorities to call upon the army to act in capturing outlaws and bringing them to civil authorities. Wallace followed the president's proclamation with his own on November 13. It stated all citizens of Lincoln County and officers and soldiers were pardoned of all offenses against the law from February 1, 1878, up to the date of the proclamation, except for those individuals indicted of crimes or those sentenced and serving time for their crimes. Lieutenant Colonel Dudley and his officers wrote a contemptuous letter to the *Santa Fe New Mexican* rejecting Governor Wallace's amnesty. Wallace was now convinced that to help bring peace to Lincoln County, Dudley had to go.[35]

The Kid and other Regulators were not welcome at Fort Stanton. On December 20, 1878, Lieutenant Colonel Dudley issued an order that the fort was off-limits to the Kid and ten other men "recognized as the murderers of Roberts, Brady, Tunstall, Bernstein, and Beckwith."[36]

The Kid wanted to go straight. He told his friend and old Tunstall clerk Sam Corbet that he was tired of fighting against the law and Jimmie Dolan's gang. Governor Wallace's proclamation did nothing to help the Kid since anyone indicted for crimes was exempt from the pardon. The Kid was indicted for two murders—a territorial indictment for the murder of Sheriff Bill Brady and a federal indictment for the murder of Buckshot Roberts.[37]

On February 18, 1879, one year to the day of John Tunstall's murder, the Kid decided to take matters into his own hands. He sent a message to Jesse Evans, who was then at Fort Stanton, asking if Dolan was for peace or war. The answer was that Dolan and his men would come to Lincoln to further discuss the situation. Later that night, both sides, possibly up to twenty men, stood behind adobe walls across the street from each other ready to fight if need be.[38]

Jesse Evans proclaimed that the Kid could not be dealt with and needed killing. The Kid answered that they had come to make peace and not start a fight. Cooler heads prevailed, and after some back and forth, the two sides agreed to a peace treaty, which they all signed. The treaty stated that no one on either side would kill those on the other side and no one would testify against anyone who signed the treaty. Before taking either of those actions, the signer would have to let the others know he was withdrawing from the treaty. Anyone who violated the treaty would be executed. They all shook hands and signed the document.[39]

That same night, the signers went together from bar to bar drinking and celebrating their treaty. The Kid went with them but did not participate in the drinking. Along with the Jimmie Dolan, Billy Mathews, and Jesse Evans gang was a newcomer,

Billy Campbell, a mean-tempered drifter. When they entered Juan Patrón's store to drink, Campbell drew his pistol and threatened to shoot Patrón, who hid behind the others.[40]

It was around 10:30 p.m.; the Kid walked with the drunken treaty signers up the street past the courthouse. Approaching in the opposite direction was Sue McSween's lawyer, Huston Chapman, unarmed and wearing a bandage around his face to ease a severe case of neuralgia.[41]

"Who are you and where are you going?" Campbell asked Chapman.

"My name is Chapman," he replied.

Campbell rammed his pistol in Chapman's chest saying, "You are the contemptible cur who has come in here and stirred up trouble. But we've settled it all now, and we are going to be friends. Now, just to show you are peaceable, too, you've got to dance."

The Kid saw that no good was going to come of this exchange and started to run, but Evans grabbed him and made him watch.

Chapman said he would not dance for a crowd of drunks, then asked, "Am I talking to Mr. Dolan?"

Jesse Evans responded, "No, but you are talking to a damned good friend of his."

A drunken Jimmie Dolan, standing ten feet behind Chapman, fired his Winchester, followed by Campbell firing point-blank into Chapman's chest.

"My God, I am killed," Chapman said as he fell to the ground dying.

Some said Campbell fired first, and then Dolan shot Chapman in the back with his Winchester.[42]

Chapman's body lay in the street, his clothes on fire from the powder burn as the mob walked away. Some said they deliberately set his body on fire to destroy any papers he might have had on him.[43]

As the men walked away from Chapman's burning body, Campbell said, "I promised my God and Colonel Dudley that I would kill Chapman and I have done it."[44]

They entered Cullum's eatery, where they continued to drink and dine on canned oysters. Dolan and Campbell decided someone needed to place a pistol in Chapman's hand, so it would look like self-defense. The Kid said he would do it. Campbell gave the Kid a pistol, he walked back down the street, placed it in Chapman's hand, and then rode out of town.[45]

Good thing the Kid left. The new sheriff, George Kimbrell, had spotted him earlier in the day and had gone to Fort Stanton where he was given a military posse of an officer and twenty cavalry troopers. The posse arrived in Lincoln around midnight. They did not find the Kid, but they did find Chapman's severely burned body lying in the street.[46]

The murder of Chapman traumatized the citizens of Lincoln. They requested Lieutenant Colonel Dudley station troops in town, which he did. Governor Lew Wallace had promised to visit Lincoln but had never gotten around to it. Now, following Chapman's murder, he said he would come and investigate the situation.[47]

On March 5, 1879, Governor Wallace and Colonel Edward Hatch, commander of the army in New Mexico, arrived in Lincoln. On March 8, Hatch replaced Lieutenant Colonel Nathan Dudley with Captain Henry Carroll as commander of Fort Stanton.[48]

Working with Justice of the Peace John Wilson, Wallace compiled a list of thirty-five men to arrest, including the Kid, Charlie Bowdre, and Fred Waite. On March 11, Wallace told Captain Carroll to track down the men on the list. Many of them were covered by the amnesty or were long gone. Wallace was especially interested in capturing anyone involved in Chapman's murder, which had taken place after his amnesty offer. Carroll's troops could not find the Kid or O'Folliard, but they did capture Dolan, Evans, Mathews, and Campbell, imprisoning them at Fort Stanton.[49]

The Kid wrote a letter to Governor Wallace dated March 13, 1879, stating he knew who killed Chapman and was willing to testify in court if the charges against him from the Lincoln County War were dropped. He wrote he had not fought since Wallace's amnesty and that there were plenty of people who would vouch for his character. He ended by saying he was called Kid Antrim, but Antrim was his stepfather's name. He signed the letter W. H. Bonncy.[50]

Wallace sent a letter back to the Kid stating he had authority to exempt him from prosecution if he testified in court. Wallace told the Kid to meet him alone at John Wilson's house on Monday, March 17, 1879, at 9 p.m. The Kid arrived on time and they discussed Chapman's murder. Wallace and the Kid worked out a plan where the Kid would allow himself to be captured and then testify in court against the murderers. Wallace later said he told the Kid, "In return for your doing this, I will let you go scot-free with a pardon in your pocket for all your misdeeds."[51]

The very next day, March 18, Jesse Evans and Billy Campbell escaped from Fort Stanton's guardhouse with the help of a guard who deserted with them. The Kid was concerned Evans and Campbell would try to kill him, but he went ahead with the plan. On March 21, he and Tom O'Folliard were arrested by Sheriff Kimbrell and brought to Lincoln where they were guarded at the home of Juan Patrón, next door to the Montaño store where Governor Wallace was staying.[52]

The Hispanos welcomed the Kid and one night serenaded him while Wallace listened. The governor met with the Kid who explained in detail what had been going on in the world of the outlaws in Lincoln County. In early April, the Kid's Regulator friend, Doc Scurlock, was arrested and housed with the Kid.[53]

Wallace left Lincoln and returned to Santa Fe before Judge Warren Bristol began the grand jury proceedings on April 14. The Kid and Tom O'Folliard both identified Campbell and Dolan as Chapman's murderers and Evans as an accessory. Campbell and Evans had escaped and disappeared into Texas, and Dolan was eventually acquitted. District Attorney William Rynerson, who had always been a Dolan man, reneged on Governor Wallace's pledge that the Kid would be released from prosecution, stating the governor did not have the right to offer immunity, and Judge Bristol sided with him.[54]

Bristol and Rynerson would not drop the charges against the Kid for Sheriff Bill Brady's murder, however, Sheriff Kimbrell allowed the Kid freedom to move about town. The Kid waited for Governor Wallace to act; he believed Wallace would remain true to his word and grant him a pardon. The Kid assisted Sue McSween in her case against Lieutenant Colonel Dudley. The army held a court of inquiry at Fort Stanton into whether Dudley assisted Dolan in the siege of the McSween house and had his men help set fire to the house. The Kid testified against Dudley, but after a lengthy court of inquiry, Dudley was exonerated on June 10, 1879.[55]

That same month, Judge Bristol convened the US district court in Mesilla, and ordered US Marshal John Sherman to arrest the Kid and Doc Scurlock for the murder of Buckshot Roberts. Believing Governor Wallace had betrayed him, the Kid rode out of Lincoln with Doc Scurlock and Tom O'Folliard on the night of June 17, 1879.[56]

On July 4, 1879, the first Santa Fe Railroad train reached Las Vegas, New Mexico, and the town boomed. The Kid spent several weeks there gambling, possibly dealing monte, and enjoying the town's rowdy lifestyle.[57]

By the first part of August, the Kid had returned to the Lincoln area. Sheriff Kimbrell learned the Kid was staying in a cabin six miles outside of Lincoln. On the night of August 9, Kimbrell with a posse of Fort Stanton soldiers surrounded the cabin and waited for dawn when they intended to capture him; but during the night, the Kid shimmied up through the cabin's chimney and escaped undetected.[58]

The Kid "skinned out" for Fort Sumner where he had friends who took him in. At the time, Fort Sumner was part of San Miguel County just over the border from Lincoln County and a hundred miles from Las Vegas, the county seat. There was no law enforcement in Fort Sumner and the San Miguel County sheriff rarely made an appearance. It was the perfect place for the Kid to make his home.[59]

Doc Scurlock left for Texas, but Tom O'Folliard and Charlie Bowdre, who was working for rancher Tom Yerby, remained. The Kid had many friends among the Hispano sheepherders and Anglo cattlemen. He gambled at Fort Sumner's two saloons, one owned by Beaver Smith and the other owned by Bob Hargrove. The Kid attended Fort Stanton's weekly *baile*, dancing and flirting with the young girls, many of whom considered him their *querido* or sweetheart. There were rumors that the Kid fathered several children. But of all the women and girls, rumor had it that the Kid was in love with the beautiful Paulita Maxwell, sister to Pete Maxwell, and she was in love with him. Paulita later denied this, saying she liked the Kid very much, but she was not his sweetheart.[60]

The Kid returned to his old profession—stealing. He, along with Charlie Bowdre, Tom O'Folliard, and others, rustled cattle from the Texas Panhandle and sold them to New Mexican buyers in Tularosa and the new gold mining town of White Oaks, New Mexico.[61]

On January 10, 1880, Jim Chisum, brother of John Chisum, along with three of his hands, were in the Fort Sumner area recovering rustled cattle. The Kid met Chisum and his men and invited them to Lincoln where he said he would treat them to a drink.[62]

Earlier that day, a Texan hard case named Joe Grant had started drinking early and challenged the Kid, "I'll bet twenty-five dollars that I kill a man today before you do."

Grant was drinking in Bob Hargrove's saloon when the Kid, along with Chisum and his men, entered. Grant walked up to Jack Finan, one of Chisum's men, took his revolver out of the holster and replaced it with his own. Finan allowed Grant to do it, not wanting to provoke any violence. The Kid saw what happened and walked over to Grant, saying, "That's a mighty nice looking six-shooter you got," lifting it out of Grant's holster. As he looked at the revolver, he spun the cylinder and saw three of the chambers were empty. He made sure the gun's hammer rested on an empty chamber and handed it back to Grant.

Grant became more belligerent, breaking bottles on the back bar and threatening to kill someone. He looked at Jim Chisum and said he was going to kill John Chisum. The Kid told him he was wrong. He had the wrong Chisum.

"That's a lie!" Grant shouted as the Kid turned away and walked toward the door. Grant reached for the revolver, aimed at the Kid, and pulled the trigger—the gun clicked as the hammer fell on the empty chamber. The Kid whirled around, firing three rapid shots, all hitting Grant in the chin and killing him. All saw it as a case of self-defense, and no lawmen came after the Kid.[63]

Las Vegas, New Mexico, then being the town at the end of the line for the Santa Fe Railroad, attracted a large criminal element. Some of these men drifted south to Fort Sumner and from time to time rode with the Kid and his friends. Three of these hard cases were Tom Pickett, Billy Wilson, and the most dangerous of all, Dave Rudabaugh, who had been a member of the Dodge City Gang, based out of Las Vegas. Back in 1878, after robbing a train in Kansas, Texas cattle rustler Rudabaugh was captured by a posse led by Bat Masterson. Testifying against his accomplices, Rudabaugh was released only to turn up in Las Vegas, New Mexico, robbing stagecoaches. After mortally wounding a deputy sheriff, he rode south to Fort Sumner where he met the Kid and his rustler friends.[64]

The Kid believed John Chisum owed him money for fighting as a Regulator. Chisum disagreed. The Kid started stealing cattle from Jim and Pitser Chisum's herd, claiming it was what was justly owed him. They filed charges against the Kid in Las Vegas, stating that on March 10, 1880, he stole twenty-two head of cattle valued at $220.[65]

Later that spring, John Chisum was in Fort Sumner when the Kid demanded his money from him.

"Billy, you know as well as I do that I never hired you to fight in the Lincoln County War," Chisum said. "I always pay my honest debts. I don't owe you anything, and you can kill me but you won't knock me out of many years. I'm an old man."

"Aw, you ain't worth killing," the Kid responded.[66]

The Kid, Bowdre, and O'Folliard continued stealing cattle from the Texas Panhandle. In May 1880, they stole sixty head, driving them to White Oaks, New Mexico, where they sold them for $700.[67]

In the spring of 1880, Texas cattlemen banded together to form the Panhandle Stock Association to put an end to the rustling. That autumn, they sent stock detective Frank Stewart and four cowboys to New Mexico to track down the rustlers. At White Oaks, they found hides with Panhandle brands as evidence of rustling, and locals blamed the Kid. Stewart reported his findings to the stock association that decided to send men to New Mexico to recover their stolen cattle and put an end to the Kid's career.[68]

The Kid had been using the name William H. Bonney. People referred to him as Billy. In the 1880s he became known as Billy the Kid, and it stuck.

Residents of Lincoln and White Oaks notified the US Treasury Department that counterfeit hundred-dollar bills were circulating in Lincoln County. In October 1880, the US Secret Service sent special operative Azariah Wild to investigate. Wild found that W. H. West and Sam Diedrick, who had bought a livery stable in White Oaks, were involved in passing the counterfeit money. It appeared that the counterfeit bills were also being passed in Beaver Smith's saloon in Fort Sumner and at John Chisum's old headquarters at Bosque Grande. Wild uncovered that West and Diedrick were also involved in buying stolen livestock. Wild was certain the Kid and his friends, including Billy Wilson, who he wrongly believed was the ringleader, were involved in circulating the counterfeit bills.[69]

Wild wouldn't trust any local law enforcement, including Sheriff Kimbrell, because he was friends with the Kid and occasionally played cards with him. Wild found two men he believed he could trust, John Hurley and Bob Olinger; both had been Dolan men during the Lincoln County War. Wild convinced US Marshal John Sherman to appoint both men deputy US marshals. With their help, he formed a posse of thirty men to apprehend the counterfeiters and, while they were at it, arrest the livestock thieves.[70]

On October 16, 1880, robbers held up the US mail outside of Fort Stanton. The soldiers had just been paid, and many were sending money to family or banks. Witnesses identified two of the robbers as Billy Wilson and Billy the Kid.[71]

Sheriff George Kimbrell was up for reelection in November 1880. Roswell businessman Joseph Lea and John Chisum believed it was time for a change—time for someone who could bring law and order to Lincoln County. They believed that person was Pat Garrett. Lea and Chisum convinced Garrett to move from Fort Sumner to Roswell in Lincoln County and run for sheriff. Garrett had lots of backers, including Jimmie Dolan and Santa Fe Ring leader Thomas Catron.[72]

At the time Garrett was thirty years old. Originally from Alabama, Garrett had worked cattle in Texas and hunted buffalo for hides before winding up in Fort Sumner in 1878, where he worked cattle for Pete Maxwell until they had a disagreement and then tended bar for Beaver Smith. Garrett married Juanita Martinez, who died of unknown causes shortly after the marriage. He then married Apolonaria Gutierrez on January 14, 1880. Chisum believed Garrett was brave and was impressed with his shooting ability and horsemanship.[73]

Pat Garrett and Billy the Kid had become friends in Fort Sumner. They ate meals and went to dances together. They gambled against each other, lending the other fellow money when he was short. They competed against each other in shooting contests. "Both were wonderful shots," Paulita Maxwell said years later. "It was a toss-up between them when it came to the rifle, but Billy was the better shot with a revolver."[74]

The friendship did not extend into politics. Billy the Kid actively supported Sheriff George Kimbrell's reelection, but it didn't do any good. The citizens of Lincoln County were ready for law and order. On November 2, 1880, Pat Garrett beat George Kimbrell 320 to 179 votes. Kimbrell was a good sport about his loss, appointing Garrett as deputy sheriff while he served out his term in office until January 1, 1881. US Marshal John Sherman had sent Azariah Wild two commissions for John Hurley to be a deputy US marshal. On one of them, Wild crossed out Hurley's name and wrote in Garrett's name as deputy US marshal.[75]

Governor Wallace had not forgotten about Billy the Kid. He entrusted further negotiations with the Kid to Las Vegas lawyer Ira Leonard. The Kid had sent a letter to Leonard stating he was tired of being on the dodge and wanted to know his status. Leonard worked with Azariah Wild to concoct a plan whereby if Billy provided evidence to convict the counterfeiters, the federal government would let his murder cases "slumber." Time dragged. Leonard and Wild had a falling out over how the case should be managed, and then events flared that ended any further negotiations.[76]

On November 15, 1880, Billy the Kid and five others rode up to Barney Mason, Pat Garrett's brother-in-law, who was caring for Pete Maxwell's cattle east of Fort Sumner. Billy Wilson asked for Pete Maxwell's rifle and another rider asked Mason to loan him a saddle. They told Mason they had come to steal Padre Polaco's horses. Padre Polaco, who had always been friendly with the Kid, was Alexander Grzelachowski, a former Catholic priest and now store owner in Puerto de Luna. The thieves took sixteen head of horses worth $1600.[77]

Billy the Kid, along with Billy Wilson, Sam Cook, Buck Edwards, and Dave Rudabaugh, herded the horses toward White Oaks where they planned to sell them. Along the way, they stopped at "Whiskey Jim" Greathouse and Fred Kuch's combination store and ranch. There the gang sold Greathouse and Kuch four of the horses.[78]

Billy the Kid and the gang rode into White Oaks the night of November 20. The Kid had heard that Ira Leonard was in town and wanted to talk with him about the progress on his pardon but was disappointed when he learned Leonard had left town. Whether the Kid condoned it or not, the gang went on a robbery spree. After stealing weapons, coats, blankets, and mules, they raced out of town.[79]

The citizens of White Oaks were outraged. Deputy Sheriff Bill Hudgens learned that the gang was camped at Blake's sawmill a few miles out of town. On November 22, Hudgens led an eight-man posse to capture the thieves.[80]

When the posse reached Blake's sawmill, the gang was gone, but they followed their tracks in the snow until they reached Coyote Springs, where the gang opened fire on the posse. The posse returned fire and got the best of the outlaws. Billy Wilson and the Kid's horses were shot out from under them as was Deputy Sheriff Hudgens's horse. The gang split up, members heading in several directions, and the posse returning to White Oaks. The Kid and Billy Wilson, both on foot, stayed together and later met up with Dave Rudabaugh, who had managed to get away on horseback.[81]

The three gang members returned to Whiskey Jim Greathouse and Fred Kuch's store and ranch. News reached White Oaks that the Kid and his friends were at Greathouse and Kuch's. A thirteen-man posse, including Deputy Sheriff Bill Hudgens and Constable Tom Longworth, rode out after the thieves.[82]

Early Saturday morning, November 27, 1880, the posse surrounded the ranch house and took cover. Joe Steck, the cook for Greathouse and Kuch, stepped outside and was quietly captured. After some questioning, Steck said the Kid, Wilson, and Rudabaugh were sleeping in the house. Hudgens wrote a note telling the Kid and the gang to surrender and sent it back into the house with Steck.[83]

Billy the Kid read the note out loud to the others. They all laughed, and the Kid wrote a response, "You can only take me a corpse," and sent it back out with Steck. Negotiations went back and forth. Greathouse and Steck came out to negotiate. The Kid and Rudabaugh asked for Jimmy Carlyle to come into the house to talk it over. Carlyle was a popular White Oaks blacksmith from whom the gang had stolen the mules on their robbery spree. Carlyle agreed to enter the house, and Greathouse said he would act as a hostage to guarantee Carlyle's safety. Hudgens thought it was a bad idea, but Carlyle entered the house anyway.[84]

Everyone but the Kid had started drinking the store's whiskey, and Carlyle joined in as they talked, but nothing got accomplished other than Carlyle drinking too much. After several hours, Carlyle wanted to leave, but the gang refused to let him go. By 2:00 p.m., the posse was getting antsy. They sent in a note declaring that if Carlyle was not released in five minutes, they would kill Greathouse. One of the posse members fired a shot. Carlyle must have thought they had killed Greathouse and the gang would kill him in retribution. He leaped through a window, his body smashing the glass panes. Carlyle got up and started running for cover as the Kid, Rudabaugh, and Wilson all fired and killed him.[85]

The posse opened fire. The Kid claimed the posse shot Carlyle. Kuch and Steck were outside the house and ran for cover as the posse shot at them.[86]

Cold, hungry, and demoralized, the posse rode back to White Oaks to get more men and provisions. After night fell, the Kid, Rudabaugh, and Wilson walked to another ranch where they met Greathouse, who the posse had released. Greathouse gave them horses and they rode off into the night.[87]

Lincoln County citizens were outraged over the death of Jimmy Carlyle, and many of Billy the Kid's supporters turned against him.[88]

DID JESSE JAMES AND BILLY THE KID MEET IN 1879?

Minnesota doctor Henry Hoyt not only led an adventurous life as a youth, but later became a respected physician serving on various state and hospital governing boards in the Minneapolis–St. Paul, Minnesota, area. He was hired as chief surgeon for two major railroads and was commissioned a major and chief surgeon in the army during the Spanish American War and the Philippine Insurrection.[89]

Hoyt had a connection to the James Younger Gang's Northfield bank robbery. After Charlie Pitts was shot and killed at Lake Hanska, Dr. Frank Murphy, Minnesota surgeon general, obtained Charlie's remains and had them embalmed for dissecting purposes. In March 1877, Hoyt was able to obtain the body and wanted to mount Charlie's skeleton to display in his office. One method to clean a skeleton for mounting was to immerse the bones underwater for a year. So, Hoyt put Charlie's bones in a wooden box and submerged it in St. Paul's Lake Como before leaving for the frontier. Months later, someone found the box with the human remains inside. There was a public uproar over the mysterious find—people speculated someone had been murdered and placed in the box. The newspapers spread the story across the country. Henry's brother knew of the bones, and when he read about the find in the newspapers, he told an uncle, who explained to the local authorities that they were Charlie Pitts's bones and they belonged to Henry. Henry's uncle gave the bones to a Chicago doctor.[90]

Hoyt drifted to the Texas Panhandle where he met Billy the Kid, and they became good friends. Hoyt left the Panhandle in late October 1878 and landed in Las Vegas, New Mexico, where he worked as a bartender.[91]

On a Sunday in late July 1879, Hoyt rode out to Scott and Minnie Moore's hotel at hot springs six miles outside Las Vegas. The springs and their bathhouses were a popular tourist attraction, and the hotel's cuisine was well worth the trip. On Sundays the meals were extra special.[92]

Entering the hotel's dining room, Hoyt found all the seats were taken except one at a corner table where sat none other than his old friend Billy the Kid with two other men. The Kid was dressed in new store-bought clothes. Hoyt sat down, and the Kid and he reminisced about their time together in Texas. The Kid introduced the man to his left, "Hoyt, meet my friend Mr. Howard from Tennessee."[93]

Hoyt described Howard in his book *A Frontier Doctor*:

> *Mr. Howard had noticeable characteristics. He had piercing steely blue eyes with a peculiar blink, and the tip of a finger on his left hand was missing. I mentally classed him as a railroad man. He proved to be congenial, was a good talker, had evidently traveled quite a bit, and the meal passed pleasantly.*[94]

Afterwards, the Kid invited Hoyt to his room where, after pledging Hoyt to secrecy, he told him Mr. Howard was none other than Jesse James. The Moores were friends of the Kid's and were also old friends of Jesse James's, so they introduced the two outlaws to each other. Jesse was in the area sizing up its possibilities. He invited the Kid to join his gang, but the Kid declined since he said he only knew horse stealing and cattle rustling and knew nothing of bank and train robbing. Besides, he had no desire to leave "his magnet at Fort Sumner."[95]

Jesse, the Kid, and Hoyt met again that evening and had quite the visit. Hoyt never let on he knew who Jesse was. At one point in the conversation, Hoyt asked "Mr. Howard" if he had ever been to St. Paul, Minnesota. Hoyt wrote in *A Frontier Doctor*:

> *[Mr. Howard] replied in the negative in the most nonchalant manner and changed the subject. It was no doubt lucky for me that he was not a mind-reader. He evidently did not know of the recent publicity that had been given his former pal, Charley [sic] Pitts, and myself. It was a case of, "where ignorance is bliss, 'twere folly to be wise."*[96]

CHAPTER 12

TRIALS AND TRIBULATIONS

The year 1881 began with the publication of two more books featuring the exploits of the James boys. The author, James William Buel, wrote them both: *The Border Outlaws* and *The Border Bandits*. They were a mixture of fact and fiction, but the reading public did not know that and took them as true histories. Sixty-five thousand copies were sold the first six months.[1]

However, real life was altogether different for the James boys. Their former bushwhacker friend Jim Cummins had been staying with Jesse. Cummins had lent a horse to Ed Miller that Miller had been riding at the time of his disappearance. Cummins discovered that Jesse had the horse he had lent to Miller in his possession. Cummins asked Jesse on several occasions what had happened to Miller. Jesse would only respond that Miller had been very ill and probably would never return. Cummins believed Miller had been killed and said if he ever found out what happened he "intended to avenge his death."[2]

Jesse worried that Cummins was going to betray them and talked with the other gang members about killing him. Toward the end of January 1881, Cummins vanished, leaving most of his clothes behind. Frank and Jesse worried Cummins had gone to the Nashville police, so the brothers left town for several weeks.

There was no manhunt, so they returned but moved their families to new locations in town.[3]

Jesse continued to scout for new targets and settled on robbing the federal payroll for the US Army Corps of Engineers Muscle Shoals Canal project in northern Alabama. The Army Corps of Engineers was building a canal and lock system along the Tennessee River to improve river traffic. With lots of workers, the payroll would be high. Jesse took with him Bill Ryan and probably his cousin Wood Hite. Riding south from Nashville, at times they followed the old Natchez Trace that had been one of the major roads in the area but by now was little used. They reached the canal near Lock No. 7 in Alabama, and Jesse learned who would be carrying the payroll and when he should arrive.[4]

On March 10, 1881, Alexander Smith rode from Florence, Alabama, toward the canal with a payroll of $5,240.18 in gold and silver coins and greenbacks. As Smith reached the canal, the three gang members joined him, riding along and having a pleasant conversation about the progress of the canal. When they reached an isolated section of the canal, Jesse and his men pulled their revolvers on Smith and took the payroll. They found a separate fifty dollars in Smith's vest pocket and asked if it was his own money. He replied it was, and they let him keep it and his gold watch. Smith later related, "They said they only wanted government money." The gang headed north, making Smith ride with them until they released him later that night. The Army Corps of Engineers sent an agent to track down the gang, but after following them for quite a ways, he lost their trail.[5]

Disaster struck on March 25, 1881. Bill Ryan, who went by the alias Tom Hill, got drunk in a saloon outside of Nashville. Claiming to be an outlaw, he waved around a revolver. He was disarmed, arrested, and hauled to jail in Nashville. There, the police discovered Ryan had $1,400, jewelry, and a gold watch. For the time being, Ryan sat in his cell, not talking.[6]

When Jesse and Frank learned about Ryan's capture in the next day's newspapers, they knew they had to leave Nashville immediately. Frank put Annie and Robert on a train to Kansas City, Missouri, that day. Zee and the children traveled to Louisville, and a few days later took the train to Kearney, Missouri.[7]

On March 31, Alexander Smith arrived in Nashville and identified Hill as one of the Muscle Shoal bandits and recognized Hill's horse as one of theirs as well.[8]

Jesse and Dick Liddil stole horses and, along with Frank, rode to Kentucky where they hid out with their Hite relatives. Frank later said, "It was with a sense of despair that I drove away from our little home . . . and again became a wanderer."[9]

J. H. Koogler, owner of the *Las Vegas Gazette*, had toured the Pecos River valley and was incensed over the extent of rustling and terrorizing. He wrote a letter to Governor Wallace about what he saw and then published an article appearing in the December 3, 1880, issue of the *Gazette*. Koogler wrote that a gang of rustlers consisting of forty to fifty hard characters were "under the leadership of 'Billy the Kid' a desperate cuss who is eligible for the post of captain of any crowd, no matter how mean or lawless."[10]

Many newspapers, including the *New York Sun*, printed the story, bringing Billy the Kid national renown. The Kid wrote a letter to Governor Wallace stating he was not the person Koogler made him out to be and he was not the leader of a gang. He was not following a life of crime, but simply earning a living as a gambler at Fort Sumner. Wallace had had enough of Billy the Kid, and on December 13, 1880, he posted a $500 reward for the capture of "William Bonny alias 'the Kid.'"[11]

After the fight at Greathouse and Kuch's ranch, the Kid, Dave Rudabaugh, and Billy Wilson returned to Fort Sumner. The Kid went back to gambling and contemplated leaving the area. Deputy

Sheriff Pat Garrett scoured the countryside looking to arrest the Kid, but the Kid was always one step ahead of him.[12]

Garrett learned the Kid and friends were back in Fort Sumner, most of them wanted by the law: Dave Rudabaugh, Billy Wilson, Charlie Bowdre, Tom Pickett, and Tom O'Folliard. He formed a posse of Texas cowboys who were employed by the Panhandle Stock Association to round up stolen cattle, his Fort Sumner brother-in-law, Barney Mason, and a few men from Puerto de Luna, totaling thirteen men.[13]

The night of December 17, Billy the Kid and his friends learned that Garrett and his posse were on the way and hightailed it out of town to spend the night at the Wilcox-Brazil ranch. Garrett and his posse reached Fort Sumner early the next morning during a heavy snowfall only to find the Kid and the others had left. Garrett hid the posse in the fort's abandoned hospital building, while he asked around and learned the Kid and the others were at the Wilcox-Brazil ranch. Working with a couple local men, Garrett sent out false information that he and the posse had left Fort Sumner and were returning to Roswell.[14]

The Kid took the bait, and after the snowstorm cleared, he and his friends rode back into town around 8:00 p.m., on December 19. Lon Chambers had been posted as a guard and let the posse know the Kid and friends were riding into town. Garrett and the others quietly spread out, taking positions in the darkness.[15]

Tom O'Folliard and Tom Pickett were in the lead, as the other riders lagged behind.

"Halt!" Garrett shouted. O'Folliard reached to draw his pistol. Both Garrett and Chambers fired their Winchesters at him. He cried out in pain as his horse reared and raced off. Other posse members shot at Wilson, but with a cry he raced away. The rest of the riders galloped off as the posse sent parting shots after them.[16]

O'Folliard's horse slowly walked back to the posse as O'Folliard, slumped in the saddle, said, "Don't shoot anymore, I am dying." One of the bullets had hit him in the chest just below the heart. They took him off his horse, carried him into the hospital, and laid him on a blanket by the wood-burning stove. Garrett and some of the posse members played poker as O'Folliard cussed Garrett and then died.[17]

Billy the Kid and the gang rode back to the Wilcox-Brazil ranch. Manuel Brazil informed Garrett of their return. On the night of December 22, Garrett led his posse out to the ranch, but the gang had left. Brazil told Garrett it should be easy to follow their trail and showed him the gang's horses' tracks in the snow.[18]

The posse tracked the gang to Stinking Spring, an abandoned sheepherder's one-room rock house with a rough opening that had once been a door. It was 3 a.m., December 23, as the posse took positions around the house. The gang had taken two horses into the house and tied the other three outside to beams supporting the roof.[19]

Garrett wanted to rush the house, but stock detective and leader of the Texans, Frank Stewart, disagreed and convinced Garrett to wait until morning. Garrett believed if they could kill the Kid that the others would give up. At dawn a man wearing a Mexican sombrero emerged from the house. Garrett, believing it was the Kid, gave the signal to shoot. The posse fired their Winchesters and the man staggered back through the door.[20]

Billy Wilson shouted from the house that Charlie Bowdre was shot and wanted to surrender. Garrett agreed he could come out. Bowdre stepped outside with his hands up. The Kid said to him, "They have murdered you, Charley [sic], but you can get revenge. Kill some of the sons-of-bitches before you die."[21]

Bowdre, hands in the air, walked out of the building and up to Garrett's position. Bowdre said, "I wish—I wish—I wish—I'm dying." Collapsing, he died almost immediately.[22]

The gang members were trying to pull the horses into the building to mount and then make their escape. Garrett shot and killed one of the horses in the doorway, blocking it. He then shot, severing the lead ropes of the other two horses, which walked away.[23]

The outlaws were trapped, and they knew it. They spent the day trying to figure out how to escape while the posse played the waiting game. The Kid and Garrett bantered back and forth, inviting each other to come visit.[24]

That afternoon, Brazil arrived with a wagonload of food, blankets, and firewood for the posse. The posse started cooking the food and by 4:00 p.m. the hungry outlaws surrendered after Garrett promised he would protect them from mob violence.[25]

The posse and prisoners stayed at the Brazil ranch that night. On December 24, the posse left for Fort Sumner, escorting the prisoners who rode in a wagon with Bowdre's body. At the fort, Garrett had the blacksmith fashion shackles on the prisoners' legs; the Kid was paired with Dave Rudabaugh. The Kid gave his horse to Frank Stewart and his Winchester to Jim East until Beaver Smith took it, saying the Kid owed him money. Paulita Maxwell gave the Kid a long-lasting kiss before he was hustled away with the others to the jail in Las Vegas.[26]

News of the capture of Billy the Kid and his gang preceded the prisoners' arrival in town. Large crowds gathered in the streets of Las Vegas on Sunday, December 26, to get a look at the outlaws. The Kid enjoyed the attention. Spotting an old acquaintance, Dr. J. H. Sutfin, the owner of the Grand View Hotel who watched from its veranda, the Kid shouted, "Hello, doc! Thought I'd jes drop in and see how you fellers in Vegas air behavin' yerselves."[27]

Rudabaugh worried. In April 1880, he had failed to break a friend out of the Las Vegas jail. During the attempt, he had shot and killed Deputy Sheriff Lino Valdez. Recognizing Rudabaugh, the crowd turned ugly. Concerned a mob might try to storm the jail and hang Rudabaugh, Garrett and his deputies stood guard at the jail through the night.[28]

The next morning, December 27, Sheriff Desiderio Romero allowed a *Las Vegas Gazette* reporter into the jail to talk with the inmates. The reporter wrote, "Bonney . . . was light and chipper and very communicative, laughing, joking and chatting with bystanders."[29]

"You appear to take it easy," the reporter said.

"Yes!" responded the Kid, "What's the use of looking on the gloomy side of everything. The laugh's on me this time."[30]

Sheriff Romero wanted Garrett to turn Rudabaugh over to him for the murder of Deputy Sheriff Lino Valdez, but Garrett said no. He explained that he had arrested Rudabaugh on the charges of robbing the US mail and would not turn him over to county authorities. Garrett also held the Kid and Wilson on federal charges, but since there were no federal charges against Tom Pickett, Garrett turned him over to Romero's custody.[31]

Garrett and his five deputies, including Deputy US Marshal Jim Bell who had been part of the posse at the Greathouse ranch, loaded the Kid and the two other gang members into public wagons. They took the prisoners to the railway station, where they boarded the train for Santa Fe.[32]

The train was delayed on a sidetrack at the station while it waited for a northbound train to pass. Sheriff Romero had not given up and led a posse of thirty-five men determined to remove Rudabaugh from the train. Defiant, Garrett stood on the train platform facing down Romero's posse. Some of Romero's men threw the switch so the train could not proceed onto the main line while others held their Winchesters on the engineer and fireman as an angry mob swelled around the car holding the prisoners.[33]

Billy the Kid's window was open. Leaning out, he struck up a conversation with the *Gazette* reporter from the previous day.

"If I only had my Winchester, I'd lick the whole crowd," the Kid said. The reporter wrote, "The prospects of a fight exhilarated him." The Kid stated he was not the leader of a gang, he hadn't stolen any stock, and he made his living by gambling. He said, "Chisum got me into all this trouble and then wouldn't help me out."[34]

The angry mob continued to grow; many carried Winchesters. Garrett and the deputies told the prisoners to lie on the floor of the car, so they would not be shot through the windows. A compromise was finally reached. The townsmen would allow the train to proceed with the prisoners. Two representatives of Sheriff Romero would go along to ensure the prisoners would be taken into federal custody in Santa Fe.[35]

The train arrived in Santa Fe that evening, and the Kid and the other prisoners were turned over to federal authorities and locked in the Santa Fe County jail. Garrett and his deputies were hailed heroes and eventually received the $500 reward.[36]

Billy the Kid was to be tried before Judge Warren Bristol in Mesilla that spring, first in US district court for the murder of Buckshot Roberts and then in territorial court for the murder of Sheriff Bill Brady.

As Billy the Kid languished in jail, he wrote a note to Governor Wallace, asking that he come see him, but Wallace was away on a trip. He tried to get legal help from the governor's attorney friend Ira Leonard, but nothing materialized. Dave Rudabaugh's attorney, Edgar Caypless, was going to represent him. The Kid gave Caypless his horse in payment until it was discovered that the Kid had given the horse to Frank Stewart who had given it to Minnie Moore.[37]

Realizing no one was going to help him other than himself, the Kid worked with Billy Wilson and Dave Rudabaugh digging a tunnel under the jailhouse wall and hiding the excavated dirt and rock in and under their mattresses. On the last day of February and just before their attempted escape, Sheriff Romulo Martinez learned of their plans and thwarted their escape. He had them separated, shackled, and placed under constant guard.[38]

Learning Governor Wallace was back in Santa Fe, the Kid sent him a letter stating he wanted to see him and threatening to release letters Wallace had sent him. Wallace did not respond. On March 4, two days later, the Kid wrote Wallace again, voicing his frustration, "I have done everything that I promised you I would, and you have done nothing that you promised me." The Kid received no response from Wallace.[39]

The Kid and Billy Wilson were scheduled to leave by train for Mesilla on March 28. The day before their departure, the Kid sent Governor Wallace another letter in which he wrote, "For the last time I ask, Will you Keep your promise." Governor Wallace did not respond in writing to the Kid, but his friend, attorney Ira Leonard, who had worked with the Kid in the past, traveled with the Kid to represent him in the federal Buckshot Roberts murder case.[40]

Dave Rudabaugh had been sent back to Las Vegas to stand trial. Monday, March 28, the Kid and Billy Wilson were escorted onto the train by Deputy US Marshals Bob Olinger, Tony Neis, and Francisco Chavez.[41]

Bob Olinger was from Seven Rivers and had been on the side of the House during the Lincoln County War. On August 29, 1879, Bob Olinger had murdered the Kid's friend John Jones by shooting him in the back. Jones was one of the first people the Kid had met when he first entered Lincoln County. Olinger was now not only a deputy US marshal but also one of Pat Garrett's deputy sheriffs.[42]

The train made a stop in Bernalillo, New Mexico. The Kid's old friend Dr. Henry Hoyt recognized the Kid through a window and entered the train car. The Kid saw Hoyt and greeted him. Hoyt introduced himself to the deputies who sat across from the shackled Kid and asked the Kid if there was anything he could do for him.

In high spirits, the Kid replied, "Sure Doc, just grab and hand me Bob's gun for a moment."

"My boy," Olinger said, "You had better tell your friend good-bye. Your days are short."

"Oh, I don't know," the Kid responded, "There's many a slip twixt the cup and the lip." The Kid and Hoyt said good-bye and never saw each other again.[43]

The guards and prisoners had to switch from the train to a stagecoach at Rincon, New Mexico. An angry mob gathered, but the deputies leveling their weapons made them back off as Deputy US Marshal Neis told them, "You don't get them fellows without somebody being killed."[44]

When the stagecoach stopped in Las Cruces, New Mexico, a crowd gathered round the travelers. Someone in the crowd asked which one of them was Billy the Kid. Maintaining his sense of humor, the Kid put his hand on Leonard's shoulder saying, "This is the man."[45]

The Kid and Billy Wilson reached the Mesilla jail safely. On March 30, the Kid was arraigned before his old nemesis Judge Warren Bristol in federal district court for the murder of Buckshot Roberts. Ira Leonard acted as his defense attorney, and on March 31, he entered a plea of not guilty.[46]

The April 2, 1881, edition of Las Cruces's *Newman's Semi-Weekly* voiced the concern that the Kid had escaped jail in the past "and has made his brags that he only wants to get free in order to kill three men—one of them being Governor Wallace."[47]

On April 5, Leonard withdrew the Kid's not-guilty plea. He now pled that the federal government had no jurisdiction over the Roberts murder case since it did not occur on federal land as Blazer's Mill was private property and not part of the reservation. On April 6, Judge Bristol ruled in favor of Leonard's argument and dismissed the case. However, the Kid would still be tried for the first-degree murder of Sheriff Bill Brady in territorial court. If the Kid was found guilty, the penalty would be death.[48]

For whatever reason, Ira Leonard did not represent the Kid in territorial court for the murder of Bill Brady. Judge Bristol appointed the partnership of attorneys John Bail and Albert Fountain to represent the Kid.[49]

The jury was entirely Hispanos. The prosecution witnesses were deputy sheriff and silent House partner Billy Mathews and two people who had been friendly with the Kid, store owner Isaac Ellis and Saturnino Baca's young son, Bonnie.[50]

On Saturday, April 9, after hearing all the testimony, Judge Bristol instructed the jury, "If he [the Kid] was present—encouraging—inciting—aiding in—abetting—advising—or commanding this killing of Brady he is as much guilty as though he fired the fatal shot." Judge Bristol went on to tell them not to worry about reasonable doubt, "Merely a vague conjecture or a bare possibility that the defendant may be innocent is not sufficient to cause a reasonable doubt of his guilt." After deliberating, the jury came back with a unanimous verdict of guilty.[51]

The following Wednesday, April 13, Judge Bristol sentenced the Kid to be returned to the jurisdiction of Lincoln County where on May 13, 1881, between the hours of 9:00 a.m. and 3:00 p.m. "the said William Bonney, alias Kid, alias William Antrim be hanged by the neck until his body be dead."[52]

On April 15, in an interview with a reporter for the *Mesilla News*, the Kid said he believed he deserved a pardon from Governor

Wallace since he had assisted him during the Lincoln County War and, of over fifty men indicted for offenses, he was "the only one to suffer the extreme penalty of the law"[53]

The next night at 10:00 p.m., the Kid was handcuffed, shackled, and chained inside a wagon and secretly hustled out of town to prevent any actions to take him—some wanted to liberate him, while others wanted to hang him. Seven men guarded the Kid, including three who had no love for him: Billy Mathews, the rustler king John Kinney, and Bob Olinger, who believed the Kid was responsible for the death of his friend Bob Beckwith who had been shot behind McSween's burning house. These three men climbed into the wagon—Olinger sat across from the Kid, facing him, Mathews sat beside Olinger, and Kinney sat beside the Kid. It took five days for the wagon and its escort to reach Fort Stanton where Lincoln County Sheriff Pat Garrett took charge of the prisoner, conducting him from there to Lincoln.[54]

Lincoln County had recently bought the House's old store building and now used it as the courthouse. Prisoners could easily escape from the old Lincoln County jail, so Sheriff Garrett was holding inmates on the second floor of the courthouse. A flight of interior stairs provided access to the second floor. At the head of the stairs was a room Garrett used as an armory. His office was down a short hallway and faced the street. To the left of his office was a room used to house prisoners, and to the right, the northeast corner of the building, was a room he placed the Kid in. Garrett kept the Kid handcuffed and restrained with leg irons. He assigned the responsibility to guard the Kid to his deputy sheriffs, Bob Olinger and Jim Bell. A chalk line was drawn across the floor dividing the Kid's room in two. He told the Kid if he crossed the line, they would kill him.[55]

Sheriff Garrett and Deputy Sheriff Bell were kind and respectful to the Kid, but Olinger hated the Kid, taunting him nonstop. He would poke the Kid with the barrel of his shotgun, telling him to go ahead and try to run so he could have the pleasure of blowing him to pieces.[56]

A friend of Olinger's told him, "If that man [the Kid] is shown the slightest chance on earth, if he is allowed the use of one hand, or if he is not watched every moment from now until the moment he is executed, he will effect some plan by which he will murder the whole lot of you before you even have time to suspect that he has any such intention." Olinger smiled and said there was no more chance of the Kid escaping than there was of him going to Heaven.[57]

On April 27, Sheriff Garrett left town on a two-day trip to Las Tablas and White Oaks to collect taxes. Before leaving, he warned Bell and Olinger to be vigilant of the Kid.[58]

The Kid still hoped Governor Wallace would pardon him, but in an April 28, 1881, interview with a *Las Vegas Gazette* reporter, Wallace said, "I can't see how a fellow like him should expect any clemency from me."[59]

The Kid was not the only prisoner in the courthouse. In the room to the left of Sheriff Garrett's office, five men were housed waiting for the grand jury to convene. These men had participated in a gun battle over water rights along the Rio Tularosa where four men wound up dead.[60]

On Thursday morning, April 28, 1881, as Bob Olinger loaded his Whitney double-barreled 10 gauge shotgun in front of the Kid, he said, "The man that gets one of these loads will feel it."

"I expect he will," the Kid said, "but be careful Bob, or you might shoot yourself accidentally."[61]

That evening, around 6:00 p.m., Olinger escorted the five Rio Tularosa prisoners across the street to the Wortley Hotel for supper. The Kid and Deputy Sheriff Jim Bell were the only ones in the courthouse. Both cuffs of the Kid's handcuffs were locked on one wrist allowing the Kid flexibility to eat and use the privy.[62]

Gottfried Gauss, who lived behind the courthouse, was outside when "[I] heard a shot fired, then a tussle upstairs in the courthouse, somebody hurrying downstairs, Deputy Sheriff Bell emerging from the door running toward me. He ran right into my arms, expired the same moment, and I laid him down, dead."[63]

The Kid had somehow got his hands on a revolver and shot Bell; one bullet entered his body on the right side and passed through the left. There are many suppositions as to what happened. One theory is that the Kid struck Bell on the head with his handcuffs, wrestled Bell's revolver from him, and shot Bell as he ran down the steps. Sheriff Pat Garrett believed the Kid raced up the steps, grabbed a pistol from the sheriff's armory on the second floor and used it to shoot Bell. A third theory is that the Kid asked Bell to take him to the privy where he retrieved a revolver one of the Kid's friends had hidden for him there and used it on Bell when they returned to the second floor of the courthouse.[64]

The Kid looked down at Bell's body through the open rear window. Slipping the handcuffs off his wrist, he tossed them at the body, shouting, "Here damn you, take these, too." Grabbing Olinger's shotgun, he returned to his room where he could watch the street from the open windows on the north and east sides of the building.[65]

Across the street at the Wortley Hotel, Bob Olinger and his prisoners had heard the gunshots. He ran out into the street toward the northeast corner of the courthouse. Gottfried Gauss called to Olinger, "Bob, the Kid has killed Bell." From the second-floor window, the Kid pulled back both hammers to full cock on Bob's shotgun and said to Olinger, "Hello old boy." As Olinger looked up, he said, "Yes, and he's killed me too." The Kid fired one barrel, hitting Olinger in the chest and face, killing him instantly.[66]

The Kid walked into Garrett's office and out onto the balcony where he fired the second barrel at Olinger's body and then smashed the shotgun on the railing, breaking it in two. Hurling the pieces at the body, the Kid shouted, "Take it damn you, you won't follow me anymore with that gun."[67]

The Kid went to the armory and took a Winchester and two revolvers. Returning, now armed, to the balcony, he controlled the

HATZELL 2019

town for an hour until he left. A mixed crowd had gathered across the street; there were those who were sympathetic and those who feared the Kid.[68]

He told Gauss to get him something to break his leg irons. Gauss found a small pick that he threw up to the Kid. He used it to remove one leg iron, but would have to wait until later to remove the other leg iron, and tied the leg iron's loose chain to his belt. He told Gauss to saddle Deputy Probate Clerk Billy Burt's horse and bring it around to the front of the courthouse. While waiting for the horse, the Kid stood on the balcony laughing and shouting as he danced about.[69]

Bob Brookshire left the Wortley Hotel and began walking away from the courthouse. The Kid aimed his Winchester at Brookshire and shouted, "Go back young fellow, go back! I don't want to hurt you, but I am fighting for my life. I don't want anybody to leave that house."[70]

The Kid told the crowd he did not want to kill Bell, but he ran, and he had to shoot him. He said he did not want to kill anyone, but if someone tried to interfere with his escape, he would kill him. He cursed his enemies and said he had not been a bad man, but now people would see just what a "bad man" could do.[71]

The Kid walked down the stairs and out the back of the courthouse to Bell's body and said, "I'm sorry I had to kill you, but couldn't help it." He walked to Olinger's body and prodding it with his boot, said, "You are not going to round me up again."[72]

Gauss had trouble saddling the horse, but finally brought it around to the front of the courthouse. As the Kid started to mount, the horse broke loose and ran off. The Kid ordered one of the prisoners, Alex Nunnelly, to retrieve the horse for him.[73]

The Kid mounted the horse and shouted, "Tell Billy Burt I will send his horse back to him." A few hundred yards down the road, he stopped at a Hispano house and bought a rope. Riding west out of town at a walk, some folks said they could hear Billy the Kid singing.[74]

LEW WALLACE AND *BEN-HUR*

Lewis Wallace was not only governor of New Mexico Territory, but he was a lawyer, warrior, and storyteller. Wallace was born April 10, 1827, in Brookville, Indiana. At the age of sixteen, he and a friend headed downriver toward New Orleans, planning to join the Texas navy, until they were caught and returned home. At the outbreak of the Mexican-American War in 1846, Wallace raised a volunteer company with the First Regiment Indiana Volunteers and was commissioned a second lieutenant. The regiment was sent to Mexico but never saw action.[75]

Trained as a lawyer, Wallace was admitted to the bar in 1849. Wallace quickly became bored with the law and began to hone his literary talents, writing an unpublished novel and working on a second, *The Fair God*, about the Spanish conquest of Mexico. This second novel would not be published until 1873, thirty years after he began it.[76]

With the onslaught of the Civil War, Wallace was appointed a colonel and raised a volunteer regiment. He advanced rapidly through the ranks, and by March 1862, he was appointed brigadier general, the youngest general in the Union army at the time. He served throughout the war, participating in a variety of major battles. After the war, he served on the military tribunal that convicted seven men and one woman of plotting with John Wilkes Booth to assassinate President Abraham Lincoln.[77]

Wallace returned to a civilian life of law and politics, when in 1875, he developed an idea to write a novel based on the Three Wise Men from the Bible's Christmas story. Later he said when he started writing his novel *Ben-Hur: A Tale of the Christ*, he "had no conviction about God or Christ. I neither believed nor disbelieved."[78]

Ben-Hur takes place during the life of Jesus and follows the adventures of the fictional character Judah Ben-Hur as he loses a fortune, is thrown into slavery, and eventually is given his freedom. It's a tale of revenge and forgiveness set against the backdrop of the Roman Empire and Jesus's mission to reconcile all people to God.

Wallace was still writing *Ben-Hur* when, in September 1878, President Rutherford B. Hayes appointed him governor of New Mexico. It was in an unadorned back room of the Palace of the Governors in Santa Fe where Wallace worked night after night to finish *Ben-Hur*, published in 1880. Wallace later wrote, "Long before I was through with my book, I became a believer in God and Christ."[79]

At first *Ben-Hur* was off to a slow start, but as the years rolled by, more and more copies were sold. In 1913, the mail-order firm of Sears, Roebuck, and Company offered a million copies of *Ben-Hur* for sale. It became the second biggest seller in America right behind the Bible until Margaret Mitchell's *Gone with the Wind* was released in 1936.[80]

Ben-Hur has been made into plays and three major motion pictures. It has been translated into many languages and remains in print today.

CHAPTER 13
BILLY THE KID'S END

Billy the Kid rode west out of Lincoln the evening of April 28, 1881. Reining his horse off the road to Fort Stanton, he rode north into the Captain Mountains where friends helped remove his shackles, fed him, and gave him shelter. At least two friends advised him to head to Mexico where he would be safe. He considered that option but instead decided to go to Fort Sumner. When the Kid told John Meadows his decision, Meadows said, "Sure as you do, Garrett will get you, or you will have to kill him."

"Don't you worry, I've got too many friends up there," the Kid replied, "Anyhow, I don't believe he will try to get me. I can stay there awhile and get enough to go to Mexico on."[1]

On his way to Fort Sumner, the Kid's horse spooked and got away from him. He had to finish the last twenty miles on foot, reaching town on May 7, 1881. There he stole a horse from black rancher Montgomery Bell and rode bareback fifteen miles downstream along the Pecos River to a sheep camp.[2]

Deputy Sheriff Barney Mason and Jim Cureton trailed the Kid on his stolen horse to the sheep camp where the Kid and four Hispano sheepherders stood ready to fight. Unarmed, Cureton approached and talked with the Kid, who promised he would either return Bell's horse or pay him for it. Realizing they were outgunned, Mason and Cureton rode back to Fort Sumner. Mason attempted to raise a posse to go after the Kid, but no one would join him. Fearing for his life because of his participation in the Kid's capture, Mason loaded his family in a wagon and left Fort Sumner, intending to reach the safety of Roswell. About six miles out of town, they met the Kid who let them pass without harming them.[3]

Over the following weeks, the Kid stayed with Hispano sheepherder friends and sympathetic ranchers. No one tried to interfere with him when he visited Fort Sumner to dance at *bailes* and spend the nights with friends.[4]

When the Kid had killed deputies Jim Bell and Bob Olinger on April 28, 1881, Sheriff Pat Garrett was in White Oaks collecting taxes. There, the next day, he learned of the Kid's murderous escape. Riding into Lincoln on April 30, he formed a posse but soon lost the Kid's trail. Garrett knew it would be difficult to track down the Kid. He knew he needed to be careful since the Kid was dangerous and had many supporters, especially among Hispanos.[5]

Newspapers across the nation demanded the Kid be apprehended and face justice, and Governor Lew Wallace offered a $500 reward for the Kid's capture. Garrett's plan was to wait and see where the Kid turned up. He sent out letters of inquiry and riders to see what they could learn. After receiving numerous false leads, he heard rumors repeated in the newspapers that the Kid was frequenting his old haunts at Fort Sumner.[6]

Finally, Sheriff Garrett received two separate pieces of information on the Kid's location. The first was a letter from rancher Manuel Brazil. Garrett had earlier sent him a letter asking if he knew the Kid's whereabouts. Brazil replied he was worried the Kid would come after him for his part in the Kid's capture. Brazil believed the Kid was still in the Fort Sumner area. Confirming Brazil's information, Deputy Sheriff John Poe rode into Lincoln, telling Garrett he had heard from a good source that the Kid was at Fort Sumner. Poe, a detective for the Panhandle Stock Association, was in New Mexico tracking down rustlers and buyers of stolen stock. Garrett was working with Poe and had deputized him.[7]

Garrett believed if he led a large posse after the Kid, informants would tip off the Kid, giving him enough time to flee. So Garrett decided to go after the Kid, taking only Poe and Deputy Sheriff Tom "Kip" McKinney.[8]

Garrett and his two men left his Roswell ranch the night of July 11, heading north along the Pecos River, staying off the road and bypassing ranch houses. He did not want to chance anyone informing the Kid of their approach. Garrett had written Brazil asking him to meet them the night of July 13 at the mouth of Taiban Creek, five miles south of Fort Sumner. They reached the rendezvous spot that night and waited until daylight, but Brazil never showed.[9]

They needed a new course of action to locate the Kid. Since Garrett and McKinney were well known in Fort Sumner and Poe had never been there, Garrett thought it best to send him alone to reconnoiter the town. If he did not find any information there, Garrett told him to ride to Sunnyside and talk with Garrett's friend Postmaster Milnor Rudolph who might be able to divulge the Kid's whereabouts.[10]

When Poe rode into Fort Sumner, he received a cool reception from wary residents. He loitered about the plaza then entered Beaver Smith's saloon for a bite to eat and a few drinks but learned nothing. He rode to Sunnyside and questioned Rudolph who appeared nervous, claiming he didn't know where the Kid was.[11]

That evening, Poe returned to Fort Sumner to a prearranged meeting site with Garrett and McKinney north of town. After hearing Poe's dismal report, Garrett decided they should approach the town to see if they could spot the Kid and, if not, watch Paulita Maxwell's room at Pete Maxwell's house. It was rumored the Kid was romantically involved with Paulita. As a final move, Garrett thought he would attempt to see Pete Maxwell, who might be able to give him information on the Kid.[12]

At about 9 p.m., under a bright moon, the three men walked through an orchard toward Fort Sumner's buildings. Hearing voices speaking in Spanish, they stopped. They couldn't make out what was being said, but the voices were coming from people in the orchard. "Soon a man arose from the ground in full view, but too far away to recognize," Garrett said. "He wore a broad-brimmed hat, a dark vest and pants, and was in his shirt sleeves." The man said something, leaped the fence, and walked into the plaza. Garrett learned later this was Billy the Kid.[13]

Sheriff Garrett and his men left the orchard and circled around to Pete Maxwell's house, originally officers' quarters. Maxwell's corner bedroom had an outside door which was open to the cool night air, as were the windows. The rooms were all dark inside. Garrett told Poe and McKinney to wait outside while he entered Maxwell's bedroom. Proceeding through the fence gate, Garrett stepped onto the porch and walked into the house. Poe sat on the edge of the porch while McKinney squatted on his heels outside the fence. A few moments later, a man approached Maxwell's house wearing no hat and in his stocking feet.[14]

It was about midnight when Garrett entered Maxwell's dark bedroom. He sat down on the edge of the bed near Maxwell's pillow, woke him, and asked if he knew where the Kid was. Maxwell replied the Kid had been around, but he didn't know if he had left or not. Just then they heard voices outside.[15]

Having left the orchard earlier, the Kid returned to where he was staying, the home of Saval and Celsa Gutierrez—Pat Garrett was their brother-in-law. The Kid asked Celsa to fix him something to eat. Maxwell had a freshly killed beef hanging outside his house, and the Kid headed there to cut off a slab for his meal. As he left the Gutierrez home, he took a knife as well as a pistol. Walking through the gate toward the porch of Maxwell's house, the Kid saw Poe and McKinney. Startled, the Kid pulled his gun asking, "*Quien es*?" (Who is it?) Not knowing it was the Kid, Poe stood and assured him everything was fine.[16]

"*Quien es*?" the Kid said again. "*Quien es*?" He backed into the doorway of Maxwell's bedroom, disappearing, then stuck his head out again saying, "*Quien es*?" and disappeared again.[17]

Hearing the voices, Maxwell and Garrett saw a person enter and approach the bed.

"Who is it Pete?" Garrett whispered to Maxwell but received no answer.

"Who are they Pete?" the Kid asked Maxwell as he leaned forward and put both hands on the bed.

"That's him!" Maxwell whispered to Garrett who swiftly drew his single-action Colt Army revolver from its holster and pulled back the hammer. The Kid jumped back, bringing up his pistol, asking, "*Quien es? Quien es*?" Garrett fired his gun, lunging to the side, then shot a second time. The Kid slumped to the floor, emitting a gurgling sound. Garrett ran out the door as Maxwell tried to run, too, only to get tangled in his sheets and blanket and fall to the floor. As he ran out the door, Garrett told his deputies not to shoot Maxwell. He then told them he thought he shot the Kid. Poe said the Kid would never come there, that Garrett must have shot the wrong man. Garrett responded it was the Kid, that he knew his voice.[18]

It was silent in the room, but no one wanted to enter and check to make sure the Kid was dead. Maxwell lit a candle, placing it in one of the bedroom's open windows. The light revealed a motionless body on the floor. Garrett and Maxwell entered the room, determined the person was dead, and identified him as Billy the Kid. One bullet had entered his body just above the heart.[19]

Hearing the gunshots, a crowd quickly gathered outside Maxwell's house. The word spread Pat Garrett had shot and killed Billy the Kid. The Kid had many friends in town and they were becoming agitated. Deluvina, a Maxwell servant and friend of the Kid, and Jesus Silva, a Maxwell cowboy and also a friend of the Kid, entered the bedroom. When Delvina saw the Kid's face, she began to cry and curse Garrett. Paulita Maxwell walked into the

bedroom and stared at the Kid's face for a long time, not saying anything. A group of women begged Garrett to allow them to remove the Kid's body, prepare it for burial, and hold a wake. Garrett consented, and Maxwell suggested they take it to the fort's carpenter shop.[20]

Garrett and his men kept watch during the night. They were concerned the Kid's friends might come after them, but no one did. The next morning, Garrett had the *alcalde* [magistrate] Alejandro Seguro hold an inquest on the killing. Garrett needed a legal document validating he had killed the Kid to make sure he would collect Wallace's $500 reward. Seguro selected six men for the inquest, including Garrett's brother-in-law Saval Gutierrez and postmaster friend Milnor Rudolph. After examining the body and Maxwell's bedroom, and interviewing the only witnesses, Garrett and Maxwell, the members of the inquest unanimously concluded Pat Garrett had shot and killed William Bonney. The men serving on the inquest board wrote, "Our judgment is that the action of said Garrett was justifiable homicide and we are united in opinion that the gratitude of all the community is due to said Garrett for his action and whom is worthy of being compensated."[21]

Garrett had his legal document validating his deed, but Governor Wallace had moved on to an ambassadorship to Turkey, and the new governor, not wanting to part so fast with the cash, would say he could do nothing until the legislature met. Garrett would get his money, but he would have to wait.[22]

Jesus Silva built the Kid's coffin, Vicente Otero dug the Kid's grave in Fort Sumner's old military cemetery, and most of the town turned out for the funeral. Billy the Kid's grave was in a row beside those of his old partners Charlie Bowdre and Tom O'Folliard—all of them brought to an end by Pat Garrett who wrote that the Kid was dead at the age of twenty-one years, seven months, and twenty-one days.[23]

DID BILLY THE KID LIVE ON?

Many years after Sheriff Pat Garrett shot and killed Billy the Kid, several men stepped forward claiming they were the Kid. The most prominent Billy the Kid claimant was William Henry Roberts, who went by the moniker Brushy Bill.

In the 1940s, William Morrison worked as a paralegal for a Beaumont, Texas, legal firm and was familiar with New Mexico history. His firm sent him to Florida to help a man named Joe Hines in his quest to receive an inheritance. The name Joe Hines was an alias, and some believe he was Jesse Evans. Hines told Morrison that Billy the Kid was alive and living in Texas. Hines would not tell Morrison the Kid's alias or the town he was living in. Morrison began investigating if, in fact, the Kid was still alive. His research led him to a man in Missouri who gave him the name of an O. L. Roberts who lived in Hamilton, Texas.[24]

In June 1948, Morrison traveled to Hamilton, Texas, and met with O. L. Roberts. On Morrison's second meeting with Roberts, Roberts confessed that he was actually William Henry Roberts and went by O. L., which was the name of a deceased relative. Roberts said over the years he had used a variety of aliases and nicknames. One he was most known by was Brushy Bill. After persistent questioning by Morrison, Brushy Bill confessed he was Billy the Kid. At first, he did not want that information revealed because of the death sentence for the murder of Sheriff Bill Brady.[25]

Brushy Bill's appearance resembled what the Kid might have looked like in old age. He knew all the details of the Lincoln County War, including information on the Kid's friends and enemies. Morrison believed Brushy Bill's story, taped interviews with him, and began promoting that Brushy Bill was Billy the Kid.

As to the Fort Sumner shooting that occurred July 14, 1881, Brushy Bill said Sheriff Pat Garrett shot the wrong man. He said that instead of shooting Billy the Kid, Garrett shot the Kid's friend Billy Barlow.[26]

Morrison arranged a meeting on November 30, 1950, with New Mexico Governor Thomas Mabry to seek a pardon for Brushy Bill, aka Billy the Kid, a pardon that Governor Lew Wallace had promised the Kid. When asked several key questions, Brushy Bill could not answer them; he had to be prompted to remember Pat Garrett's name, and he claimed he did not kill Garrett's deputies,

Jim Bell and Bob Olinger. Most historians have written him off as a fraud.[27]

Supporters of Brushy Bill being Billy the Kid point to a 1990 facial-recognition study conducted by the University of Texas using the tintype of Billy the Kid and a photo of Brushy Bill as an old man that provide strong data showing the Kid and Brushy Bill are the same man. The Lincoln County Heritage Trust commissioned Oklahoma forensic pathologist Clyde Snow to conduct a computer analysis of the two photos, and the test results showed that out of 150 people compared to Billy the Kid's tintype, there were forty who looked more like Billy the Kid than Brushy Bill did. Opponents state that Billy the Kid had buckteeth and Brushy Bill did not. Proponents counter that Brushy Bill's front teeth were pulled in 1931.[28]

In 2003, Lincoln County Sheriff Tom Sullivan opened an investigation into the deaths of the deputies the Kid shot and the Kid's own death. People, including New Mexico Governor Bill Richardson, joined in. The investigation included attempting to obtain DNA material from the Kid, his mother, Brushy Bill, John Miller—another Billy the Kid claimant—and others, but it became tied up in legal wrangling. To make matters worse, no one actually knows for sure the exact location of the Kid's grave in Fort Sumner's graveyard. Over the years, the Pecos River has flooded, washing away parts of the cemetery including headstones and human remains.[29]

Roberts said it was his friend Billy Barlow who Garrett killed, but there is no record of a Billy Barlow anywhere in New Mexico Territory. Brushy Bill proponents say Billy Barlow was most likely an alias. The biggest problem with Brushy Bill's story is that if Sheriff Pat Garrett shot the wrong man and it was all a cover-up, then Garrett, Pete Maxwell, Paulita Maxwell, John Poe, Kip McKinney, the members of the coroner's inquest, and all the Fort Sumner residents would have to be in on it. Knowing human nature, someone should have spilled the beans.

CHAPTER 14
JESSE JAMES'S END

The James boys read of fellow gang member Bill Ryan's capture in the March 26, 1881, newspapers. They knew they had to leave their Nashville, Tennessee, homes immediately. Jesse and Frank, accompanied by Dick Liddil, traveled to Kentucky where, for a few days, they hid out with their Hite relatives.[1]

According to Bardstown, Kentucky, resident Ben Johnson, who would later become a state legislator and US congressman, detective and bounty hunter George Hunter and Louisville detective Delos "Yankee" Bligh heard rumors that the James boys were in the Bardstown area. Upon the two detectives' arrival in town, they learned the James boys and two of their friends were eating in a hotel dining room. Recruiting two local residents, they planned to capture the outlaws. Warned that detectives were waiting for them in the hotel lobby, Frank, Jesse, and the others walked out of the dining room one by one into the lobby with hands on weapons covering each other and watching for any movement from the detectives. Intimidated, the detectives made no moves to apprehend the gang. The outlaws' horses were brought to the front of the hotel. They mounted up, gave a rebel yell, and rode away.[2]

The James boys left Kentucky, returning to Missouri. Frank's wife and son traveled to California to visit her brother in Sonora. Frank later claimed he went to the Henrietta, Texas, area to visit his sister and brother-in-law while Jesse and his family rented a small house in Kansas City, Missouri.[3]

Meanwhile, the legend of the James boys continued to build. In June 1881, Frank Tousey, based in New York City, published his first nickel novel about the James boys in *The Five Cent Wide Awake Library*. It was entitled *The Train Robbers: Or, A Story of the James Boys*. It was complete fiction, but the public loved nickel and dime novels and *The Train Robbers* was a hit, unleashing a flood of fictional dime novels featuring the exploits of the James boys. The only character who appeared more in dime novels than Jesse James was Buffalo Bill Cody.[4]

Not about to give up his outlaw ways, Jesse continued to plan robberies, always being meticulous and careful. If he spotted a flaw in a robbery plan, he discarded the target. He settled on robbing the Chicago, Rock Island and Pacific Railroad near Gallatin, Missouri. Twice a week, trains transported cash to Gallatin's Farmers' Exchange Bank. Jesse recruited brother Frank, cousins Wood and Clarence Hite, and Dick Liddil.[5]

On the evening of July 15, 1881, the James Gang put into motion their planned robbery of the Kansas City train, bound northeast toward Gallatin. Some gang members boarded the train at Cameron and others at Winston, Missouri. It was dark when the train pulled out of the Winston station. Dick Liddil and Clarence Hite took positions on the outside platform of the baggage car. The James boys and Wood Hite were seated in the smoking car. Several miles outside Winston, they made their move.[6]

The conductor, William Westfall, was collecting tickets toward the rear of the smoking car when the three gang members began shooting their revolvers in the air. Jesse killed Westfall, shooting him twice in the back. Stories varied why Jesse killed Westfall: It was an accident; Jesse thought Westfall was reaching for a gun; and Jesse believed he recognized Westfall as one of those who had taken part in the attack on the Samuel farm that killed little Archie.[7]

Passengers John Penn and Frank McMillan slipped out the back of the car to the platform. The robbers saw them, one shouting, "Down! Down!" as they shot at the two. McMillan's father was still inside the car. Thinking he heard his father's voice, McMillan peeked in the window. An outlaw saw him and shot, the bullet penetrating McMillan's head above one eye.[8]

Frank made his way to the engine where he forced the engineer to stop the train at a point where the gang had left their horses. Gang members fired shots into the baggage/express car. United States Express Company agent Charles Murray surrendered and opened the safe for them. The safe contained less than $700. It was much less than the gang had expected. They badgered Murray, demanding to know where the rest of the cash was, but he claimed it was on a different train. One robber hit Murray on the head with his pistol, knocking him out.[9]

The robbery took only fifteen to twenty minutes. The gang left the train, mounted their horses, and rode off into the Crooked River country, familiar to the James boys. They rode downriver five to six miles, stopped along a bluff, and divided the loot.[10]

The newspapers expressed the public's outrage over the murders and speculated the robbery was the work of the James Gang. Zerelda Samuel traveled to Kansas City where she stated her boys couldn't have committed the murders and robbery because they were dead. John Edwards went to work defending the James boys, writing there was no proof they committed the murders and robbery. He stated newspapers just wanted to use the James boys' names, creating more sensation to sell more papers.[11]

Missouri Governor Thomas Crittenden was furious. A Democrat who had fought for the Union, Crittenden had campaigned on the promise to bring the James Gang to justice. Missouri law forbade the governor from offering large rewards for the capture of bandits, so he turned to the railroads for financial help. They agreed to provide reward money up to $50,000. Crittenden issued a proclamation that $5,000 would be awarded for the capture of each participant in the Winston train robbery and that $5,000 bonuses would be awarded upon the conviction of either Frank or Jesse James. One of his hopes was that a James Gang member would betray the brothers.[12]

When Jesse learned of the reward, he was angry, and according to Clarence Hite, "Jesse said . . . if he only knew on what train Gov. Crittenden was he would take him off and hold him for a ransom. Thought he could get about $25,000."[13]

The James Gang wasted no time preparing for a follow-up train robbery. The gang consisted of the same members who participated in the Winston train robbery with the addition of a new recruit, Charlie Ford. They planned to target a train on the east-west–running Chicago and Alton Railroad which they had hit back on October 8, 1879, at Glendale. The site they selected for the robbery was called Rocky Cut (also known as Blue Cut), about three miles from Lexington and one mile from Glendale. It was an excellent spot to stop a train. The railroad track curved through a thirty-foot cut in the terrain, requiring trains to slow down to go through it.[14]

Wednesday night, September 7, 1881, five years to the day after the Northfield, Minnesota, raid, the James Gang stopped a westbound train. They had piled rocks across the tracks and one of them waved a red warning lantern at the approaching train. Seeing the lantern, the engineer, "Choppey" Foote, applied the brakes. He saw the man with the lantern was masked and realized they were about to be robbed.[15]

Gang members captured Foote and the fireman while others covered the passenger cars from above the cut. One gang member introduced himself to Foote, saying he was Jesse James. They told Foote to get a coal pick and marched him to the express car where they ordered him to bash in the door, which he did. H. A. Fox, the messenger for the United States Express Company, had left the car and was hiding in the weeds. Foote was told to get the messenger back or he would be shot. He called for Fox to come out, which he did. The robbers forced Fox to open the safe and place its contents in their sack. They were disappointed at the small amount of cash, and in frustration Charlie Ford beat Fox over the head twice with his revolver. Fox never revealed there was a second safe with a larger amount of cash that was covered under a pile of chicken coops.[16]

Jesse told the gang members to rob the passengers, who numbered nearly one hundred. The conductor, Joel Hazelbaker, had told people to hide their valuables. Many did so, even stuffing cash into spittoons. The gang members ordered the passengers to hold up their hands and took enough watches, jewelry, and cash to nearly fill a two-bushel sack. The outlaws overlooked robbing some passengers and, in a few cases, gave watches back to the owners. They gave a silver watch back to a boy, saying it wasn't worth enough to steal. When a gang member took a dollar from a woman, she fainted. Jesse took care of her, wetting a cloth and applying it to her face. After she was revived, he gave her the dollar back.[17]

A freight train was scheduled to soon arrive at their position. Hoping to prevent a wreck, conductor Hazelbaker and the brakeman jumped off the train and ran back along the tracks to warn the oncoming train. Gang members began firing at them. Engineer Foote quickly explained to Jesse what the conductor and brakeman were doing, and Jesse ordered his men to stop shooting. Successfully warning the oncoming train to stop, the conductor and brakeman returned to their train.[18]

Jesse waved his pistol under Hazelbaker's nose and said, "Damn you, smell of that! That's the pistol I shot Westfall with at Winston! Now, listen, all you dogs, the next reward that is offered we'll burn your damn train, and don't forget it." Jesse cursed the railroads and the governor and threatened to burn the trains. He was constantly talking during the robbery, quoting scripture, and telling the passengers that it was just as evil to lie as steal. "If we are going to be wicked, we might as well make a good job of it." At the end of the robbery, Jesse gave a deep bow and said, "Good-bye, this is the last time you will ever see Jesse James."[19]

Jesse escorted Foote and the brakeman back to the engine. "Now get back there, we will remove the stones. You have been a bully boy and here is a little present for you," Jesse said as he handed Foote two silver dollars. Jesse added Foote should use the money to drink to Jesse James, and if he didn't, he would be killed. He added a second warning to quit working for the Chicago and Alton Railroad or he would be killed. Foote said he would take care of the obstructions on the tracks. With that, the James Gang disappeared on foot.[20]

Law enforcement officers formed several posses to pursue the robbers. Suspects were arrested but found to be innocent. The James Gang had divided the loot and made a clean getaway.[21]

Meanwhile, James Gang member Bill Ryan, who had been arrested outside Nashville, Tennessee, back in March 1881, had been extradited to Missouri to stand trial for his participation in the robbery of the Chicago and Alton Railroad train at Glendale, Missouri, on October 8, 1879. Tucker Bassham, who had also participated in the robbery, had been arrested, convicted, and was serving a ten-year sentence in the Missouri penitentiary. Bassham agreed to testify against Ryan and, in exchange, Governor Crittenden would pardon him.[22]

Ryan's trial was held during late September 1881 in Independence. The town was flooded with armed James Gang supporters from the nearby Cracker Neck region. Many of them slept at night on the courthouse lawn and posted guards. The prosecutors were threatened, and witnesses were warned not to testify, forcing Governor Crittenden to rush to the scene to preserve order. Bassham's Cracker Neck home was burned down. It was said that Jesse and his men were close by Independence in the woods, planning to rescue Ryan. The gang relented when they found that the man in charge of guarding Ryan was a determined fighter, Captain Maurice Langhorne, a former Confederate officer in Jo Shelby's brigade.[23]

Tucker Bassham was not intimidated and identified the gang's leader as Jesse James and his fellow robbers as Ed Miller,

Dick Liddil, Wood Hite, and Bill Ryan. On September 28, Ryan was convicted and sentenced to twenty-five years in prison, and Bassham was pardoned but received so many death threats he moved away, telling no one where he was going.[24]

After the Rocky Cut train robbery, Jesse returned to his family in Kansas City, and Frank visited his mother at the Samuel farm. From there Frank traveled by rail with Clarence Hite and Charlie Ford to Cincinnati, Ohio, where the three went their separate ways. Frank met his wife and son in Nelson County, Kentucky, and took them traveling east. They eventually settled in Lynchburg, Virginia, where Frank went by the alias James Warren.[25]

Trouble had been brewing between James Gang members Dick Liddil and James cousin Wood Hite. Wood's mother had died, and his father married a young widow named Sarah Norris Peck. The Hite family disapproved of Sarah, and Wood believed she was a loose woman. While Dick Liddil was at the Hite's Kentucky farm in October 1881, Wood believed Sarah was romantically involved with Liddil. Wood also believed Liddil had stolen a hundred dollars from him while they were splitting the loot from the Rocky Cut robbery.[26]

The two chose to settle the score by a duel. They walked out near the barn, stood back to back and strode to where they were to turn and fire, but Liddil turned early and shot at Wood, missing him. Wood ducked behind a tree as Liddil emptied his pistol at him. Liddil then ran toward the house as Wood shot at him several times, missing. Hite family members broke up the affair, and Liddil quickly rode away.[27]

A few weeks after the duel, John Tabor, a black man who worked on the Hite farm, was delivering a love letter from Sarah Hite to another one of her admirers. Wood Hite caught Tabor with the letter and told him never to act as Sarah's messenger again. Catching Tabor a second time with a love note from Sarah, Wood shot and killed him, hiding his body under some bushes. When Tabor's body was found, stepmother Sarah swore out a warrant for Wood's arrest. Law enforcement officers apprehended him and placed him under guard in Adairville, Kentucky. He managed to escape custody, found a horse, and rode out of town.[28]

On November 5, 1881, Jesse packed up the family and left Kansas City for St. Joseph, Missouri. Charlie Ford, who had returned from Cincinnati, accompanied them. Along the way, they stopped at the Samuel farm to visit Zerelda. Charlie's brother, Bob, was also there but did not travel with them. Arriving in St. Joseph on November 9, Jesse rented a house and went by the name of Thomas Howard.[29]

The evening of December 3, Dick Liddil and Bob Ford rode into the Harbison place, which was home to Bob and Charlie Ford as well as their widowed sister, Martha Bolton. Harbison's farm, located a few miles outside of Richmond, Missouri, was one of the safe places for James Gang members.[30]

When Liddil woke the next morning, he came downstairs for breakfast to find brothers Bob, Charlie, and Capline Ford, and of all people, Wood Hite, in the dining room. Hite had been at Harbison's for several days. Besides arguing over the take from the Rocky Cut robbery, Liddil and Hite were most likely rivals for Martha Bolton's affections. Hite tried to talk with Liddil about the hundred dollars he accused him of taking. Liddil called him a liar. The argument escalated. They both drew their revolvers and began shooting at each other. Gun smoke quickly filled the small dining room. Liddil fired five shots to Hite's four. Hite was hit in the right arm and Liddil was hit in the right thigh. Bob Ford drew his revolver, aimed at Hite, and fired one shot, hitting him in the head. Wood Hite died twenty minutes later.[31]

Stripping any usable clothing from Hite's body, they wrapped it in an old horse blanket and buried it in a shallow grave in the woods about a mile from the house. Liddil and the Fords had always been suspicious that Jesse had killed fellow gang member Ed Miller. Now they feared if Jesse ever learned they had killed his cousin Wood Hite, they would be next on his hit list.[32]

Charlie Ford returned to St. Joseph to live with Jesse and his family, saying nothing of Wood Hite's killing. On Christmas Eve, Jesse moved his family, along with Charlie, to 1318 Lafayette Street, situated on a high hill where Jesse had an excellent view of his surroundings.[33]

On December 29, Jesse and Charlie visited Harbison's place to talk to Dick Liddil. Jesse was still unaware that Liddil had killed Wood Hite. Jesse wanted Liddil to join with them. Liddil, sullen and noncommittal, believed Jesse wanted to take him out and kill him. Liddil quietly left Harbison's the next day. Jesse now believed Liddil had turned against him. On his return to St. Joseph, Jesse wrote a letter to his cousin Clarence Hite, warning him to leave home. He believed Liddil was working with detectives and they would soon be coming for Clarence.[34]

Liddil returned to Harbison's after Jesse and Charlie left. Clay County Sheriff James Timberlake was bound and determined to put an end to the James Gang. He learned that the Harbison place in neighboring Ray County was a James Gang refuge. As he conducted his investigations, he overheard that Dick Liddil and Bob Ford had killed Wood Hite. On the night of January 6, 1882, Timberlake led a posse to Harbison's place looking to capture James Gang members. Liddil just barely escaped. This was the last straw for him. He had to make a choice between the mercy of Jesse James or the mercy of the law. He chose the law.[35]

Martha Bolton met with Governor Crittenden on Liddil's behalf. The governor promised if Liddil surrendered to Sheriff Timberlake and testified against the James boys, he would not be prosecuted. Bolton then told the governor that her brother, Bob Ford, was willing to cooperate in the matter of Jesse James as long as the governor could offer him assurances. The governor was interested and wanted to meet with Ford.[36]

On January 13, Governor Crittenden was attending a ball at the St. James Hotel in Kansas City. He slipped away from the festivities and met Bob Ford in a private room where it was agreed if Ford took care of Jesse James, the governor would give him a pardon and the reward money. Crittenden later said he had told Ford that Jesse needed to be brought in alive. Ford later remembered the governor saying he wanted Jesse dead or alive. Governor Crittenden told Ford to work with Sheriff Timberlake and Kansas City Police Commissioner Captain Henry Craig, which he agreed to do.[37]

On January 24, 1882, Dick Liddil surrendered to Clay County Sheriff James Timberlake and began telling what he knew of the James Gang members and activities. Liddil's arrest was kept secret to prevent Frank and Jesse from learning.[38]

Sheriff Timberlake and Commissioner Craig traveled to Kentucky, taking with them Dick Liddil as guide. At 2:00 a.m., on February 11, 1882, without informing local law enforcement, they arrested Clarence Hite at the farm, charging him for his participation in the Winston, Missouri, train robbery. They took Hite to Missouri, where he was presented with Liddil's detailed testimony. He confessed to his part in the robbery and was sentenced to twenty-five years in prison. Rumors flew that Hite had implicated others in the robbery, but government authorities held the information tight.[39]

During mid-March, Jesse took Charlie Ford on a tour of eastern Kansas towns, looking for a good bank to rob. Jesse asked Charlie if he knew anyone who would want to participate in a robbery. Charlie replied that his brother Bob would be a good choice.[40]

They rode to Harbison's place to recruit Bob. With Bob's knowledge, Sheriff Timberlake had been watching Harbison's for the possibility of Jesse's appearance. The weather had turned bad, and Timberlake left just before Jesse and Charlie arrived at the farm. Before leaving with Jesse and Charlie, Bob told his sister Martha that if no one heard from him in ten days he was probably dead.[41]

Jesse and the Ford brothers went to the Samuel farm where Jesse visited his half-brother John who had been shot at a party after drinking too much and becoming belligerent. When Jesse and Zerelda were alone he confided to her, "I am not feeling well tonight; I am a little low spirited—maybe I'll never see you again." She tried to cheer him up and then said, "I have noticed Charlie since he has been here this last time; he has greatly changed; he does not look at me as honestly as he used to; I fear he is meditating treachery."

"Bob Ford, I don't trust," Jesse said, "I think he is a sneak; but Charlie Ford is as true as steel."

Later Zerelda caught Bob Ford alone and challenged him, asking if he was still Jesse's friend. Bob took Zerelda's hand in one of his and raised his other hand to heaven swearing he would sooner die than see her son harmed.[42]

From this time on, both Ford brothers lived at Jesse's house with the family in St. Joseph. They kept in contact with the authorities and notified them as to where Jesse was living, but no one made a move to arrest him. The brothers made up their minds to kill Jesse, but they had to wait for the right time. He was watchful like a hawk. Jesse and Zee took the Ford brothers in as part of the family. They slept in the James's house, ate their food, and played with their two little children.[43]

Jesse was puzzled by Dick Liddil's disappearance. Since Liddil had been frequenting Harbison's place, Bob Ford's home, Jesse asked Bob what had become of Liddil. Bob responded by saying Jesse knew as much as he did. Sheriff Timberlake had instructed Bob not to let Jesse know that Liddil had surrendered. Timberlake also told Bob to try to keep newspapers away from Jesse as reporters were hearing rumors that Liddil had surrendered and the news was bound to get out. On March 31, 1882, it was official: Law enforcement released to the press that Dick Liddil had surrendered, but Jesse was still unaware.[44]

Jesse settled on a plan to rob the bank in Platte City, Missouri. A murder trial was in progress, and the attention of the town's citizens would be riveted to the proceedings at the courthouse while Jesse and the Ford brothers robbed the bank. They planned to leave for Platte City the night of April 3 and rob the bank the next morning.[45]

Monday morning, April 3, 1882, was bright and balmy. Zee was in the kitchen preparing breakfast when Bob Ford brought the latest newspapers into the front room. He handed Jesse the *St. Louis Republican* and sat down across from him. As they began to look through the papers, Bob saw the *Kansas City Times* headline announced Dick Liddil's surrender. Panicked, he tried to hide the paper under a shawl draped on a chair, but Jesse spied the paper, and tucking it under his arm, walked into the kitchen for breakfast. As Bob followed, he checked his revolver, making sure it was positioned on his belt near his right hand.[46]

Zee poured coffee as Bob sat down across from Jesse. Charlie and the two children were already seated. Jesse spread the newspaper on the table, exclaiming, "Hello, here! Surrender of Dick Liddil!" Jesse looked up and across the table at Bob.

"Young man," Jesse said, "I thought you told me you didn't know anything about Dick."

"I didn't."

"Well it's very strange. He surrendered three weeks ago, and you were right here in the neighborhood. It looks fishy to me."[47]

Jesse glared at Bob who left the kitchen and walked into the front room. Jesse followed him there and spoke in a reassuring voice, "Well, it's all right anyway, Bob." Bob believed Jesse was on to him but would not kill him in front of his wife and children; he would probably do that when they were out of town.[48]

After breakfast, Jesse and the Ford brothers went out to the stable to feed and curry the horses. The day was becoming hot. When they returned to the house, Jesse left the front-room door open to let in a cool breeze. He complained he was hot, and removing his coat, he laid it on a bed in the room. Not wanting passersby to see his guns, he took off his gun belt and guns and laid them on the bed. Charlie left Jesse and Bob in the front room, wandering into the kitchen where Zee was cleaning up from breakfast and the children were playing.[49]

A picture of a horse hanging on one of the walls of the front room caught Jesse's eye. He was either thinking of rehanging it, adjusting it, or dusting the frame, as he placed a straight-back chair under the picture and stood on it to reach the picture. This was Bob's chance. Jesse was unarmed with his back to him—vulnerable. Bob pulled his Smith & Wesson .44 New Model No. 3 revolver, a gift from Jesse, and aimed it at the back of Jesse's head. As Bob cocked the revolver's hammer, Jesse's head began to turn at the sound. Bob pulled the trigger, firing a bullet into the back of his head. Jesse fell lifeless to the floor. Charlie rushed into the room and then Zee. The earliest accounts placed Charlie in the kitchen, and then later accounts had him in the front room with Bob, maybe so Charlie could share in the reward.[50]

"It was an accident!" Bob said as Zee knelt by Jesse's head, trying to wipe the blood away.

"Yes, an accident on purpose," Zee said. "You traitor. Bob Ford, traitor! Traitor!"[51]

The Ford brothers ran from the house, yelling to a passerby to inform the police they had killed Jesse James. They raced to the telegraph station where they sent messages of Jesse's death to Governor Crittenden, Sheriff Timberlake, and Commissioner Craig. They found St. Joseph Marshal Enos Craig and informed him they had killed Jesse James. Craig arrested them and placed them in jail.[52]

Jesse's body was taken to Buchanan County Coroner Dr. James Heddens's establishment where reporters examined his body, finding two bullet wound scars on the right side of his chest, a portion of the left-hand middle finger missing, as well as other distinguishing marks that confirmed the body was Jesse James. Crowds of people showed up to view the body of the famous outlaw. An autopsy was performed by four doctors, who surgically removed part of Jesse's skull to examine the bullet damage to his brain.[53]

Six citizens were impaneled for the coroner's inquest, which began at 3 p.m. that same day and lasted into the next. An immense crowd was on hand listening to the witnesses who were there to testify as to the identity of the body. Zee James, the Ford brothers, and Zerelda Samuel, who arrived the second day, all testified it was Jesse James. Friends and former bushwhackers who had ridden with Jesse identified the body as his.[54]

Kansas City Police Commissioner Captain Henry Craig testified, "The body corresponds with the description of Jesse James. I know the Fords. Bob Ford assisted Sheriff Timberlake and myself. He was not commissioned. Robert Ford acted through our instructions, and Charles was not acting under our instructions."[55]

Clay County Sheriff James Timberlake testified about Jesse, "We were personally acquainted. I saw him last in 1870. I knew his face. He had part of a finger shot off. I told Ford to get his brother to assist him."[56]

Dick Liddil was brought in and testified, "I have seen the body and recognize it as the body of Jesse James. I have no doubt of it."[57]

Governor Crittenden asked Dr. George W. James, no relation to Jesse, to identify the body. Dr. James had treated Jesse after he had accidently shot off the tip of his finger. Dr. James said, "Yes, it was Jesse, all right. The finger I attended was easy to identify."[58]

The coroner's jury determined the deceased was Jesse James, who Robert Ford intentionally killed. Zee swore out a warrant for the arrest of the Ford brothers in the murder of her husband, Jesse James. Law enforcement arrested them, and they remained in the St. Joseph jail.[59]

Jesse's body traveled by train to Kearney. A viewing was held at the Kearney Hotel, where hundreds passed by the body to pay their last respects. It was the largest number of people in Kearney up to that time.[60]

On April 6, 1882, Jesse's funeral service was held at the Mt. Olivet Baptist Church. About two thousand people attended, friend and foe alike, including Captain Henry Craig and Sheriff James Timberlake, who was a pallbearer. After the service, the funeral procession went to the Samuel farm, where a deep grave had been dug under a large coffee bean tree in the yard near the house. Jesse's body was buried at 5 p.m. that evening.[61]

It was the end of the line for Jesse James the man but not Jesse James the legend.

DID JESSE JAMES LIVE ON?

In January 1932, John James arrived in Excelsior Springs near Frank and Jesse James's family farm in Missouri. John James revealed he was actually Jesse James and had returned to visit his old haunts. He stated the man the Ford brothers killed in Jesse James's home in St. Joseph was a man named Charlie Bigelow. Some prominent residents believed him, and the national news media began proclaiming Jesse James was alive and well.[62]

Jesse James's son, Jesse Jr., and his wife, Stella, were living in California at the time. Jesse Jr. was disturbed by John James's claim but was unwell and not able to leave home. Stella traveled to Missouri to investigate John James.[63]

When questioned, John James could not remember Jesse's half-brother Archie's name or which of Zerelda's arms had been injured in the Pinkerton attack. When Stella met with John James, she brought along a pair of Jesse's boots as well as Frank Milburn, who had made them for Jesse. Jesse had small feet, size six and a half. Stella asked John James to try them on, but he couldn't—his feet were too big for the boots.[64]

Stella learned John James was on parole from Menard Penitentiary in Illinois, where he had served time for killing a man. She found John James's sister, Dr. Bessie James Garver, who wrote an affidavit stating his name was William John James and that he was mentally unbalanced and a potential threat to society. Undeterred, John James continued to proclaim he was Jesse James and appeared across the country in shows and circuses as Jesse James.[65]

It's not known how many men claimed to be Jesse James, but his son, Jesse Jr., said he knew of twenty-six Jesse James claimants. One of these, a man named J. Frank Dalton, revealed himself on national radio in May 1948.[66]

Dalton was from Lawton, Oklahoma, and the day after the radio show, the local newspapers picked up the story as thirty thousand curiosity seekers descended upon the town. Dalton claimed many things, among them, piloting an airplane at age sixty-nine in World War I.[67]

Dalton's story was similar to John James's tale. He said a man named Charlie Bigelow had been shot and killed while Dalton hid in a nearby stable. The James family was upset with this imposter and refused to talk with him.[68]

In 1948, Dalton began earning a living at carnivals and fairs, proclaiming he was Jesse James. He appeared on stage with "Colonel" James Russell Davis, who claimed he was Cole Younger, as well as with William Henry "Brushy Bill" Roberts, who claimed he was Billy the Kid. On January 13, 1950, all three claimants appeared on NBC's national *We the People* radio and television show.[69]

On July 17, 1995, Jesse James's remains were exhumed for DNA testing alongside James family descendants. Ironically, the exhumation was guarded by Pinkerton's Incorporated. Not only were human bones and teeth found in Jesse James's second grave, but also a .36-caliber bullet in the area of the right rib cage. In addition, a .38-caliber bullet had earlier been found in the original grave at the Samuel farm.[70]

A forensic team, led by Professor James Starrs, analyzed the remains found in Jesse James's grave. On February 23, 1996, Starrs held a press conference at the Forty-Eighth Annual Meeting of the American Academy of Forensic Sciences in Nashville, Tennessee. After conducting DNA tests and reviewing artifacts found with the human remains, Professor Starrs stated, "I feel a reasonable degree of scientific certainty that we have the remains of Jesse James."[71]

CHAPTER 15

END OF THE TRAIL

Billy the Kid and Jesse James were in their graves, but life went on. Newspapers continued to print tales about them, and publishers continued to churn out books and dime novels keeping their memories alive.

Representatives for Frank James, including his wife, Annie, his mother, Zerelda Samuel, and mouthpiece John Edwards worked behind the scenes negotiating with state officials for Frank's surrender. On October 5, 1882, Frank walked into Missouri Governor Thomas Crittenden's office and surrendered. Unbuckling his gun belt with his holstered revolver, Frank said, "Governor Crittenden, I want to hand over to you that which no living man except myself has been permitted to touch since 1861, and to say that I am your prisoner."[1]

Over the next several years, Frank was tried in court after court for the murder of Pinkerton agent Joseph Whicher and a variety of bank, train, and payroll robberies. By February 1885, the many cases against Frank were either dismissed or Frank was acquitted by juries, making him a free man. The state of Minnesota made noise to have him extradited, claiming he was involved in the botched Northfield bank robbery, but the new governor of Missouri, former Confederate general John Marmaduke, told Frank's friend John Edwards that he would never extradite Frank to Minnesota.[2]

Frank held a variety of jobs over the years, farming and ranching, working as a store clerk, horse-race starter, racehorse manager, and doorman at the Standard Theater in St. Louis.[3]

The Younger brothers had been in the Minnesota State Prison at Stillwater since 1876. On September 16, 1889, Bob died of tuberculosis. In July 1901, Cole and Jim were paroled but with restrictions that included they must remain in the state. Jim wanted to marry, but he needed permission from the state. It was denied. Despondent, he shot and killed himself.[4]

After Jim's death, the state government removed Cole's restrictions, and he returned to Missouri. Cole contacted Frank James, and after finding financial backers, they started their own wild west show in 1903 called "The Great Cole Younger and Frank James Historical Wild West." They put on a good show, reenacting scenarios from the Old West. Cowboys and Indians displayed feats of horsemanship and marksmanship while the band played, and the crowds cheered. However, the show was plagued by poor management and out-of-control employees drinking, brawling, and stealing. Frank had enough and was done by the end of the season.[5]

He appeared in a play, *The Fatal Scar*, performing throughout the country. In later years, Frank managed the Samuel farm as a tourist attraction and working farm. Frank died February 18, 1915 and instructed that his remains be cremated.[6]

Soon after Jesse's assassination, tourists began arriving at the Samuel farm to look around. One of them wanted to buy a picture hanging on the wall inside the house. At first Zerelda said no, but then thought better of it and sold it to the man for ten dollars. "I must have money now," she said. "They have killed him on whom I depended." She made money by charging tourists to visit the farm and selling them mementos. Zerelda and Jesse's wife, Zee, were paid royalties from profits generated from Frank Triplett's book published in 1882, *Jesse James: The Life, Times, and Treacherous Death of the Most Infamous Outlaw of All Time*. After the book was released, Zerelda and Zee read it and did not like its content. They disavowed Triplett's book, but took the money anyway. Zerelda died on February 10, 1911.[7]

Zee James raised her children, Jesse Jr. and Mary, as a single parent. By 1900, she was in poor health and died November 13 of that year. Before she died, Zee requested that Jesse's body be reburied beside her in Mount Olivet Cemetery in Kearney. In 1902, the family honored her wishes, and Jesse's remains were dug up and reburied beside her.[8]

On September 23, 1898, a gang dynamited an express car in a robbery attempt eight miles outside Kansas City, Missouri. One arrested suspect confessed to being part of the gang and named Jesse James Jr. as one of the gang members. James was arrested and stood trial. The jury found him not guilty. This experience sent him on the path to become an attorney. In 1899, he wrote a book, *Jesse James, My Father*, and in 1907, he graduated with honors from law school.[9]

Bob and Charlie Ford were indicted for first-degree murder of Jesse James, on April 17, 1882. They both pled guilty, and the judge handed down the punishment of hanging until dead. Later that day, Governor Crittenden pardoned them both. Bob was eventually acquitted of murdering Wood Hite. No one knows how much of the reward money the Ford brothers were paid, but it was not the full amount. Whatever happened to all the money raised by the railroads and express companies remains a mystery.[10]

The Ford brothers toured the country with a show called *How I Killed Jesse James* in which they reenacted the murder. When they appeared to Missouri audiences, they were booed and threatened with lynching. Charlie developed a terminal case of tuberculosis and became addicted to morphine. Returning to Missouri, on May 4, 1884, he shot himself.[11]

Dick Liddil, who was released from prison, and Bob Ford teamed up, opening a saloon in Las Vegas, New Mexico. It was a failure, and over the next several years Bob held a variety of jobs in different towns. On June 8, 1892, he was running a saloon in

Creede, Colorado, when in walked Ed O'Kelly with a sawed-off shotgun. Kelly, a low-life bad man, had been feuding with Ford. He pointed the shotgun at Ford and pulled the trigger, killing him.[12]

And what about those left behind when Billy the Kid was killed? His friends and some of his enemies kept his memory alive.

After Sheriff Pat Garrett shot and killed Billy the Kid, many people grumbled about ambushing the Kid in the dark. People said it wasn't a fair fight. Wanting to tell his side of the story, Garrett collaborated with Ash Upson to write a book about the Kid. In February or March 1882, they worked with Charles Green, editor of the *Santa Fe New Mexican* and Santa Fe Ring member, to publish *The Authentic Life of Billy the Kid, the Noted Desperado of the Southwest, Whose Deeds of Daring and Blood Made His Name a Terror in New Mexico, Arizona and Northern Mexico.* The launch of the book was not a success. It did not become a best seller until after Garrett and Upson were dead.[13]

Pat Garrett worked at a variety of projects and jobs in New Mexico and Texas over the years, including sheriff of Doña Ana County, New Mexico. President Theodore Roosevelt appointed him as customs collector at El Paso, Texas, but he was not reappointed in 1905. He ranched near Las Cruces, New Mexico, where he became embroiled in a dispute with neighbors. On February 29, 1908, he was driving his team of horses along a lonely stretch of road and stopped to urinate. He was ambushed, shot in the back of the head. A couple of neighbors were suspected, but no one was ever convicted of his murder.[14]

After the Lincoln County War, John Chisum brought his herds back to his South Spring River ranch. In the summer of 1884, he made a trip to Kansas City to have a tumor removed from his neck. The operation was a success, but the tumor soon reappeared and Chisum died December 22, 1884.[15]

Sue McSween remained in New Mexico managing her late husband's estate. She started her own ranch in the Three Rivers area west of the Sierra Blanca mountains. In 1884, she married

George Barber but divorced him in 1891. Her ranching operation was a success. In 1892, she was running eight thousand head of cattle. She died at her White Oaks home in 1931.[16]

Jimmie Dolan was elected Lincoln County treasurer in 1884, and then in 1888, he was elected to the New Mexico territorial senate. Along with William Rynerson and Numa Raymond, he formed the Feliz Land and Cattle Company, which took control of John Tunstall's old cattle range. Dolan died in 1898.[17]

After the July 1878 fight in Lincoln, Johnny Riley spent little time there. He ran a cattle operation with William Rynerson and then later had business interests with Thomas Catron. He was involved in a major land dispute and the Tularosa Water War. By 1898, Riley had separated from his family and moved to Colorado where he prospered raising cattle and hogs. He died of pneumonia in Colorado Springs on February 10, 1916.[18]

Even though the leader of the Santa Fe Ring, Thomas Catron, lost his appointment as US attorney for the district of New Mexico in 1878, he was still a successful politician, being elected to the New Mexico Territorial Council several times. During his career, he was president of the New Mexico bar and mayor of Santa Fe. When New Mexico became a state in 1912, the legislature elected him as one of the state's first US senators. Catron acquired three million acres of land, becoming the largest landowner in New Mexico. On May 15, 1921, Catron died in Santa Fe.[19]

Gang leader John Kinney was arrested for cattle rustling and sent to prison in 1883. After his release in 1886, there is no record of him committing any more crimes. He served with the army during the Spanish-American War in 1898 and was successful at mining in Arizona, where he died in Prescott on August 25, 1919.[20]

The Kid's antagonist, Jesse Evans, had left New Mexico for Texas to continue his cattle rustling operations. In 1880, he and his gang were pursued by Texas Rangers. In a shoot-out with them, Evans killed a Ranger and was sentenced to ten years in the penitentiary. In 1882, he escaped from a work gang and disappeared.[21]

AFTERWORD

Writers have created hundreds of books, both fiction and nonfiction, about Jesse James and Billy the Kid. I recommend three nonfiction books on Jesse James: Mark Lee Gardner's *Shot All to Hell*, T. J. Stiles's *Jesse James: Last Rebel of the Civil War*, and Ted P. Yeatman's *Frank and Jesse James: The Story behind the Legend*. I recommend three nonfiction books on Billy the Kid: Mark Lee Gardner's *To Hell on a Fast Horse*, Frederick Nolan's *The West of Billy the Kid*, and Robert Utley's *Billy the Kid: A Short and Violent Life*. Sometimes books about Jesse James and Billy the Kid, fiction and nonfiction, have interacted with well-known people's lives.

In March 1886, outlaw "Red-headed" Mike Finnigan and his gang of two stole Theodore Roosevelt's boat and took off down Dakota Territory's Little Missouri River. Roosevelt and his men chased after them and caught them six days later. A voracious reader, Roosevelt had finished Tolstoy's nine-hundred-page *Anna Karenina*. He asked the gang members if they had any reading material and borrowed a Jesse James dime novel from them.[1]

After lawmen ambushed and killed the outlaws Bonnie and Clyde on May 23, 1934, they found a copy of Walter Noble Burns's *The Saga of Billy the Kid* in their bullet-riddled car.[2]

When future president Harry S. Truman was a boy, his teacher caught him with a Jesse James dime novel hidden in a schoolbook. She reported it to his parents who gave him one of the "soundest licken's [sic]."[3]

Many songs and ballads have been written about Jesse and Billy. The most popular ballad about Jesse is "Jesse James" by an unknown composer. Bentley Ball first recorded it in 1919 and many recording artists have sung it ever since. Woody Guthrie, Pete Seeger, The Kingston Trio, Van Morrison, Bob Seger, The Nitty Gritty Dirt Band, Sons of the Pioneers, Johnny Cash, and Bruce Springsteen have all sung the lyrics, "He stole from the rich and he gave to the poor." Members of Western Writers of America listed it as one of the top one hundred Western songs.[4]

Marty Robbins performed his song "Billy the Kid" (1959) and Billy Joel's "Ballad of Billy the Kid" (1975) is a great song but has little to do with the reality of Billy the Kid. There was even a one-act ballet written about the Kid. Composer Aaron Copland's *Billy the Kid* (1938) is one of his most popular compositions.

Both Jesse James and Billy the Kid have been portrayed on radio and television shows. Their memories live on in the movies; although all the films miss the mark of truth, some come closer to it than others.

How many movies have been made about Jesse James and Billy the Kid? Johnny Boggs, author of *Jesse James and the Movies* and *Billy the Kid on Film*, says, "There's no telling, and an exact number will probably never be known." One of the problems is that there is no record of how many silent films were made and many have disappeared. "But if you want to limit this to American-produced movies in the sound era, including serials and made-for-TV films, there are roughly forty about Jesse James," Boggs says. "Regarding Billy the Kid movies, the total is more like fifty-five films in the sound era."

Jesse James (1939), starring Tyrone Power as Jesse and Henry Fonda as Frank James, was probably one of the most important movies about Jesse. "*Jesse James* redefined how Jesse was portrayed," Boggs says. "He went from thug outlaw to farm boy turned to crime by corrupt banks and railroads, a flawed hero for the common man."

Two of the most popular movies about Jesse James are *The Long Riders* (1980), and *The Assassination of Jesse James by the*

Coward Robert Ford (2007), starring Brad Pitt as Jesse and Casey Affleck, who received an Oscar nomination for Best Supporting Actor, as Bob Ford. Johnny Boggs picks *The Assassination of Jesse James* as "the best blend of history and cinema," but he says it might not be to everyone's taste.

As for movies about Billy the Kid, *Young Guns* (1988) is one of the most popular. Sam Peckinpah's *Pat Garrett and Billy the Kid* (1973) is my favorite Billy the Kid movie not based on accuracy but just plain fun. Johnny Boggs agrees it's probably the best Billy the Kid movie, "but it's a train wreck, with a handful of incredibly great scenes . . . surrounded by a ton of garbage and poor history." The cast is loaded with a who's who of old-time cowboy actors. Bob Dylan, who wrote and played the songs for the film, can be found in several scenes. Dylan's "Knocking on Heaven's Door" plays during one of the most powerful scenes as Slim Pickens's character, Sheriff Baker, is dying. Western Writers of America rated this song one of the top one hundred Western songs.

Johnny Boggs believes Jesse James and Billy the Kid saved Western movies from extinction. By 1939, serious Westerns were not being filmed, but with the success of *Jesse James*, there was a resurgence. By 1988, Westerns were dead, but with the release of *Young Guns*, they became popular again. "So as weak as most movies about those two outlaws are, you can't dismiss them," Boggs says. "It took Jesse James to bring back the A-Western in 1939, and almost fifty years later, it took a movie about Billy the Kid to raise, again, the Western from Hollywood's grave."[5]

Why do Americans love Billy the Kid and Jesse James? Why do we remember their names but can't remember the names of presidents of the United States?

Americans love an underdog, a person who stands up against perceived tyranny. After all, our underdog forefathers and foremothers rebelled against Great Britain, the greatest superpower of its time, and won. Jesse James and Billy the Kid personify that rebellious spirit. That's why they remain popular even though they were criminals and killed people. Many Americans overlook the crimes and see the romance of the rebel.

Jesse became the American version of Robin Hood, robbing the rich and giving to the poor. Billy became the symbol of the American loner: the little guy fighting against all odds; the misunderstood youth who battled the combined corrupt government and business forces hell-bent on his destruction. Both were fearless, devil-may-care, audacious, pulling off extraordinary feats of daring.

Many attributed robberies to Jesse when he wasn't even there. If you're going to be robbed, you might as well be robbed by the best—Jesse James. Everyone wanted to be associated with Billy the Kid—he stayed at their ranch or he stole one of their horses.

Leading even more to their status as outlaw heroes, both Billy the Kid and Jesse James were killed in ways the American public disapproved. Case in point, after Jesse's assassination by "that dirty little coward" Bob Ford, he remained popular and his stature grew through time, while Frank, who had surrendered and committed no major crimes after that, lessened in the public view. And Sheriff Pat Garrett was never lauded for ambushing the Kid in a dark bedroom.

After studying Jesse James and Billy the Kid, I've come to view them both as likeable criminals. They could be pleasant company and they enjoyed a good joke. They were true to their friends—unless they believed their friends were double-crossing them—courteous to women, made time for children, and were kind to animals. That being said, I do not condone their murders and crimes. They justified their violent actions in their own minds. When they killed, they believed it was for self-preservation, revenge, or just plain business. They needed to face the full consequences for breaking the law.

In my mind, Jesse was the greatest outlaw. He had a longer outlaw career. He was audacious, planning and robbing banks in the middle of the day and stopping the most powerful machines of the time—railroad engines—to rob their trains and successfully get away.

Billy was a successful small-time horse thief and cattle rustler. There was nothing spectacular about his robberies, but Billy was an excellent gunman. He was successful in eluding pursuing posses and, when captured, escaping.

I don't believe Jesse James and Billy the Kid will be replaced anytime soon as America's greatest outlaws. They strike a chord in Americans' fiber—the little guy taking on overwhelming odds and winning. They each had hair-raising adventures and escapes. Jesse James and Billy the Kid will continue to ride across the landscape of America's imagination, always on the run—never to be caught.

ACKNOWLEDGMENTS

First, thanks to Billy the Kid and Jesse James for living extraordinary lives that I could explore and tell about. Thanks to all the folks who recorded the events during those two outlaws' lifetimes and to those who preserve those records. Thanks to all the researchers, writers, and authors who have dug into the Jesse James and Billy the Kid stories seeking the truth.

Thank you, Erin Turner and the folks at TwoDot and Rowman & Littlefield for giving me the opportunity to write this book. Jim Hatzell, thank you for your outstanding illustrations.

A big thank-you to freelance wordsmith Barry Keith Williams for an excellent job polishing the manuscript and fact-checking—you are a master. Another big thank-you to fellow Delta Kappa Epsilon Brother Phil "Theta" Bowden for the detailed review and no-nonsense critique—Friends from the Heart Forever. Mike Pellerzi, as always thanks for providing your cowboy point of view. Bro-in-Law Ron Swift, thank you for your review and Missouri location fact-checking.

Brenda DeVore, director, Prairie Trails Museum of Wayne County, Corydon, Iowa, thank you for providing information and insight into the James Younger Gang robbery of the Ocobock Bank. Jim Clark, manager of operations, James Clark & Company Railroad Motion Pictures Services, thank you for providing your expertise with railroads, track, and engines, and your railroad-robberies review. Johnny Boggs, author of *Jesse James and the Movies* and *Billy the Kid on Film*, thank you for your critique of Jesse James and Billy the Kid films.

I thank my fellow Most Intrepid Western Author Posse members for their support: Chris Enss, Sherry Monahan, Monty McCord, and Kellen Cutsforth. Thanks to the members of Western Writers of America—without them my writing career would not be where it is today.

A big thank-you to my wife, Liz, for putting up with my long hours in the basement plunking away on the computer keyboard, helping with the occasional spelling of a word—I am the world's worst speller—and for traveling with me to Billy the Kid's gravesite and other obscure places on my research trips. Thanks to my entire family for their support. Thanks to all the critters who distracted me by peeking in my window to see what I was doing. Most of all, thanks to the Lord for giving me this opportunity and for the ability to think and write.

NOTES

CHAPTER 1: THE EARLY YEARS

1 David Wolfe Eaton, "How Missouri Counties, Towns and Streams Were Named," *Missouri Historical Review*, vol. 10, no. 3, April 1916, 277.
2 Edwards Brothers, *An Illustrated Historical Atlas of Clay County, Missouri* (Philadelphia: Edwards Brothers of Missouri, 1877), 9.
3 T. J. Stiles, *Jesse James: Last Rebel of the Civil War* (New York: Random House, 2002), 19.
4 Ted P. Yeatman, *Frank and Jesse James: The Story behind the Legend* (Naperville, IL: Sourcebooks, 2000), 25.
5 Ibid., 26.
6 Phil Stewart, "History of the James Farm," Friends of the James Farm website, 2, accessed April 16, 2018, http://n.b5z.net/i/u/10126339/f/Article Archive/stewart_article.pdf.
7 T. J. Stiles, *Jesse James*, 20.
8 T. J. Stiles, *Jesse James*, 18, 22, 23; Find a Grave, "Jesse James," accessed April 16, 2018, https://www.findagrave.com/memorial/539/jesse-woodson-james.
9 Find a Grave, "Susan Lavenia James Parmer," accessed April 16, 2018, https://www.findagrave.com/memorial/10700891/susan-lavenia-parmer.
10 T. J. Stiles, *Jesse James*, 25, 26.
11 Ted P. Yeatman, *Frank and Jesse James*, 26.
12 Ibid.
13 T. J. Stiles, *Jesse James*, 28–31.
14 Ibid., 30, 31.
15 Ibid., 31, 32.
16 J. A. Dacus, *Life and Adventures of Frank and Jesse James, the Noted Western Outlaws* (St. Louis: N. D. Thompson & Co., 1881), 18, 19.
17 Ibid., 21, 22.
18 Ted P. Yeatman, *Frank and Jesse James*, 28.
19 James R. Ross, *I, Jesse James* (Thousand Oaks, CA: Dragon Books, 1989), xi, 1.
20 T. J. Stiles, *Jesse James*, 36.
21 Frederick Nolan, *The West of Billy the Kid* (Norman: University of Oklahoma Press, 1998), 3–6.

22 Mark Lee Gardner, *To Hell on a Fast Horse: Billy the Kid, Pat Garrett, and the Epic Chase to Justice in the Old West* (New York: HarperCollins Publishers, 2010), 36.
23 Pat Garrett, *The Authentic Life of Billy the Kid, the Noted Desperado of the Southwest* (Santa Fe: New Mexico Printing and Publishing Co., 1882), 8; Mark Lee Gardner, *To Hell on a Fast Horse,* 36.
24 Pat Garrett, *The Authentic Life of Billy the Kid*, 8; Mark Lee Gardner, *To Hell on a Fast Horse*, 36.
25 Frederick Nolan, *The West of Billy the Kid* (Norman: University of Oklahoma Press, 1998), 3–6.
26 Ancestry.com, 1880 United States Federal Census, accessed April 17, 2018, https://www.ancestry.com/interactive/6742/4242010-00881?pid=15438484&backurl=https://search.ancestry.com/cgi-bin/sse.dll?indiv%3D1%26dbid%3D6742%26h%3D15438484%26tid%3D%26pid%3D%26usePUB%3Dtrue%26_phsrc%3DuBu3%26_phstart%3DsuccessSource&treeid=&personid=&hintid=&usePUB=true&_phsrc=uBu3&_phstart=successSource&usePUBJs=true.
27 Kansaspedia, "Thomas W. Barber," Kansas Historical Society, accessed May 17, 2018, https://www.kshs.org/kansapedia/thomas-w-barber/11730.
28 James M. McPherson, *Battle Cry of Freedom: The Civil War Era* (New York, NY: Ballantine Books, 1988), 148, 149.
29 Ibid., 152, 153.

Chapter 2: Civil War

1 Ibid., 290, 292.
2 Ted P. Yeatman, *Frank and Jesse James*, 29.
3 E. B. Long, *The Civil War Day by Day: An Almanac 1861–1865* (Garden City, NY: Doubleday & Co., 1971), 56–60.
4 Lawrence O. Christensen, William E. Foley, and Gary Kremer, eds., *Dictionary of Missouri Biography*, (Columbia: University of Missouri Press, 1999), 425.
5 Ted P. Yeatman, *Frank and Jesse James*, 30.
6 Jesse James Jr., *Jesse James, My Father* (Cleveland: Buckeye Publishing Co., 1899), 28.
7 Ted P. Yeatman, *Frank and Jesse James*, 30.
8 *History of Clay and Platte Counties, Missouri* (St. Louis: National Historical Company, 1885), 266.
9 William A. Settle Jr., *Jesse James Was His Name or, Fact and Fiction Concerning the Careers of the Notorious James Brothers of Missouri* (Lincoln: University of Nebraska Press, 1966), 20, 21; *History of Clay and Platte Counties, Missouri*, 266; Ted P. Yeatman, *Frank and Jesse James*, 35.
10 Ted P. Yeatman, *Frank and Jesse James*, 35.
11 Thomas Coleman Younger, *The Story of Cole Younger, By Himself* (St. Paul, MN: Minnesota Historical Society, 2000), 5, 6.
12 T. J. Stiles, *Jesse James*, 87, 88; Ted P. Yeatman, *Frank and Jesse James*, 36–38.

13 Ted P. Yeatman, *Frank and Jesse James*, 38–40; T. J. Stiles, *Jesse James*, 88, 89, 417n29.
14 T. J. Stiles, *Jesse James*, 90.
15 Ted P. Yeatman, *Frank and Jesse James*, 41.
16 James M. McPherson, *Battle Cry of Freedom*, 785, 786; T. J. Stiles, *Jesse James*, 93–95.
17 T. J. Stiles, *Jesse James*, 100.
18 William A. Settle Jr., *Jesse James Was His Name*, 32.
19 T. J. Stiles, *Jesse James*, 101.
20 Ted P. Yeatman, *Frank and Jesse James*, 50, 51; T. J. Stiles, *Jesse James*, 102, 103.
21 Ted P. Yeatman, *Frank and Jesse James*, 51.
22 Ibid., 53.
23 "William 'Bloody Bill' Anderson," American Experience, accessed May 14, 2018, http://www.pbs.org/wgbh/americanexperience/features/james-anderson/; Ted P. Yeatman, *Frank and Jesse James*, 52, 53.
24 Geoffrey C. Ward, *The Civil War: An Illustrated History* (New York: Alfred A. Knopf, 1990), 246; T. J. Stiles, *Jesse James*, 111, 112.
25 T. J. Stiles, *Jesse James*, 112, 113.
26 "William 'Bloody Bill' Anderson."
27 John N. Edwards, *Noted Guerrillas, or the Warfare of the Border* (St. Louis, MO: Bryan Brand & Co., 1877), 176.
28 T. J. Stiles, *Jesse James*, 116–118.
29 *History of Boone County, Missouri* (St. Louis: Western Historical Co., 1882), 442; T. J. Stiles, *Jesse James*, 119.
30 *History of Boone County, Missouri*, 441; T. J. Stiles, *Jesse James*, 120.
31 *History of Boone County, Missouri*, 443, 444; T. J. Stiles, *Jesse James*, 120.
32 *History of Boone County, Missouri*, 446–450; T. J. Stiles, *Jesse James*, 120–122.
33 *History of Boone County, Missouri*, 452–455.
34 Ibid., 455.
35 *History of Boone County, Missouri*, 456; Ted P. Yeatman, *Frank and Jesse James*, 56.
36 *History of Boone County, Missouri*, 459; Ted P. Yeatman, *Frank and Jesse James*, 56.
37 *History of Boone County, Missouri*, 458, 459.
38 Ibid., 458, 461.
39 William A. Settle Jr., *Jesse James Was His Name*, 28; Ted P. Yeatman, *Frank and Jesse James*, 56; T. J. Stiles, *Jesse James*, 126; J. A. Dacus, *Life and Adventures of Frank and Jesse James*, 52; Jesse James Jr., *Jesse James, My Father*, 35.
40 *History of Boone County, Missouri*, 460.
41 Ted P. Yeatman, *Frank and Jesse James*, 56.
42 T. J. Stiles, *Jesse James*, 123.
43 Ibid., 133–135.
44 Ted P. Yeatman, *Frank and Jesse James*, 57, 58; T. J. Stiles, *Jesse James*, 136–138; William A. Settle Jr., *Jesse James Was His Name*, 28; Robert Barr Smith, "The

James Boys Go to War," *Civil War Times Illustrated Magazine*, January/February 1994, John N. Edwards, *Noted Guerrillas, or the Warfare of the Border*, 166.
45 T. J. Stiles, *Jesse James*, 139.
46 William A. Settle Jr., *Jesse James Was His Name*, 29.
47 William A. Settle Jr., *Jesse James Was His Name*, 30; Jesse James Jr., *Jesse James, My Father*, 50; J. A. Dacus, *Life and Adventures of Frank and Jesse James*, 57.
48 T. J. Stiles, *Jesse James*, 140, 141.
49 Ted P. Yeatman, *Frank and Jesse James*, 72; T. J. Stiles, *Jesse James*, 143.
50 John N. Edwards, *Noted Guerrillas, or the Warfare of the Border*, 332; J. A. Dacus, *Life and Adventures of Frank and Jesse James*, 61.
51 John N. Edwards, *Noted Guerrillas, or the Warfare of the Border*, 332, 333; J. A. Dacus, *Life and Adventures of Frank and Jesse James*, 61; T. J. Stiles, *Jesse James*, 151; Ted P. Yeatman, *Frank and Jesse James*, 74.
52 T. J. Stiles, *Jesse James*, 151; Ted P. Yeatman, *Frank and Jesse James*, 74, 75.
53 John N. Edwards, *Noted Guerrillas, or the Warfare of the Border*, 333.
54 T. J. Stiles, *Jesse James*, 153, 154.
55 Ted P. Yeatman, *Frank and Jesse James*, 76, 77; T. J. Stiles, *Jesse James*, 153, 154.
56 Frederick Nolan, *The West of Billy the Kid*, 4, 5.

CHAPTER 3: BANKS ARE WHERE THE MONEY'S AT

1 Ted P. Yeatman, *Frank and Jesse James*, 72, 77, 83; T. J. Stiles, *Jesse James*, 154.
2 Jesse James Jr., *Jesse James, My Father*, 63, 64; Ted P. Yeatman, *Frank and Jesse James*, 83, 84; T. J. Stiles, *Jesse James*, 154, 155, 165.
3 T. J. Stiles, *Jesse James*, 166; Ted P. Yeatman, *Frank and Jesse James*, 71, 81, 84.
4 T. J. Stiles, *Jesse James*, 166.
5 T. J. Stiles, *Jesse James*, 166, 167; *History of Clay and Platte Counties, Missouri*, 268.
6 T. J. Stiles, *Jesse James*, 129; William A. Settle, *Jesse James Was His Name*, 16; John N. Edwards, *Noted Guerrillas, or the Warfare of the Border*, 167, 168.
7 William Allan Pinkerton, *Train Robberies, Train Robbers and the "Holdup" Men*, reprint (Andesite Press, 1907), 20.
8 Jesse James Jr., *Jesse James, My Father*, 39.
9 T. J. Stiles, *Jesse James*, 298, 340.
10 Ted P. Yeatman, *Frank and Jesse James*, 88.
11 T. J. Stiles, *Jesse James*, 167.
12 Ibid., 167, 173, 174.
13 *History of Clay and Platte Counties, Missouri*, 259; William A. Settle, *Jesse James Was His Name*, 33; Ted P. Yeatman, *Frank and Jesse James*, 85.
14 *History of Clay and Platte Counties, Missouri*, 259; T. J. Stiles, *Jesse James*, 172; William A. Settle, *Jesse James Was His Name*, 33.
15 *History of Clay and Platte Counties, Missouri*, 260; T. J. Stiles, *Jesse James*, 171, 172; William A. Settle, *Jesse James Was His Name*, 33; Ted P. Yeatman, *Frank and Jesse James*, 85.

16 Carl W. Breihan, *Saga of Jesse James* (Caldwell, ID: Caxton Printers, 1991), 30; *History of Clay and Platte Counties, Missouri*, 260; T. J. Stiles, *Jesse James*, 172; Ted P. Yeatman, *Frank and Jesse James*, 86.
17 *History of Clay and Platte Counties, Missouri*, 259–261; T. J. Stiles, *Jesse James*, 172; William A. Settle, *Jesse James Was His Name*, 34.
18 *History of Clay and Platte Counties, Missouri*, 259; T. J. Stiles, *Jesse James*, 172, 173; Ted P. Yeatman, *Frank and Jesse James*, 86, 101, 402n10; Ted P. Yeatman, "Two Great Myths about Jesse James: Setting the Record Straight," *True West Magazine*, August 2002.
19 William A. Settle, *Jesse James Was His Name*, 34, 35; T. J. Stiles, *Jesse James*, 181, 182.
20 T. J. Stiles, *Jesse James*, 183, 184.
21 Ted P. Yeatman, "Two Great Myths about Jesse James: Setting the Record Straight"; Ted P. Yeatman, *Frank and Jesse James*, 89, 91; William Allan Pinkerton, *Train Robberies, Train Robbers and the "Holdup" Men*, 18.
22 T. J. Stiles, *Jesse James*, 174, 186, 187.
23 *History of Ray County, Missouri* (Saint Louis: Missouri Historical Company, 1881), 388, 389; Ted P. Yeatman, *Frank and Jesse James*, 91, 92; William A. Settle, *Jesse James Was His Name*, 35; T. J. Stiles, *Jesse James*, 194; Linda Emley, "Postcards: Word of Mouth, Local Lore Add to Bank Robbery Story," *Richmond Daily News*, 2013, accessed May 23, 2018, https://www.richmond-dailynews.com/2013/08/postcards-word-of-mouth-local-lore-add-to-bank-robbery-story/.
24 Ted P. Yeatman, *Frank and Jesse James*, 92, 93; William A. Settle, *Jesse James Was His Name*, 54.
25 Ted P. Yeatman, *Frank and Jesse James*, 93, 95; T. J. Stiles, *Jesse James*, 196.
26 Ted P. Yeatman, *Frank and Jesse James*, 93–95; T. J. Stiles, *Jesse James*, 196, 197; William A. Settle, *Jesse James Was His Name*, 35, 36.
27 William A. Settle, *Jesse James Was His Name*, 54, 55; Ted P. Yeatman, *Frank and Jesse James*, 95; Jesse James Jr., *Jesse James, My Father*, 67; David Middlecamp, "Paso Robles' Founders: A Vigilante, a Capitalist and Jesse James' Uncle," *The Tribune*, accessed May 25, 2018, http://www.sanluisobispo.com/news/local/news-columns-blogs/photos-from-the-vault/article39472611.html.
28 William A. Settle, *Jesse James Was His Name*, 54, 55; Ted P. Yeatman, *Frank and Jesse James*, 95; Jesse James Jr., *Jesse James, My Father*, 66.
29 T. J. Stiles, *Jesse James*, 203.
30 Ibid., 203, 204.
31 Ibid.
32 T. J. Stiles, *Jesse James*, 203; Ted P. Yeatman, *Frank and Jesse James*, 96.
33 T. J. Stiles, *Jesse James*, 203, 204.
34 Stephanie Francis Ward, "The Lawyer Who Took on Jesse James . . . and Won," *American Bar Association Journal*, March 2008, accessed June 1, 2018, http://www.abajournal.com/magazine/article/

the_lawyer_who_took_on_jesse_james_and_won/; T. J. Stiles, *Jesse James*, 204; Ted P. Yeatman, *Frank and Jesse James*, 96.
35 T. J. Stiles, *Jesse James*, 204, 205; Ted P. Yeatman, *Frank and Jesse James*, 96, 97.
36 T. J. Stiles, *Jesse James*, 205; Ted P. Yeatman, *Frank and Jesse James*, 97.
37 T. J. Stiles, *Jesse James*, 205.
38 Ibid., 205, 206.
39 Ted P. Yeatman, *Frank and Jesse James*, 97; T. J. Stiles, *Jesse James*, 206.
40 Stephanie Francis Ward, "The Lawyer Who Took on Jesse James . . . and Won."
41 T. J. Stiles, *Jesse James*, 207, 209, 211.
42 T. J. Stiles, *Jesse James*, 211; William A. Settle, *Jesse James Was His Name*, 41.
43 T. J. Stiles, *Jesse James*, 166, 211, 212.
44 Ted P. Yeatman, *Frank and Jesse James*, 97, 98.
45 Stephanie Francis Ward, "The Lawyer Who Took on Jesse James . . . and Won."
46 T. J. Stiles, *Jesse James*, 212, 213; Ted P. Yeatman, *Frank and Jesse James*, 99; William A. Settle, *Jesse James Was His Name*, 207n31.
47 T. J. Stiles, *Jesse James*, 213.
48 T. J. Stiles, *Jesse James*, 213; William A. Settle, *Jesse James Was His Name*, 43. Ted P. Yeatman, *Frank and Jesse James*, 99; John Koblas, "Robbing the Yankees: The James Brothers and Their Gang Were the Right Bandits for Their Time," *True West Magazine*, March 2007; *Biographical and Historical Record of Wayne and Appanoose Counties, Iowa* (Chicago: Interstate Publishing Co., 1886), 535, 536.
49 Brenda DeVore, "The Trial of Clelland Miller," *Newsletter of the Wayne County Historical Society*, Corydon, IA, December 2012; T. J. Stiles, *Jesse James*, 213; William A. Settle, *Jesse James Was His Name*, 43.
50 *Biographical and Historical Record of Wayne and Appanoose Counties, Iowa*, 535, 536.
51 Sources state Oscar Ocobock was the cashier, but the transcripts of Clell Miller's trial show that the teller that day was Ted Wock, who testified at the trial.
52 Brenda DeVore, "The Trial of Clelland Miller"; T. J. Stiles, *Jesse James*, 213; William A. Settle, *Jesse James Was His Name*, 43; Ted P. Yeatman, *Frank and Jesse James*, 99; John Koblas, "Robbing the Yankees"; *Biographical and Historical Record of Wayne and Appanoose Counties, Iowa*, 535, 536.
53 T. J. Stiles, *Jesse James*, 213, 214; Ted P. Yeatman, *Frank and Jesse James*, 99; John Koblas, "Robbing the Yankees"; *Biographical and Historical Record of Wayne and Appanoose Counties, Iowa*, 536.
54 T. J. Stiles, *Jesse James*, 214.
55 *Biographical and Historical Record of Wayne and Appanoose Counties, Iowa*, 536; Brenda DeVore, "The Trial of Clelland Miller."

56 T. J. Stiles, *Jesse James*, 214; Brenda DeVore, director, Prairie Trails Museum of Wayne County, Corydon, IA, personal e-mail communication to Bill Markley, June 4, 2018.
57 T. J. Stiles, *Jesse James*, 214; Brenda DeVore, "The Trial of Clelland Miller."
58 T. J. Stiles, *Jesse James*, 214.
59 *The Trial of Frank James for Murder* (Kansas City: George Miller Jr., 1898), 109; T. J. Stiles, *Jesse James*, 217, 218.
60 T. J. Stiles, *Jesse James*, 215.
61 T. J. Stiles, *Jesse James*, 215; Ted P. Yeatman, *Frank and Jesse James*, 100.
62 Brenda DeVore, "The Trial of Clelland Miller."
63 Mark Lee Gardner, *Shot All to Hell: Jesse James, the Northfield Raid, and the Wild West's Greatest Escape* (New York, NY: HarperCollins Publishers, 2013), 36.
64 Brenda DeVore, "The Trial of Clelland Miller."
65 Brenda DeVore, "The Trial of Clelland Miller"; *Biographical and Historical Record of Wayne and Appanoose Counties, Iowa*, 536.
66 William A. Settle, *Jesse James Was His Name*, 44; T. J. Stiles, *Jesse James*, 218, 219.
67 William A. Settle, *Jesse James Was His Name*, 44; T. J. Stiles, *Jesse James*, 219.
68 The Lowry gang was a North Carolina robber gang made up of Lumbee Indians; Ted P. Yeatman, *Frank and Jesse James*, 406n47.
69 T. J. Stiles, *Jesse James*, 219; Ted P. Yeatman, *Frank and Jesse James*, 102.
70 Ted P. Yeatman, *Frank and Jesse James*, 102; T. J. Stiles, *Jesse James*, 220.
71 T. J. Stiles, *Jesse James*, 173, 197, 220.
72 Ibid., 220.
73 T. J. Stiles, *Jesse James*, 218, 219; William A. Settle, *Jesse James Was His Name*, 44.
74 William A. Settle, *Jesse James Was His Name*, 44, 45; Ted P. Yeatman, *Frank and Jesse James*, 103; T. J. Stiles, *Jesse James*, 223.
75 Ted P. Yeatman, *Frank and Jesse James*, 103; William A. Settle, *Jesse James Was His Name*, 45; T. J. Stiles, *Jesse James*, 223, 224.
76 Ted P. Yeatman, *Frank and Jesse James*, 344, 345.
77 Ibid., 344.
78 Ibid., 344, 345.
79 American Experience, "Jesse James Primary Source Newspaper Accounts," Public Broadcasting Service, accessed June 3, 2018, https://www.pbs.org/wgbh/americanexperience/features/james-newspapers/; Ted P. Yeatman, *Frank and Jesse James*, 105; T. J. Stiles, *Jesse James*, 224, 225.
80 T. J. Stiles, *Jesse James*, 226.
81 Ted P. Yeatman, *Frank and Jesse James*, 106.
82 Samuel S. Hildebrand was a well-known bushwhacker leader in southeast Missouri. Several months before the robbery, he had been shot and killed for a $300 reward; T. J. Stiles, *Jesse James*, 228.
83 "Bank Robbery; Particulars of the Daylight Outrage in Ste. Genevieve, Mo.," *New York Times Archives*, May 31, 1873, accessed June 3, 2018, https://

timesmachine.nytimes.com/timesmachine/1873/05/31/82408551.pdf ; T. J. Stiles, *Jesse James*, 228, 229; William A. Settle, *Jesse James Was His Name*, 47; "The Ste. Genevieve, Missouri Robbery," *Civil War St. Louis*, accessed June 3, 2018, http://www.civilwarstlouis.com/History/jamesstegenevieve.htm.
84 T. J. Stiles, *Jesse James*, 228-289; William A. Settle, *Jesse James Was His Name*, 47.
85 Frederick Nolan, *The West of Billy the Kid*, 8–10; Mark Lee Gardner, *To Hell on a Fast Horse*, 37, 38.
86 Frederick Nolan, *The West of Billy the Kid*, 15; Mark Lee Gardner, *To Hell on a Fast Horse*, 38.
87 Frederick Nolan, *The West of Billy the Kid*, 16; Mark Lee Gardner, *To Hell on a Fast Horse*, 39.
88 Frederick Nolan, *The West of Billy the Kid*, 18, 19. Mark Lee Gardner, *To Hell on a Fast Horse*, 39.
89 Frederick Nolan, *The West of Billy the Kid*, 19–21.
90 David Nevin, *The Expressmen* (Alexandria, VA: Time-Life Books, 1974), 16.
91 S. Paul O'Hara, *Inventing the Pinkertons or Spies, Sleuths, Mercenaries, and Thugs* (Baltimore: Johns Hopkins University Press, 2016), 18; David Nevin, *The Expressmen*, 188, 192; Wikipedia, "Adams Express Company," accessed August 3, 2018, https://en.wikipedia.org/wiki/Adams_Express_Company.
92 T. J. Stiles, *Jesse James*, 230.
93 Adams Funds, accessed January 2, 2019, https://www.adamsfunds.com/about/history/.
94 Wells Fargo Today, 3rd Quarter 2018, Quarterly Fact Sheet, accessed January 2, 2019, https://www08.wellsfargomedia.com/assets/pdf/about/corporate/wells-fargo-today.pdf.

Chapter 4: Trains Are Where the Money's At

1 Jim Clark, manager of operations, James Clark & Company Railroad Motion Pictures Services, personal communication July 26, 2018; Ted P. Yeatman, *Frank and Jesse James*, 106; T. J. Stiles, *Jesse James*, 233.
2 T. J. Stiles, *Jesse James*, 233, 235.
3 T. J. Stiles, *Jesse James*, 233, 234; Jim Clark, personal communication, August 22, 2018.
4 Ted P. Yeatman, *Frank and Jesse James*, 106.
5 T. J. Stiles, *Jesse James*, 234, 236; William A. Settle, *Jesse James Was His Name*, 48.
6 T. J. Stiles, *Jesse James*, 234; Ted P. Yeatman, *Frank and Jesse James*, 106, 107.
7 T. J. Stiles, *Jesse James*, 234, 235; Ted P. Yeatman, *Frank and Jesse James*, 107.
8 Ted P. Yeatman, *Frank and Jesse James*, 108; T. J. Stiles, *Jesse James*, 235.
9 Robertus Love, *The Rise and Fall of Jesse James* (Lincoln: University of Nebraska Press, 1925), 129; T. J. Stiles, *Jesse James*, 235, 445n30.

10 Ted P. Yeatman, *Frank and Jesse James*, 108; William A. Settle, *Jesse James Was His Name*, 48.
11 Ted P. Yeatman, *Frank and Jesse James*, 109; William A. Settle, *Jesse James Was His Name*, 51, 56; T. J. Stiles, *Jesse James*, 241, 242.
12 Ted P. Yeatman, *Frank and Jesse James*, 109.
13 Ken Robison, *Yankees & Rebels on the Upper Missouri: Steamboats, Gold and Peace* (Charleston, SC: History Press, 2016), 201; William A. Settle, *Jesse James Was His Name*, 48; T. J. Stiles, *Jesse James*, 242n48, 446.
14 Ken Robison, *Yankees & Rebels on the Upper Missouri*, 199.
15 Ibid., 199–201.
16 Ibid., 201, 202.
17 J. A. Dacus, *Life and Adventures of Frank and Jesse James*, 158; Thomas Coleman Younger, *The Story of Cole Younger, By Himself*, 59, 62; James R. Ross, *I, Jesse James*, 144; William A. Settle, *Jesse James Was His Name*, 49, 50; Ted P. Yeatman, *Frank and Jesse James*, 109, 110; T. J. Stiles, *Jesse James*, 243; Sue Eakin and Manie Culbertson, *Louisiana: The Land and Its People* (Gretna, LA: Pelican Publishing, 1998), 370.
18 Ted P. Yeatman, *Frank and Jesse James*, 19, 21.
19 Ted P. Yeatman, *Frank and Jesse James*, 19, 20; T. J. Stiles, *Jesse James*, 243, 244; Stephen Orgel and A. R. Braunmuller, eds., *William Shakespeare: The Complete Works* (New York: Penguin Books, 2002), 1047, 1053, 1054.
20 Ted P. Yeatman, *Frank and Jesse James*, 20; T. J. Stiles, *Jesse James*, 243, 244.
21 Ted P. Yeatman, *Frank and Jesse James*, 19; T. J. Stiles, *Jesse James*, 224, 245.
22 Ted P. Yeatman, *Frank and Jesse James*, 20; T. J. Stiles, *Jesse James*, 244.
23 Ibid.
24 Ibid.
25 Ibid.
26 Ted P. Yeatman, *Frank and Jesse James*, 20, 21; T. J. Stiles, *Jesse James*, 244, 245.
27 Ted P. Yeatman, *Frank and Jesse James*, 21.
28 Ted P. Yeatman, *Frank and Jesse James*, 21; T. J. Stiles, *Jesse James*, 245.
29 Ted P. Yeatman, *Frank and Jesse James*, 21.
30 Ibid., 21, 378n7.
31 Ibid., 21.
32 Ibid., 21, 378n10.
33 Henry Gannett, *The Origin of Certain Place Names in the United States* (Washington, DC: US Government Printing Office, 1905), 197; E. B. Long, *The Civil War Day by Day: An Almanac 1861–1865* (Garden City, NY: Doubleday & Co., 1971), 235, 236; Ted P. Yeatman, *Frank and Jesse James*, 109; William Salt Brassington, *Shakespeare's Homeland: Sketches of Stratford-upon-Avon, the Forest of Arden, and the Avon Valley* (London: J. M. Dent & Co., 1903), 94.
34 Ted P. Yeatman, *Frank and Jesse James*, 22; T. J. Stiles, *Jesse James*, 246.
35 Ted P. Yeatman, *Frank and Jesse James*, 21; T. J. Stiles, *Jesse James*, 245.
36 Ted P. Yeatman, *Frank and Jesse James*, 21.
37 Ibid., 22.

38 Ibid.
39 Ted P. Yeatman, *Frank and Jesse James*, 22, 112–114; T. J. Stiles, *Jesse James*, 246.
40 Ted P. Yeatman, *Frank and Jesse James*, 22, 23.
41 Ted P. Yeatman, *Frank and Jesse James*, 112, 113; T. J. Stiles, *Jesse James*, 249, 252.
42 T. J. Stiles, *Jesse James*, 252.
43 Ibid.
44 Ibid., 252, 253.
45 Ibid., 253, 254.
46 Ibid., 254.
47 T. J. Stiles, *Jesse James*, 254; William Allan Pinkerton, *Train Robberies, Train Robbers and the "Holdup" Men*, 24; Ted P. Yeatman, *Frank and Jesse James*, 114, 115.
48 Ted P. Yeatman, *Frank and Jesse James*, 115.
49 T. J. Stiles, *Jesse James*, 258.
50 T. J. Stiles, *Jesse James*, 253; Ted P. Yeatman, *Frank and Jesse James*, 115, 116; William A. Settle, *Jesse James Was His Name*, 61.
51 Ted P. Yeatman, *Frank and Jesse James*, 116.
52 Ted P. Yeatman, *Frank and Jesse James*, 116; T. J. Stiles, *Jesse James*, 255, 256.
53 T. J. Stiles, *Jesse James*, 256.
54 Ibid., 257.
55 Ibid., 261, 262.
56 Ibid., 259.
57 T. J. Stiles, *Jesse James*, 213; Ted P. Yeatman, *Frank and Jesse James*, 121.
58 Ted P. Yeatman, *Frank and Jesse James*, 121–123; T. J. Stiles, *Jesse James*, 263.
59 Ted P. Yeatman, *Frank and Jesse James*, 121–123; T. J. Stiles, *Jesse James*, 264.
60 Ted P. Yeatman, *Frank and Jesse James*, 121, 123; T. J. Stiles, *Jesse James*, 264, 265.
61 Ted P. Yeatman, *Frank and Jesse James*, 122, 123; T. J. Stiles, *Jesse James*, 264, 265.
62 Ted P. Yeatman, *Frank and Jesse James*, 123; T. J. Stiles, *Jesse James*, 265, 450n59; William A. Settle, *Jesse James Was His Name*, 71.
63 Ted P. Yeatman, *Frank and Jesse James*, 123; T. J. Stiles, *Jesse James*, 265.
64 T. J. Stiles, *Jesse James*, 267, 268; Ted P. Yeatman, *Frank and Jesse James*, 123; William A. Settle, *Jesse James Was His Name*, 72, 73.
65 T. J. Stiles, *Jesse James*, 265.
66 Ibid., 265, 266.
67 Ibid., 266.
68 Ibid.
69 T. J. Stiles, *Jesse James*, 266; Ted P. Yeatman, *Frank and Jesse James*, 124.
70 T. J. Stiles, *Jesse James*, 267.
71 Ted P. Yeatman, *Frank and Jesse James*, 124–126; T. J. Stiles, *Jesse James*, 271, 274.

72 William A. Settle, *Jesse James Was His Name*, 74.
73 William A. Settle, *Jesse James Was His Name*, 75; Carl W. Breihan, "Did Cole Younger Rob the Bank at Corinth?" *Real West Magazine*, vol. XIV, no. 98, November 1971, 17.
74 T. J. Stiles, *Jesse James*, 272, 273; Ted P. Yeatman, *Frank and Jesse James*, 126.
75 T. J. Stiles, *Jesse James*, 273; Ted P. Yeatman, *Frank and Jesse James*, 127.
76 Ibid.
77 T. J. Stiles, *Jesse James*, 273, 274; Ted P. Yeatman, *Frank and Jesse James*, 127, 128.
78 T. J. Stiles, *Jesse James*, 272, 275; Ted P. Yeatman, *Frank and Jesse James*, 128; William A. Settle, *Jesse James Was His Name*, 75.
79 S. Paul O'Hara, *Inventing the Pinkertons*, 42.
80 Mark Lee Gardner, *To Hell on a Fast Horse*, 40, 41; Robert M. Utley, *Billy the Kid: A Short and Violent Life* (Lincoln: University of Nebraska Press, 1989), 6.
81 Mark Lee Gardner, *To Hell on a Fast Horse*, 40, 41; Robert M. Utley, *Billy the Kid: A Short and Violent Life*, 6; Frederick Nolan, *The West of Billy the Kid*, 24.
82 Mark Lee Gardner, *To Hell on a Fast Horse*, 40, 41; Robert M. Utley, *Billy the Kid: A Short and Violent Life*, 6; Frederick Nolan, *The West of Billy the Kid*, 23.
83 Mark Lee Gardner, *To Hell on a Fast Horse*, 40, 41; Robert M. Utley, *Billy the Kid: A Short and Violent Life*, 6, 7; Frederick Nolan, *The West of Billy the Kid*, 27.
84 Carl Sandburg, *Abraham Lincoln: The War Years*, vol. 1 (New York, NY: Harcourt, Brace & World, 1939), 66.
85 Chris Enss, *The Pinks: The First Women Detectives, Operatives, and Spies with the Pinkerton National Detective Agency* (Guilford, CT: Globe Pequot, 2017), 60, 61, 67, 72.
86 Carl Sandburg, *Abraham Lincoln*, 77.
87 S. Paul O'Hara, *Inventing the Pinkertons*, 15, 16, 18, 21–23; Chris Enss, *The Pinks*, 38, 39.
88 S. Paul O'Hara, *Inventing the Pinkertons*, 35, 36.
89 Ibid., 38–41.
90 S. Paul O'Hara, *Inventing the Pinkertons*, 58, 62; Joseph Bloom, "Molly MacGuires in Pennsylvania Coal Regions," *American History Magazine*, June 12, 2006, HistoryNet, accessed August 3, 2018, http://www.historynet.com/molly-macguires-in-pennsylvania-coal-regions.htm.
91 S. Paul O'Hara, *Inventing the Pinkertons*, 57, 62; Joseph Bloom, "Molly MacGuires in Pennsylvania Coal Regions."
92 S. Paul O'Hara, *Inventing the Pinkertons*, 62; Joseph Bloom, "Molly MacGuires in Pennsylvania Coal Regions"; T. J. Stiles, *Jesse James*, 279.

Chapter 5: Pinkerton Raid on the James Farm

1 S. Paul O'Hara, *Inventing the Pinkertons*, 42; T. J. Stiles, *Jesse James*, 277.
2 T. J. Stiles, *Jesse James*, 278; Ted P. Yeatman, *Frank and Jesse James*, 128, 129.
3 T. J. Stiles, *Jesse James*, 279; Ted P. Yeatman, *Frank and Jesse James*, 129–131.

4 T. J. Stiles, *Jesse James*, 279.
5 T. J. Stiles, *Jesse James*, 279, 280.
6 Ibid., 280, 453n28.
7 Ibid., 280.
8 Ibid., 281.
9 T. J. Stiles, *Jesse James*, 281, 282; Ted P. Yeatman, *Frank and Jesse James*, 136; Robertus Love, *The Rise and Fall of Jesse James*, 153.
10 T. J. Stiles, *Jesse James*, 282; Ted P. Yeatman, *Frank and Jesse James*, 136, 360, 361; Robertus Love, *The Rise and Fall of Jesse James*, 153.
11 Robertus Love, *The Rise and Fall of Jesse James*, 153, 154.
12 Ted P. Yeatman, *Frank and Jesse James*, 361.
13 Ted P. Yeatman, *Frank and Jesse James*, 136, 141; T. J. Stiles, *Jesse James*, 454n38.
14 T. J. Stiles, *Jesse James*, 282, 283; Ted P. Yeatman, *Frank and Jesse James*, 136.
15 T. J. Stiles, *Jesse James*, 283, 286; Ted P. Yeatman, *Frank and Jesse James*, 136, 137; William A. Settle, *Jesse James Was His Name*, 76.
16 Ted P. Yeatman, *Frank and Jesse James*, 137.
17 T. J. Stiles, *Jesse James*, 288, 289; Ted P. Yeatman, *Frank and Jesse James*, 140, 360–362.
18 T. J. Stiles, *Jesse James*, 291, 292; Ted P. Yeatman, *Frank and Jesse James*, 143, 144.
19 T. J. Stiles, *Jesse James*, 289; Ted P. Yeatman, *Frank and Jesse James*, 363.
20 Mark Lee Gardner, *Shot All to Hell*, 37; Ted P. Yeatman, *Frank and Jesse James*, 144.
21 T. J. Stiles, *Jesse James*, 292; William A. Settle, *Jesse James Was His Name*, 80.
22 T. J. Stiles, *Jesse James*, 292, 293.
23 T. J. Stiles, *Jesse James*, 293; Ted P. Yeatman, *Frank and Jesse James*, 145.
24 William A. Settle, *Jesse James Was His Name*, 85, 86; T. J. Stiles, *Jesse James*, 293; Ted P. Yeatman, *Frank and Jesse James*, 145.
25 T. J. Stiles, *Jesse James*, 294; Ted P. Yeatman, *Frank and Jesse James*, 147.
26 Michael Wallis, *Billy the Kid: The Endless Ride* (New York: W. W. Norton & Co., 2007), 82, 83, 85, 86; Robert M. Utley, *Billy the Kid*, 7; Frederick Nolan, *The West of Billy the Kid*, 28, 29.
27 Michael Wallis, *Billy the Kid*, 84, 85.
28 Robert M. Utley, *Billy the Kid*, 7; Frederick Nolan, *The West of Billy the Kid*, 32; Michael Wallis, *Billy the Kid*, 87.

Chapter 6: Plenty of Ways to Get into Trouble

1 T. J. Stiles, *Jesse James*, 298; Ted P. Yeatman, *Frank and Jesse James*, 150; Frank Triplett, *Jesse James: The Life, Times, and Treacherous Death of the Most Infamous Outlaw of All Time* (New York: Skyhorse Publishing, 2013), 167.
2 Ted P. Yeatman, *Frank and Jesse James*, 150.
3 Ibid., 151.

4 T. J. Stiles, *Jesse James*, 296.
5 Ibid., 297.
6 Ted P. Yeatman, *Frank and Jesse James*, 151, 152; T. J. Stiles, *Jesse James*, 300, 301.
7 Ted P. Yeatman, *Frank and Jesse James*, 152; T. J. Stiles, *Jesse James*, 301.
8 Ted P. Yeatman, *Frank and Jesse James*, 153; T. J. Stiles, *Jesse James*, 301, 302.
9 Ted P. Yeatman, *Frank and Jesse James*, 161; T. J. Stiles, *Jesse James*, 302; Jesse James Jr., *Jesse James, My Father*, 9.
10 Ted P. Yeatman, *Frank and Jesse James*, 156.
11 Ibid., 155.
12 Ted P. Yeatman, *Frank and Jesse James*, 156; Carl W. Breihan, *Saga of Jesse James*, 74.
13 Ted P. Yeatman, *Frank and Jesse James*, 156, 157.
14 Ibid., 157.
15 Ted P. Yeatman, *Frank and Jesse James*, 159; T. J. Stiles, *Jesse James*, 303; Thomas Coleman Younger, *The Story of Cole Younger, By Himself*, 72.
16 Ted P. Yeatman, *Frank and Jesse James*, 160.
17 Ibid., 159, 160.
18 Ibid., 161, 162.
19 Ted P. Yeatman, *Frank and Jesse James*, 163; Wikipedia, "Centennial Exposition," accessed August 11, 2018, https://en.wikipedia.org/wiki/Centennial_Exposition.
20 Ted P. Yeatman, *Frank and Jesse James*, 162.
21 Mark Lee Gardner, *Shot All to Hell*, 23; Ted P. Yeatman, *Frank and Jesse James*, 166, 167; T. J. Stiles, *Jesse James*, 313.
22 Mark Lee Gardner, *Shot All to Hell*, 6, 7; Carl W. Breihan, *Saga of Jesse James*, 74, 75; William A. Settle, *Jesse James Was His Name*, 88.
23 Ted P. Yeatman, *Frank and Jesse James*, 166; Mark Lee Gardner, *Shot All to Hell*, 7.
24 Mark Lee Gardner, *Shot All to Hell*, 7, 8; Ted P. Yeatman, *Frank and Jesse James*, 166.
25 Mark Lee Gardner, *Shot All to Hell*, 8, 9; Carl W. Breihan, *Saga of Jesse James*, 75.
26 Mark Lee Gardner, *Shot All to Hell*, 8, 9, 11; Ted P. Yeatman, *Frank and Jesse James*, 166.
27 Mark Lee Gardner, *Shot All to Hell*, 11.
28 Mark Lee Gardner, *Shot All to Hell*, 9, 10; Carl W. Breihan, *Saga of Jesse James*, 75.
29 Mark Lee Gardner, *Shot All to Hell*, 10.
30 Ibid., 11–13.
31 Ibid., 13.
32 Ibid., 14.
33 Ibid.

34 Mark Lee Gardner, *Shot All to Hell*, 15; Carl W. Breihan, *Saga of Jesse James*, 75, 76.
35 Mark Lee Gardner, *Shot All to Hell*, 15.
36 Mark Lee Gardner, *Shot All to Hell*, 21–24; Carl W. Breihan, *Saga of Jesse James*, 76.
37 Carl W. Breihan, *Saga of Jesse James*, 76, 77.
38 Michael Wallis, *Billy the Kid*, 87.
39 Michael Wallis, *Billy the Kid*, 87; Robert M. Utley, *Billy the Kid*, 7; Frederick Nolan, *The West of Billy the Kid*, 32, 33.
40 Michael Wallis, *Billy the Kid*, 88; Frederick Nolan, *The West of Billy the Kid*, 33.
41 Ibid.
42 Michael Wallis, *Billy the Kid*, 88; Frederick Nolan, *The West of Billy the Kid*, 33; Mark Lee Gardner, *To Hell on a Fast Horse*, 43.
43 Michael Wallis, *Billy the Kid*, 89; Frederick Nolan, *The West of Billy the Kid*, 33.
44 Michael Wallis, *Billy the Kid*, 89; Robert M. Utley, *Billy the Kid*, 8; Frederick Nolan, *The West of Billy the Kid*, 33, 34.
45 Frederick Nolan, *The West of Billy the Kid*, 34; Michael Wallis, *Billy the Kid*, 91–93.
46 Mark Lee Gardner, *To Hell on a Fast Horse*, 45; Michael Wallis, *Billy the Kid*, 95.
47 Frederick Nolan, *The West of Billy the Kid*, 49; Michael Wallis, *Billy the Kid*, 97.
48 Michael Wallis, *Billy the Kid*, 95, 96, 101.
49 Michael Wallis, *Billy the Kid*, 104, 105; Robert M. Utley, *Billy the Kid*, 10, 11; Frederick Nolan, *The West of Billy the Kid*, 49.

CHAPTER 7: THE NORTHFIELD RAID

1 Ted P. Yeatman, *Frank and Jesse James*, 143, 418n22.
2 Mark Lee Gardner, *Shot All to Hell*, 57, 262n52.
3 T. J. Stiles, *Jesse James*, 307–310.
4 Ibid., 307–311, 322, 325.
5 Hans Louis Trefousse, *Ben Butler: The South Called Him Beast!* (New York, NY: Twayne Publishers, 1957), 212.
6 Trefousse, *Ben Butler*, 111, 114.
7 Ibid., 123, 124, 133.
8 Wikipedia, "Benjamin Butler," accessed August 13, 2018, https://en.wikipedia.org/wiki/Benjamin_Butler.
9 T. J. Stiles, *Jesse James*, 324.
10 Mark Lee Gardner, *Shot All to Hell*, 23, 53.
11 Ibid., 36–40.
12 There are also reports that they rode to Minnesota on horseback.

13 Mark Lee Gardner, *Shot All to Hell*, 53, 54, 56; Thomas Coleman Younger, *The Story of Cole Younger, By Himself*, 75.
14 Mark Lee Gardner, *Shot All to Hell*, 53–55, 59.
15 John Koblas, *Faithful unto Death: The James-Younger Raid on the First National Bank, Northfield, Minnesota, September 7, 1876* (Northfield, MN: Northfield Historical Society Press, 2001), 32, 34; Mark Lee Gardner, *Shot All to Hell*, 55, 56.
16 Mark Lee Gardner, *Shot All to Hell*, 57, 58.
17 Ibid., 59, 61, 62.
18 Ibid., 63, 65, 66.
19 Ibid., 63–65.
20 Ibid., 65, 67.
21 Ibid., 67.
22 *The Northfield Bank Raid*, reprinted in 2008 by *The Northfield News* from *The Northfield News*, August 27, September 3, 10, and 17, 1926, 10th edition, 19.
23 Mark Lee Gardner, *Shot All to Hell*, 68, 72, 73; Thomas Coleman Younger, *The Story of Cole Younger, By Himself*, 78.
24 Thomas Coleman Younger, *The Story of Cole Younger, By Himself*, 78; *The Northfield Bank Raid*, 6.
25 Several people said they saw four riders at the bridge, leading to speculation: Was there a fourth rider and, if so, who was he? John Koblas, *Faithful unto Death*, 54–56.
26 John Koblas, *Faithful unto Death*, 71; Mark Lee Gardner, *Shot All to Hell*, 71.
27 The James boys never admitted they took part in the robbery, and the Younger brothers refused to name them, but most historians believe they were involved. Researchers dispute whether it was Jesse or Frank who entered the First National Bank. In his book, Cole Younger said the gang member in the bank was a man named Howard, and the outside man's name was Woods; Thomas Coleman Younger, *The Story of Cole Younger, By Himself*, 75. Jesse used the alias "Howard" and Frank used the alias "Woodson"; Mark Lee Gardner, *Shot All to Hell*, 215. I believe Jesse entered the bank, but I also admit I might be entirely wrong.
28 Mark Lee Gardner, *Shot All to Hell*, 77, 78.
29 *The Northfield Bank Raid*, 7; John Koblas, *Faithful unto Death*, 72.
30 *The Northfield Bank Raid*, 7.
31 John Koblas, *Faithful unto Death*, 73; Mark Lee Gardner, *Shot All to Hell*, 83, 84.
32 *The Northfield Bank Raid*, 8; Mark Lee Gardner, *Shot All to Hell*, 85.
33 John Koblas, *Faithful unto Death*, 62, 63, 66; Mark Lee Gardner, *Shot All to Hell*, 79.
34 John Koblas, *Faithful unto Death*, 65–67; *The Northfield Bank Raid*, 9, 15.
35 Mark Lee Gardner, *Shot All to Hell*, 80, 82, 83.
36 Ibid., 81, 82.
37 Ibid., 87–89.

38 Ibid., 90.
39 Ibid., 85, 86.
40 Mark Lee Gardner, *Shot All to Hell*, 91, 92. John Koblas, *Faithful unto Death*, 75.
41 Mark Lee Gardner, *Shot All to Hell*, 90.
42 Cole Younger said Charlie Pitts shot Heywood. Thomas Coleman Younger, *The Story of Cole Younger, By Himself*, 81. Six years after the robbery, Frank Wilcox paid Frank James a brief visit in the Jackson County jail in Independence, Missouri, and claimed Frank James was the shooter; Mark Lee Gardner, *Shot All to Hell*, 224. Other researchers have believed the description and actions fit Jesse James; T. J. Stiles, *Jesse James*, 334. If Cole Younger was telling the truth when he said the man in the bank was Howard, and based on "Howard" being Jesse's alias, then I believe Jesse James killed Joseph Heywood.
43 T. J. Stiles, *Jesse James*, 334.
44 Mark Lee Gardner, *Shot All to Hell*, 71, 85, 96.
45 Bob Boze Bell, "Cole Younger, American Outlaw," *True West Magazine*, September 2018, 28; Mark Lee Gardner, *Shot All to Hell*, 106; Ted P. Yeatman, *Frank and Jesse James*, 177.
46 Mark Lee Gardner, *Shot All to Hell*, 104, 191, 193.
47 Thomas Coleman Younger, *The Story of Cole Younger, By Himself*, 81; Mark Lee Gardner, *Shot All to Hell*, 101, 102.
48 Mark Lee Gardner, *Shot All to Hell*, 105, 107.
49 Minnesota Department of Natural Resources, "Big Woods Subsection," accessed August 22, 2018, https://www.dnr.state.mn.us/ecs/222Mb/index.html; Wikipedia, "Big Woods," accessed August 22, 2018, https://en.wikipedia.org/wiki/Big_Woods.
50 Mark Lee Gardner, *Shot All to Hell*, 107, 108.
51 Ibid., 108.
52 Ibid.
53 Mark Lee Gardner, *Shot All to Hell*, 108, 109.
54 Mark Lee Gardner, *Shot All to Hell*, 109; Thomas Coleman Younger, *The Story of Cole Younger, By Himself*, 82.
55 Mark Lee Gardner, *Shot All to Hell*, 110, 111; Bob Boze Bell, "Cole Younger, American Outlaw," 29.
56 Mark Lee Gardner, *Shot All to Hell*, 117.
57 Mark Lee Gardner, *Shot All to Hell*, 111; Bob Boze Bell, "Cole Younger, American Outlaw," 32.
58 Mark Lee Gardner, *Shot All to Hell*, 121–124.
59 Ted P. Yeatman, *Frank and Jesse James*, 178; Mark Lee Gardner, *Shot All to Hell*, 132, 133.
60 Mark Lee Gardner, *Shot All to Hell*, 133, 134.
61 Ibid., 133–135.
62 Mark Lee Gardner, *Shot All to Hell*, 136–138 ; T. J. Stiles, *Jesse James*, 342; Thomas Coleman Younger, *The Story of Cole Younger, By Himself*, 83.

63 Mark Lee Gardner, *Shot All to Hell*, 138–140; T. J. Stiles, *Jesse James*, 342.
64 Mark Lee Gardner, *Shot All to Hell*, 141–143.
65 Ibid., 143.
66 Ibid., 144.
67 Ibid., 145.
68 Ibid., 146.
69 Mark Lee Gardner, *Shot All to Hell*, 148, 149; John Koblas, *Faithful unto Death*, 119, 120.
70 Mark Lee Gardner, *Shot All to Hell*, 149; T. J. Stiles, *Jesse James*, 343, 344; Ted P. Yeatman, *Frank and Jesse James*, 180.
71 Mark Lee Gardner, *Shot All to Hell*, 181, 283n180; T. J. Stiles, *Jesse James*, 344; Ted P. Yeatman, *Frank and Jesse James*, 180.
72 T. J. Stiles, *Jesse James*, 344; John Koblas, *Faithful unto Death*, 121, 122.
73 John Koblas, *Faithful unto Death*, 123; Mark Lee Gardner, *Shot All to Hell*, 182, 183.
74 Mark Lee Gardner, *Shot All to Hell*, 183, 184.
75 Ibid., 184.
76 Ibid.
77 Mark Lee Gardner, *Shot All to Hell*, 184, 185.
78 Ibid., 185.
79 Ibid.
80 Mark Lee Gardner, *Shot All to Hell*, 186.
81 John Koblas, *Faithful unto Death*, 125, 126; Mark Lee Gardner, *Shot All to Hell*, 186, 187.
82 John Koblas, *Faithful unto Death*, 126; Mark Lee Gardner, *Shot All to Hell*, 189, 190.
83 Mark Lee Gardner, *Shot All to Hell*, 190, 191.
84 Wayne Fanebust, *Chasing Frank and Jesse James: The Bungled Northfield Bank Robbery and the Long Manhunt* (Jefferson, NC: McFarland & Co., 2018), 141; Mark Lee Gardner, *Shot All to Hell*, 192.
85 John Koblas, *Faithful unto Death*, 126, 127; Mark Lee Gardner, *Shot All to Hell*, 192, 193.
86 John Koblas, *Faithful unto Death*, 126, 127; Mark Lee Gardner, *Shot All to Hell*, 193.
87 Mark Lee Gardner, *Shot All to Hell*, 155.
88 T. J. Stiles, *Jesse James*, 346; Mark Lee Gardner, *Shot All to Hell*, 157, 158.
89 Mark Lee Gardner, *Shot All to Hell*, 158, 159.
90 Ibid., 159, 160.
91 Ibid., 160, 161.
92 Ibid., 163.
93 Ibid., 162.
94 Ibid., 162, 163.
95 Ibid., 164.
96 Ibid.

97 Mark Lee Gardner, *Shot All to Hell*, 194, 195.
98 Ibid., 131, 276n131.

CHAPTER 8: THE KID SPILLS BLOOD

1 Frederick Nolan, *The West of Billy the Kid*, 51; Michael Wallis, *Billy the Kid*, 106.
2 Robert M. Utley, *Billy the Kid*, 11; Frederick Nolan, *The West of Billy the Kid*, 51, 52; Michael Wallis, *Billy the Kid*, 107.
3 Michael Wallis, *Billy the Kid*, 110.
4 Frederick Nolan, *The West of Billy the Kid*, 52.
5 Ibid.
6 Michael Wallis, *Billy the Kid*, 111.
7 Mark Lee Gardner, *To Hell on a Fast Horse*, 46; Frederick Nolan, *The West of Billy the Kid*, 53; Michael Wallis, *Billy the Kid*, 111.
8 Frederick Nolan, *The West of Billy the Kid*, 53; Mark Lee Gardner, *To Hell on a Fast Horse*, 46.
9 Frederick Nolan, *The West of Billy the Kid*, 53; Michael Wallis, *Billy the Kid*, 112.
10 Frederick Nolan, *The West of Billy the Kid*, 54; Michael Wallis, *Billy the Kid*, 112.
11 Ibid.
12 Frederick Nolan, *The West of Billy the Kid*, 54, 55; Michael Wallis, *Billy the Kid*, 112, 113.
13 Robert M. Utley, *Billy the Kid*, 12; Michael Wallis, *Billy the Kid*, 113.
14 Frederick Nolan, *The West of Billy the Kid*, 55; Michael Wallis, *Billy the Kid*, 113.
15 Michael Wallis, *Billy the Kid*, 113.
16 Frederick Nolan, *The West of Billy the Kid*, 59; Michael Wallis, *Billy the Kid*, 113.
17 Michael Wallis, *Billy the Kid*, 114.
18 Mark Lee Gardner, *To Hell on a Fast Horse*, 48.
19 Mark Lee Gardner, *To Hell on a Fast Horse*, 48, 49; Frederick Nolan, *The West of Billy the Kid*, 59–61.
20 Frederick Nolan, *The West of Billy the Kid*, 60; Michael Wallis, *Billy the Kid*, 113.
21 Frederick Nolan, *The West of Billy the Kid*, 61.
22 Robert M. Utley, *Billy the Kid*, 13; Frederick Nolan, *The West of Billy the Kid*, 68.
23 Michael Wallis, *Billy the Kid*, 129.
24 Bill O'Neal, *Encyclopedia of Western Gunfighters* (Norman: University of Oklahoma Press, 1979), 105.
25 Frederick Nolan, *The West of Billy the Kid*, 64, 65.

26 Maurice Garland Fulton, *History of the Lincoln County War* (Tucson: University of Arizona Press, 1968), 67; Frederick Nolan, *The West of Billy the Kid*, 66.
27 Frederick Nolan, *The West of Billy the Kid*, 68, 69.
28 Frederick Nolan, *The West of Billy the Kid*, 69; Maurice Garland Fulton, *History of the Lincoln County War*, 103, 104.
29 Mark Lee Gardner, *To Hell on a Fast Horse*, 52, 53; Michael Wallis, *Billy the Kid*, 143, 144.

Chapter 9: Safe Harbors

1 Ted P. Yeatman, *Frank and Jesse James*, 187.
2 Ted P. Yeatman, *Frank and Jesse James*, 187–189; William A. Settle, *Jesse James Was His Name*, 98.
3 Ted P. Yeatman, *Frank and Jesse James*, 190, 191.
4 Ibid., 191, 192.
5 William A. Settle, *Jesse James Was His Name*, 101, 102; Mark Lee Gardner, *Shot All to Hell*, 286n202; Carl W. Breihan, *Saga of Jesse James*, 97–99.
6 William A. Settle, *Jesse James Was His Name*, 182, 183.
7 Ibid., 101.
8 Ibid.
9 Ted P. Yeatman, *Frank and Jesse James*, 198; T. J. Stiles, *Jesse James*, 339.
10 Marley Brant, *Jesse James: The Man and the Myth* (New York: Berkley Books, 1998), 196, 197.
11 Robertus Love, *The Rise and Fall of Jesse James*, 278, 279.
12 Robert M. Utley, *Billy the Kid*, 24.
13 Michael Wallis, *Billy the Kid*, 129; Mark Lee Gardner, *To Hell on a Fast Horse*, 52.
14 Maurice Garland Fulton, *History of the Lincoln County War*, 13; Robert M. Utley, *Billy the Kid*, 17, 18.
15 Richard Weddle, "Chisum: 'Cattle King of the Pecos,'" *Wild West Magazine*, August 2014, HistoryNet, accessed August 31, 2018, http://www.historynet.com/chisum-cattle-king-pecos.htm; Robert M. Utley, *Billy the Kid*, 19.
16 Richard Weddle, "Chisum: 'Cattle King of the Pecos'"; Michael Wallis, *Billy the Kid*, 143.
17 Robert M. Utley, *Billy the Kid*, 19.
18 Maurice Garland Fulton, *History of the Lincoln County War*, 45, 46, 50, 51; Mark Lee Gardner, *To Hell on a Fast Horse*, 58.
19 Maurice Garland Fulton, *History of the Lincoln County War*, 46, 47.
20 Maurice Garland Fulton, *History of the Lincoln County War*, 47; Frederick Nolan, *The West of Billy the Kid*, 154.
21 Maurice Garland Fulton, *History of the Lincoln County War*, 47.
22 Maurice Garland Fulton, *History of the Lincoln County War*, 48; Mark Lee Gardner, *To Hell on a Fast Horse*, 58; Michael Wallis, *Billy the Kid*, 174, 175.

23 Maurice Garland Fulton, *History of the Lincoln County War*, 48; Frederick Nolan, *The West of Billy the Kid*, 41.
24 Maurice Garland Fulton, *History of the Lincoln County War*, 48, 49.
25 Maurice Garland Fulton, *History of the Lincoln County War*, 49, 51–53, 73, 74, 228; Frederick Nolan, *The West of Billy the Kid*, 74.
26 Maurice Garland Fulton, *History of the Lincoln County War*, 51.
27 Frederick Nolan, *The West of Billy the Kid*, 71–73.
28 Ibid.
29 Maurice Garland Fulton, *History of the Lincoln County War*, 38, 39; Frederick Nolan, *The West of Billy the Kid*, 74.
30 Frederick Nolan, *The West of Billy the Kid*, 75, 76.
31 Ibid., 76.
32 Maurice Garland Fulton, *History of the Lincoln County War*, 54, 55; Frederick Nolan, *The West of Billy the Kid*, 38.
33 Frederick Nolan, *The West of Billy the Kid*, 44; Maurice Garland Fulton, *History of the Lincoln County War*, 55.
34 Maurice Garland Fulton, *History of the Lincoln County War*, 57; Frederick Nolan, *The West of Billy the Kid*, 44, 45.
35 Frederick Nolan, *The West of Billy the Kid*, 46; Maurice Garland Fulton, *History of the Lincoln County War*, 57.
36 Frederick Nolan, *The West of Billy the Kid*, 47; Maurice Garland Fulton, *History of the Lincoln County War*, 63.
37 Frederick Nolan, *The West of Billy the Kid*, 47, 48. Maurice Garland Fulton, *History of the Lincoln County War*, 27, 28, 83.
38 Maurice Garland Fulton, *History of the Lincoln County War*, 83; Frederick Nolan, *The West of Billy the Kid*, 78.
39 Maurice Garland Fulton, *History of the Lincoln County War*, 54.
40 Ibid.
41 Maurice Garland Fulton, *History of the Lincoln County War*, 63.
42 Maurice Garland Fulton, *History of the Lincoln County War*, 59–61; Richard Weddle, "Chisum: 'Cattle King of the Pecos.'"
43 Maurice Garland Fulton, *History of the Lincoln County War*, 82, 83; Frederick Nolan, *The West of Billy the Kid*, 67, 68.
44 Michael Wallis, *Billy the Kid*, 143.
45 Eve Ball, *Ma'am Jones of the Pecos* (Tucson: University of Arizona Press, 1969), 116–119; Mark Lee Gardner, *To Hell on a Fast Horse*, 53.
46 Eve Ball, *Ma'am Jones of the Pecos*, 115–119.
47 Ibid., 118.
48 Eve Ball, *Ma'am Jones of the Pecos*, 119; Michael Wallis, *Billy the Kid*, 144; Frederick Nolan, *The West of Billy the Kid*, 78.
49 Michael Wallis, *Billy the Kid*, 146.
50 Michael Wallis, *Billy the Kid*, 147; Frederick Nolan, *The West of Billy the Kid*, 83.
51 Frederick Nolan, *The West of Billy the Kid*, 82, 83.

52 Maurice Garland Fulton, *History of the Lincoln County War*, 84–87.
53 Maurice Garland Fulton, *History of the Lincoln County War*, 85; Frederick Nolan, *The West of Billy the Kid*, 80.
54 Maurice Garland Fulton, *History of the Lincoln County War*, 87.
55 Maurice Garland Fulton, *History of the Lincoln County War*, 87; Frederick Nolan, *The West of Billy the Kid*, 80; Robert M. Utley, *Billy the Kid*, 27.
56 Robert M. Utley, *Billy the Kid*, 27; Maurice Garland Fulton, *History of the Lincoln County War*, 88
57 Mark Lee Gardner, *To Hell on a Fast Horse*, 55, 57; Maurice Garland Fulton, *History of the Lincoln County War*, 88.
58 Frederick Nolan, *The West of Billy the Kid*, 85.
59 Ibid.
60 Frederick Nolan, *The West of Billy the Kid*, 86.
61 Frederick Nolan, *The West of Billy the Kid*, 86; Maurice Garland Fulton, *History of the Lincoln County War*, 90.
62 Mark Lee Gardner, *To Hell on a Fast Horse*, 57, 58; Maurice Garland Fulton, *History of the Lincoln County War*, 90; Frederick Nolan, *The West of Billy the Kid*, 73, 86.
63 Robert M. Utley, *Billy the Kid*, 30, 219n27.
64 Ibid., 30.
65 Robert M. Utley, *Billy the Kid*, 30; Frederick Nolan, *The West of Billy the Kid*, 87.
66 Frederick Nolan, *The West of Billy the Kid*, 87, 88; Mark Lee Gardner, *To Hell on a Fast Horse*, 58; Michael Wallis, *Billy the Kid*, 182.
67 Robert M. Utley, *Billy the Kid*, 32; Michael Wallis, *Billy the Kid*, 182.
68 Frederick Nolan, *The West of Billy the Kid*, 92, 93.
69 Robert M. Utley, *Billy the Kid*, 32; Michael Wallis, *Billy the Kid*, 194, 195.
70 Robert M. Utley, *Billy the Kid*, 33, 35; Michael Wallis, *Billy the Kid*, 195.
71 Robert M. Utley, *Billy the Kid*, 37; Michael Wallis, *Billy the Kid*, 195.

Chapter 10: Lincoln County War

1 Maurice Garland Fulton, *History of the Lincoln County War*, 89.
2 Ibid., 92.
3 Maurice Garland Fulton, *History of the Lincoln County War*, 95; Robert M. Utley, *Billy the Kid*, 39.
4 Maurice Garland Fulton, *History of the Lincoln County War*, 95, 96; Frederick Nolan, *The West of Billy the Kid*, 95; Robert M. Utley, *Billy the Kid*, 39.
5 Maurice Garland Fulton, *History of the Lincoln County War*, 96, 97; Frederick Nolan, *The West of Billy the Kid*, 89, 90.
6 Frederick Nolan, *The West of Billy the Kid*, 94.
7 Ibid., 95.
8 Maurice Garland Fulton, *History of the Lincoln County War*, 101; Robert M. Utley, *Billy the Kid*, 40; Frederick Nolan, *The West of Billy the Kid*, 97.

9 Maurice Garland Fulton, *History of the Lincoln County War*, 102; Frederick Nolan, *The West of Billy the Kid*, 97, 98.
10 Robert M. Utley, *Billy the Kid*, 40; Frederick Nolan, *The West of Billy the Kid*, 98.
11 Maurice Garland Fulton, *History of the Lincoln County War*, 103–105.
12 Robert M. Utley, *Billy the Kid*, 40; Maurice Garland Fulton, *History of the Lincoln County War*, 110.
13 Robert M. Utley, *Billy the Kid*, 40, 41; Frederick Nolan, *The West of Billy the Kid*, 100, 101.
14 Frederick Nolan, *The West of Billy the Kid*, 100; Maurice Garland Fulton, *History of the Lincoln County War*, 109.
15 Robert M. Utley, *Billy the Kid*, 41; Maurice Garland Fulton, *History of the Lincoln County War*, 112.
16 Robert M. Utley, *Billy the Kid*, 41, 42; Maurice Garland Fulton, *History of the Lincoln County War*, 112.
17 Robert M. Utley, *Billy the Kid*, 42; Frederick Nolan, *The West of Billy the Kid*, 101.
18 Robert M. Utley, *Billy the Kid*, 42, 43; Maurice Garland Fulton, *History of the Lincoln County War*, 113; Frederick Nolan, *The West of Billy the Kid*, 101, 102.
19 Robert M. Utley, *Billy the Kid*, 43; Maurice Garland Fulton, *History of the Lincoln County War*, 113, 114.
20 Robert M. Utley, *Billy the Kid*, 43; Maurice Garland Fulton, *History of the Lincoln County War*, 114.
21 Robert M. Utley, *Billy the Kid*, 43.
22 Robert M. Utley, *Billy the Kid*, 44; Maurice Garland Fulton, *History of the Lincoln County War*, 114.
23 Robert M. Utley, *Billy the Kid*, 44; Maurice Garland Fulton, *History of the Lincoln County War*, 115.
24 Ibid.
25 Robert M. Utley, *Billy the Kid*, 44, 45.
26 Robert M. Utley, *Billy the Kid*, 45; Frederick Nolan, *The West of Billy the Kid*, 104, 105.
27 Robert M. Utley, *Billy the Kid*, 45; Maurice Garland Fulton, *History of the Lincoln County War*, 115; Frederick Nolan, *The West of Billy the Kid*, 105.
28 Robert M. Utley, *Billy the Kid*, 45.
29 Ibid.
30 Robert M. Utley, *Billy the Kid*, 46; Frederick Nolan, *The West of Billy the Kid*, 105, 106.
31 Robert M. Utley, *Billy the Kid*, 46; Frederick Nolan, *The West of Billy the Kid*, 106.
32 Robert M. Utley, *Billy the Kid*, 46; Maurice Garland Fulton, *History of the Lincoln County War*, 116.
33 Robert M. Utley, *Billy the Kid*, 46; Maurice Garland Fulton, *History of the Lincoln County War*, 118.

34 Maurice Garland Fulton, *History of the Lincoln County War*, 117; Robert M. Utley, *Billy the Kid*, 46.
35 Maurice Garland Fulton, *History of the Lincoln County War*, 117.
36 Ibid., 118.
37 Maurice Garland Fulton, *History of the Lincoln County War*, 118; Frederick Nolan, *The West of Billy the Kid*, 106.
38 Maurice Garland Fulton, *History of the Lincoln County War*, 118.
39 Frederick Nolan, *The West of Billy the Kid*, 106; Robert M. Utley, *Billy the Kid*, 46.
40 Frederick Nolan, *The West of Billy the Kid*, 107; Maurice Garland Fulton, *History of the Lincoln County War*, 122, 123.
41 Maurice Garland Fulton, *History of the Lincoln County War*, 123.
42 Frederick Nolan, *The West of Billy the Kid*, 107, 108; Maurice Garland Fulton, *History of the Lincoln County War*, 127; Robert M. Utley, *Billy the Kid*, 225n4.
43 Frederick Nolan, *The West of Billy the Kid*, 108.
44 Robert M. Utley, *Billy the Kid*, 48, 49.
45 Robert M. Utley, *Billy the Kid*, 49, 50, 225n4; Maurice Garland Fulton, *History of the Lincoln County War*, 125.
46 Frederick Nolan, *The West of Billy the Kid*, 108; Maurice Garland Fulton, *History of the Lincoln County War*, 125.
47 Robert M. Utley, *Billy the Kid*, 50, 51.
48 Maurice Garland Fulton, *History of the Lincoln County War*, 125, 126; Frederick Nolan, *The West of Billy the Kid*, 108.
49 Robert M. Utley, *Billy the Kid*, 51.
50 Ibid., 51, 52.
51 Ibid., 52.
52 Robert M. Utley, *Billy the Kid*, 52, 53; Maurice Garland Fulton, *History of the Lincoln County War*, 126, 159; Frederick Nolan, *The West of Billy the Kid*, 109.
53 Robert M. Utley, *Billy the Kid*, 52, 53; Maurice Garland Fulton, *History of the Lincoln County War*, 126.
54 Robert M. Utley, *Billy the Kid*, 53; Frederick Nolan, *The West of Billy the Kid*, 109.
55 Robert M. Utley, *Billy the Kid*, 53.
56 Robert M. Utley, *Billy the Kid*, 53, 54; Frederick Nolan, *The West of Billy the Kid*, 109, 111; Maurice Garland Fulton, *History of the Lincoln County War*, 127.
57 Robert M. Utley, *Billy the Kid*, 54; Maurice Garland Fulton, *History of the Lincoln County War*, 129; Frederick Nolan, *The West of Billy the Kid*, 111.
58 Robert M. Utley, *Billy the Kid*, 54; Frederick Nolan, *The West of Billy the Kid*, 111.
59 Robert M. Utley, *Billy the Kid*, 54, 55; Maurice Garland Fulton, *History of the Lincoln County War*, 137.
60 Robert M. Utley, *Billy the Kid*, 56; Frederick Nolan, *The West of Billy the Kid*, 111; Maurice Garland Fulton, *History of the Lincoln County War*, 137, 138.

61 Robert M. Utley, *Billy the Kid*, 56; Frederick Nolan, *The West of Billy the Kid*, 111.
62 Robert M. Utley, *Billy the Kid*, 56, 57. Frederick Nolan, *The West of Billy the Kid*, 111, 112.
63 Robert M. Utley, *Billy the Kid*, 57; Frederick Nolan, *The West of Billy the Kid*, 112; Maurice Garland Fulton, *History of the Lincoln County War*, 140.
64 Robert M. Utley, *Billy the Kid*, 57, 58; Frederick Nolan, *The West of Billy the Kid*, 112.
65 Pat Garrett, *The Authentic Life of Billy the Kid*, 44; Robert M. Utley, *Billy the Kid*, 57, 58; Frederick Nolan, *The West of Billy the Kid*, 112, 113.
66 Pat Garrett, *The Authentic Life of Billy the Kid*, 44.
67 Robert M. Utley, *Billy the Kid*, 57, 58; Frederick Nolan, *The West of Billy the Kid*, 113; Maurice Garland Fulton, *History of the Lincoln County War*, 141.
68 Pat Garrett, *The Authentic Life of Billy the Kid*, 44.
69 Maurice Garland Fulton, *History of the Lincoln County War*, 141.
70 Robert M. Utley, *Billy the Kid*, 59; Frederick Nolan, *The West of Billy the Kid*, 114.
71 Pat Garrett, *The Authentic Life of Billy the Kid*, 45.
72 Frederick Nolan, *The West of Billy the Kid*, 114.
73 Ibid., 115.
74 Maurice Garland Fulton, *History of the Lincoln County War*, 143, 144; Frederick Nolan, *The West of Billy the Kid*, 115.
75 Maurice Garland Fulton, *History of the Lincoln County War*, 141, 147; Robert M. Utley, *Billy the Kid*, 58, 59.
76 Robert M. Utley, *Billy the Kid*, 63.
77 Maurice Garland Fulton, *History of the Lincoln County War*, 149; Frederick Nolan, *The West of Billy the Kid*, 117.
78 Robert M. Utley, *Billy the Kid*, 62, 63.
79 Robert M. Utley, *Billy the Kid*, 64; Frederick Nolan, *The West of Billy the Kid*, 118, 120.
80 Robert M. Utley, *Billy the Kid*, 64; Maurice Garland Fulton, *History of the Lincoln County War*, 158, 159.
81 Robert M. Utley, *Billy the Kid*, 65.
82 Robert M. Utley, *Billy the Kid*, 64; Maurice Garland Fulton, *History of the Lincoln County War*, 158; Frederick Nolan, *The West of Billy the Kid*, 120.
83 Robert M. Utley, *Billy the Kid*, 65; Maurice Garland Fulton, *History of the Lincoln County War*, 159; Frederick Nolan, *The West of Billy the Kid*, 121.
84 Robert M. Utley, *Billy the Kid*, 65; Frederick Nolan, *The West of Billy the Kid*, 121; Maurice Garland Fulton, *History of the Lincoln County War*, 159.
85 Robert M. Utley, *Billy the Kid*, 65; Michael Wallis, *Billy the Kid*, 202.
86 Robert M. Utley, *Billy the Kid*, 66.
87 Robert M. Utley, *Billy the Kid*, 66, 67. Maurice Garland Fulton, *History of the Lincoln County War*, 159; Frederick Nolan, *The West of Billy the Kid*, 123, 124.

88 Robert M. Utley, *Billy the Kid*, 67; Frederick Nolan, *The West of Billy the Kid*, 119, 120, 123.
89 Frederick Nolan, *The West of Billy the Kid*, 123, 124; Maurice Garland Fulton, *History of the Lincoln County War*, 162.
90 Robert M. Utley, *Billy the Kid*, 67.
91 Mark Lee Gardner, *To Hell on a Fast Horse*, 77; Frederick Nolan, *The West of Billy the Kid*, 126; Maurice Garland Fulton, *History of the Lincoln County War*, 208.
92 Robert M. Utley, *Billy the Kid*, 70, 71; Frederick Nolan, *The West of Billy the Kid*, 127; Maurice Garland Fulton, *History of the Lincoln County War*, 173.
93 Robert M. Utley, *Billy the Kid*, 71; Frederick Nolan, *The West of Billy the Kid*, 127.
94 Robert M. Utley, *Billy the Kid*, 69; Maurice Garland Fulton, *History of the Lincoln County War*, 175.
95 Robert M. Utley, *Billy the Kid*, 69, 70; Frederick Nolan, *The West of Billy the Kid*, 127.
96 Mark Lee Gardner, *To Hell on a Fast Horse*, 70; Robert M. Utley, *Billy the Kid*, 71, 72, 234n35.
97 Robert M. Utley, *Billy the Kid*, 72. Maurice Garland Fulton, *History of the Lincoln County War*, 175.
98 Robert M. Utley, *Billy the Kid*, 72, 73; Frederick Nolan, *The West of Billy the Kid*, 128.
99 Robert M. Utley, *Billy the Kid*, 73.
100 Robert M. Utley, *Billy the Kid*, 73; Frederick Nolan, *The West of Billy the Kid*, 129.
101 Ibid.
102 Robert M. Utley, *Billy the Kid*, 74; Frederick Nolan, *The West of Billy the Kid*, 133.
103 Robert M. Utley, *Billy the Kid*, 74.
104 Ibid.
105 Maurice Garland Fulton, *History of the Lincoln County War*, 177; Frederick Nolan, *The West of Billy the Kid*, 133; Robert M. Utley, *Billy the Kid*, 74, 75.
106 Frederick Nolan, *The West of Billy the Kid*, 136.
107 Frederick Nolan, *The West of Billy the Kid*, 136; Maurice Garland Fulton, *History of the Lincoln County War*, 195.
108 Maurice Garland Fulton, *History of the Lincoln County War*, 196, 197; Frederick Nolan, *The West of Billy the Kid*, 136.
109 Frederick Nolan, *The West of Billy the Kid*, 136.
110 Maurice Garland Fulton, *History of the Lincoln County War*, 200, 201; Frederick Nolan, *The West of Billy the Kid*, 136.
111 Maurice Garland Fulton, *History of the Lincoln County War*, 203; Robert M. Utley, *Billy the Kid*, 77.
112 Frederick Nolan, *The West of Billy the Kid*, 137; Maurice Garland Fulton, *History of the Lincoln County War*, 204.

113 Robert M. Utley, *Billy the Kid*, 77, 78.
114 Ibid., 78.
115 Ibid.
116 Frederick Nolan, *The West of Billy the Kid*, 139, 140; Robert M. Utley, *Billy the Kid*, 78, 79.
117 Robert M. Utley, *Billy the Kid*, 79.
118 Robert M. Utley, *Billy the Kid*, 79; Frederick Nolan, *The West of Billy the Kid*, 141.
119 Robert M. Utley, *Billy the Kid*, 79; Frederick Nolan, *The West of Billy the Kid*, 141, 142.
120 Robert M. Utley, *Billy the Kid*, 79; Frederick Nolan, *The West of Billy the Kid*, 142.
121 Robert M. Utley, *Billy the Kid*, 79–81; Frederick Nolan, *The West of Billy the Kid*, 143, 144.
122 Robert M. Utley, *Billy the Kid*, 81.
123 Robert M. Utley, *Billy the Kid*, 82; Maurice Garland Fulton, *History of the Lincoln County War*, 225.
124 Robert M. Utley, *Billy the Kid*, 83, 84; Maurice Garland Fulton, *History of the Lincoln County War*, 227, 232.
125 Robert M. Utley, *Billy the Kid*, 83; Maurice Garland Fulton, *History of the Lincoln County War*, 236, 240, 241.
126 Robert M. Utley, *Billy the Kid*, 84; Frederick Nolan, *The West of Billy the Kid*, 146; Maurice Garland Fulton, *History of the Lincoln County War*, 232.
127 Robert M. Utley, *Billy the Kid*, 84. Frederick Nolan, *The West of Billy the Kid*, 146.
128 Robert M. Utley, *Billy the Kid*, 84.
129 Ibid., 85.
130 Ibid.
131 Robert M. Utley, *Billy the Kid*, 86; Maurice Garland Fulton, *History of the Lincoln County War*, 234.
132 Robert M. Utley, *Billy the Kid*, 86.
133 Robert M. Utley, *Billy the Kid*, 86; Frederick Nolan, *The West of Billy the Kid*, 148.
134 Frederick Nolan, *The West of Billy the Kid*, 148; Robert M. Utley, *Billy the Kid*, 87; Maurice Garland Fulton, *History of the Lincoln County War*, 235.
135 Robert M. Utley, *Billy the Kid*, 87.
136 Robert M. Utley, *Billy the Kid*, 87; Frederick Nolan, *The West of Billy the Kid*, 148, 149.
137 Pat Garrett, *The Authentic Life of Billy the Kid*, 50; Robert M. Utley, *Billy the Kid*, 89, 103.
138 Robert M. Utley, *Billy the Kid*, 88–90.
139 Mark Lee Gardner, *To Hell on a Fast Horse*, 75; Frederick Nolan, *The West of Billy the Kid*, 151; Robert M. Utley, *Billy the Kid*, 90.

140 Frederick Nolan, *The West of Billy the Kid*, 151; Maurice Garland Fulton, *History of the Lincoln County War*, 249.
141 Ibid.
142 Frederick Nolan, *The West of Billy the Kid*, 151.
143 Frederick Nolan, *The West of Billy the Kid*, 150, 151; Maurice Garland Fulton, *History of the Lincoln County War*, 250.
144 Maurice Garland Fulton, *History of the Lincoln County War*, 250, 251.
145 Mark Lee Gardner, *To Hell on a Fast Horse*, 76; Robert M. Utley, *Billy the Kid*, 91.
146 Frederick Nolan, *The West of Billy the Kid*, 155; Maurice Garland Fulton, *History of the Lincoln County War*, 255; Robert M. Utley, *Billy the Kid*, 90.
147 Maurice Garland Fulton, *History of the Lincoln County War*, 251; Frederick Nolan, *The West of Billy the Kid*, 156.
148 Maurice Garland Fulton, *History of the Lincoln County War*, 252; Frederick Nolan, *The West of Billy the Kid*, 156, 158; Robert M. Utley, *Billy the Kid*, 90.
149 Maurice Garland Fulton, *History of the Lincoln County War*, 253; Frederick Nolan, *The West of Billy the Kid*, 157.
150 Frederick Nolan, *The West of Billy the Kid*, 158; Maurice Garland Fulton, *History of the Lincoln County War*, 253, 254.
151 Frederick Nolan, *The West of Billy the Kid*, 158; Maurice Garland Fulton, *History of the Lincoln County War*, 254.
152 Frederick Nolan, *The West of Billy the Kid*, 158; Maurice Garland Fulton, *History of the Lincoln County War*, 255.
153 Frederick Nolan, *The West of Billy the Kid*, 158, 159.
154 Frederick Nolan, *The West of Billy the Kid*, 158, 159; Maurice Garland Fulton, *History of the Lincoln County War*, 257.
155 Maurice Garland Fulton, *History of the Lincoln County War*, 255, 256.
156 Ibid., 258.
157 Maurice Garland Fulton, *History of the Lincoln County War*, 259; Frederick Nolan, *The West of Billy the Kid*, 159; Robert M. Utley, *Billy the Kid*, 93.
158 Frederick Nolan, *The West of Billy the Kid*, 159; Maurice Garland Fulton, *History of the Lincoln County War*, 260.
159 Frederick Nolan, *The West of Billy the Kid*, 160.
160 Ibid.
161 Maurice Garland Fulton, *History of the Lincoln County War*, 260; Frederick Nolan, *The West of Billy the Kid*, 160, 161.
162 Frederick Nolan, *The West of Billy the Kid*, 160; Maurice Garland Fulton, *History of the Lincoln County War*, 262.
163 Ibid.
164 Maurice Garland Fulton, *History of the Lincoln County War*, 263.
165 Ibid., 259, 262.
166 Maurice Garland Fulton, *History of the Lincoln County War*, 262; Frederick Nolan, *The West of Billy the Kid*, 160, 161; Robert M. Utley, *Billy the Kid*, 95.

167 Frederick Nolan, *The West of Billy the Kid*, 162; Robert M. Utley, *Billy the Kid*, 95.
168 Robert M. Utley, *Billy the Kid*, 95; Frederick Nolan, *The West of Billy the Kid*, 162, 163; Maurice Garland Fulton, *History of the Lincoln County War*, 264.
169 Frederick Nolan, *The West of Billy the Kid*, 162; Robert M. Utley, *Billy the Kid*, 95, 96; Maurice Garland Fulton, *History of the Lincoln County War*, 264.
170 Frederick Nolan, *The West of Billy the Kid*, 162; Robert M. Utley, *Billy the Kid*, 96; Maurice Garland Fulton, *History of the Lincoln County War*, 264.
171 Maurice Garland Fulton, *History of the Lincoln County War*, 264; Frederick Nolan, *The West of Billy the Kid*, 162.
172 Frederick Nolan, *The West of Billy the Kid*, 163; Maurice Garland Fulton, *History of the Lincoln County War*, 264.
173 Frederick Nolan, *The West of Billy the Kid*, 163. Maurice Garland Fulton, *History of the Lincoln County War*, 267, 268.
174 Frederick Nolan, *The West of Billy the Kid*, 162.
175 Frederick Nolan, *The West of Billy the Kid*, 163; Robert M. Utley, *Billy the Kid*, 97.
176 Frederick Nolan, *The West of Billy the Kid*, 163.
177 Frederick Nolan, *The West of Billy the Kid*, 164; Robert M. Utley, *Billy the Kid*, 98.
178 Frederick Nolan, *The West of Billy the Kid*, 164.
179 Frederick Nolan, *The West of Billy the Kid*, 164; Maurice Garland Fulton, *History of the Lincoln County War*, 271.
180 Maurice Garland Fulton, *History of the Lincoln County War*, 271, 272; Robert M. Utley, *Billy the Kid*, 98.
181 Maurice Garland Fulton, *History of the Lincoln County War*, 271, 272; Frederick Nolan, *The West of Billy the Kid*, 166.
182 Maurice Garland Fulton, *History of the Lincoln County War*, 273; Frederick Nolan, *The West of Billy the Kid*, 166.
183 Maurice Garland Fulton, *History of the Lincoln County War*, 273, 274, 278.
184 Frederick Nolan, *The West of Billy the Kid*, 166; Robert M. Utley, *Billy the Kid*, 99.
185 Robert M. Utley, *Billy the Kid*, 102.
186 Robert M. Utley, *Billy the Kid*, 102, 103; Maurice Garland Fulton, *History of the Lincoln County War*, 282.
187 Robert M. Utley, *Billy the Kid*, 104; Maurice Garland Fulton, *History of the Lincoln County War*, 283.
188 Frederick Nolan, *The West of Billy the Kid*, 168; Robert M. Utley, *Billy the Kid*, 104.
189 Robert M. Utley, *Billy the Kid*, 104.
190 Ibid.
191 Robert M. Utley, *Billy the Kid*, 104, 105; Frederick Nolan, *The West of Billy the Kid*, 169.

192 Robert M. Utley, *Billy the Kid*, 105; Frederick Nolan, *The West of Billy the Kid*, 170, 171.
193 Robert M. Utley, *Billy the Kid*, 105, 106; Frederick Nolan, *The West of Billy the Kid*, 171.
194 Frederick Nolan, *The West of Billy the Kid*, 171, 172.
195 Miguel Antonio Otero Jr., *The Real Billy the Kid: With New Light on the Lincoln County War* (Houston: Arte Publico Press, 1998), 61; Robert M. Utley, *Billy the Kid*, 107; Frederick Nolan, *The West of Billy the Kid*, 173.
196 Miguel Antonio Otero Jr., *The Real Billy the Kid*, 60, 61; Robert M. Utley, *Billy the Kid*, 108; Frederick Nolan, *The West of Billy the Kid*, 174, 175.
197 Mark Boardman, "The Holy Grail for Sale," *True West Magazine*, June 2011, 27.
198 Ibid., 28.
199 Ibid., 26.
200 Ibid.
201 Mark Boardman, "The Holy Grail for Sale," 26; "The Billy the Kid Wannabe Yearbook," *True West Magazine*, June 2015, 26.
202 "The Billy the Kid Wannabe Yearbook," *True West Magazine*, June 2015, 26.
203 Mark Boardman, "The Croquet Kid," *True West Magazine*, February 2016, 22, 24.
204 Ibid.
205 Jeff Aiello, "The Claim," *True West Magazine*, February 2016, 23.
206 Mark Boardman, "The Croquet Kid," 25–27.

CHAPTER 11: OUTLAWS

1 Ted P. Yeatman, *Frank and Jesse James*, 203–209.
2 Ibid., 211.
3 Ted P. Yeatman, *Frank and Jesse James*, 209–211; William A. Settle, *Jesse James Was His Name*, 102.
4 Ted P. Yeatman, *Frank and Jesse James*, 212; William A. Settle, *Jesse James Was His Name*, 102; T. J. Stiles, *Jesse James*, 354.
5 William A. Settle, *Jesse James Was His Name*, 102; Ted P. Yeatman, *Frank and Jesse James*, 213; T. J. Stiles, *Jesse James*, 353.
6 Ted P. Yeatman, *Frank and Jesse James*, 213, 214; William A. Settle, *Jesse James Was His Name*, 102.
7 T. J. Stiles, *Jesse James*, 354.
8 T. J. Stiles, *Jesse James*, 354; Ted P. Yeatman, *Frank and Jesse James*, 215.
9 Ibid.
10 William A. Settle, *Jesse James Was His Name,* 103–105; Ted P. Yeatman, *Frank and Jesse James*, 215–217.
11 Ted P. Yeatman, *Frank and Jesse James*, 223, 224.
12 Ibid., 217, 218.
13 Ibid., 218.

14 Ibid., 220.
15 Ted P. Yeatman, *Frank and Jesse James*, 219, 220; T. J. Stiles, *Jesse James*, 358.
16 T. J. Stiles, *Jesse James*, 358; Ted P. Yeatman, *Frank and Jesse James*, 221.
17 Ted P. Yeatman, *Frank and Jesse James*, 227–229, T. J. Stiles, *Jesse James*, 358, 359.
18 Robertus Love, *The Rise and Fall of Jesse James*, 289–291.
19 Ralph Ganis, "A Knight with the Widow Benton: Did the Robin Hood-Bandit Save a Widow's Home?" *True West Magazine*, August 1, 2002, accessed October 14, 2018, https://truewestmagazine.com/a-knight-with-the-widow-benton/.
20 Miguel Antonio Otero Jr., *The Real Billy the Kid*, 60, 61; Robert M. Utley, *Billy the Kid*, 108; Frederick Nolan, *The West of Billy the Kid*, 174, 175.
21 Henry F. Hoyt, *A Frontier Doctor*, reprint (New York, NY: Houghton Mifflin Co., 1929), 89.
22 Ibid., xii.
23 Ibid., 90, 91.
24 Ibid., 91, 92.
25 Ibid.
26 Henry F. Hoyt, *A Frontier Doctor*, 114.
27 Ibid., 49, 93.
28 Ibid., 94, 95. In 1923, Hoyt corresponded with old cowboy friend Charles Siringo about Dandy Dick. Hoyt sent him a copy of the bill of sale. Siringo showed it to James Brady, son of Sheriff Bill Brady, who said Dandy Dick was his father's horse which he had ridden into Lincoln the day he was shot and killed.
29 Pat Garrett, *The Authentic Life of Billy the Kid*, 63.
30 Robert M. Utley, *Billy the Kid*, 110.
31 Some sources spell Kimbrell as Kimball.
32 Maurice Garland Fulton, *History of the Lincoln County War*, 290–293; Robert M. Utley, *Billy the Kid*, 112.
33 Maurice Garland Fulton, *History of the Lincoln County War*, 298, 299; Frederick Nolan, *The West of Billy the Kid*, 179.
34 Robert M. Utley, *Billy the Kid*, 111; Frederick Nolan, *The West of Billy the Kid*, 181.
35 Maurice Garland Fulton, *History of the Lincoln County War*, 299–301, 307; Frederick Nolan, *The West of Billy the Kid*, 181.
36 Robert M. Utley, *Billy the Kid*, 110.
37 Ibid., 111, 112.
38 Robert M. Utley, *Billy the Kid*, 113; Maurice Garland Fulton, *History of the Lincoln County War*, 324.
39 Ibid.
40 Robert M. Utley, *Billy the Kid*, 113; Maurice Garland Fulton, *History of the Lincoln County War*, 326.

41 Frederick Nolan, *The West of Billy the Kid*, 186; Robert M. Utley, *Billy the Kid*, 113.
42 Robert M. Utley, *Billy the Kid*, 114; Maurice Garland Fulton, *History of the Lincoln County War*, 326–329.
43 Maurice Garland Fulton, *History of the Lincoln County War*, 327, 328.
44 Ibid., 329.
45 Robert M. Utley, *Billy the Kid*, 114; Frederick Nolan, *The West of Billy the Kid*, 186.
46 Robert M. Utley, *Billy the Kid*, 114; Frederick Nolan, *The West of Billy the Kid*, 189.
47 Robert M. Utley, *Billy the Kid*, 115; Frederick Nolan, *The West of Billy the Kid*, 189.
48 Robert M. Utley, *Billy the Kid*, 115; Frederick Nolan, *The West of Billy the Kid*, 194.
49 Robert M. Utley, *Billy the Kid*, 115, 116; Frederick Nolan, *The West of Billy the Kid*, 194.
50 Robert M. Utley, *Billy the Kid*, 117; Frederick Nolan, *The West of Billy the Kid*, 194, 195.
51 Frederick Nolan, *The West of Billy the Kid*, 195, 196; Robert M. Utley, *Billy the Kid*, 117, 118.
52 Frederick Nolan, *The West of Billy the Kid*, 196, 198; Robert M. Utley, *Billy the Kid*, 118, 119.
53 Robert M. Utley, *Billy the Kid*, 119; Frederick Nolan, *The West of Billy the Kid*, 198.
54 Robert M. Utley, *Billy the Kid*, 120, 121; Frederick Nolan, *The West of Billy the Kid*, 200.
55 Robert M. Utley, *Billy the Kid*, 120–122; Frederick Nolan, *The West of Billy the Kid*, 200, 201, 203.
56 Frederick Nolan, *The West of Billy the Kid*, 203; Robert M. Utley, *Billy the Kid*, 123.
57 Robert M. Utley, *Billy the Kid*, 124; Frederick Nolan, *The West of Billy the Kid*, 205, 208.
58 Frederick Nolan, *The West of Billy the Kid*, 209; Robert M. Utley, *Billy the Kid*, 124.
59 Robert M. Utley, *Billy the Kid*, 126; Frederick Nolan, *The West of Billy the Kid*, 211.
60 Walter Noble Burns, *The Saga of Billy the Kid: The Thrilling Life of America's Original Outlaw*, reprint (New York: Skyhorse Publishing, 2014), 183, 184; Mark J. Dworkin, *American Mythmaker: Walter Noble Burns and the Legends of Billy the Kid, Wyatt Earp, and Joaquin Murrieta* (Norman: University of Oklahoma Press, 2015), 29–34; Robert M. Utley, *Billy the Kid*, 126, 127; Frederick Nolan, *The West of Billy the Kid*, 211.
61 Frederick Nolan, *The West of Billy the Kid*, 213, 214; Robert M. Utley, *Billy the Kid*, 128, 129.

62 Robert M. Utley, *Billy the Kid*, 131; Frederick Nolan, *The West of Billy the Kid*, 217, 218.
63 Robert M. Utley, *Billy the Kid*, 132; Frederick Nolan, *The West of Billy the Kid*, 219.
64 Bill O'Neal, *Encyclopedia of Western Gunfighters*, 269, 270; Robert M. Utley, *Billy the Kid*, 130, 131.
65 Robert M. Utley, *Billy the Kid*, 133.
66 Frederick Nolan, *The West of Billy the Kid*, 217; Robert M. Utley, *Billy the Kid*, 133.
67 Robert M. Utley, *Billy the Kid*, 133, 134.
68 Robert M. Utley, *Billy the Kid*, 134; Frederick Nolan, *The West of Billy the Kid*, 222.
69 Robert M. Utley, *Billy the Kid*, 134; Frederick Nolan, *The West of Billy the Kid*, 223, 225, 226.
70 Robert M. Utley, *Billy the Kid*, 134, 135; Frederick Nolan, *The West of Billy the Kid*, 226, 227.
71 Mark Lee Gardner, *To Hell on a Fast Horse*, 105; Robert M. Utley, *Billy the Kid*, 138.
72 Michael Wallis, *Billy the Kid*, 235; Robert M. Utley, *Billy the Kid*, 135.
73 Bill O'Neal, *Encyclopedia of Western Gunfighters*, 115; Robert M. Utley, *Billy the Kid*, 135, 136; Frederick Nolan, *The West of Billy the Kid*, 230.
74 Walter Noble Burns, *The Saga of Billy the Kid*, 196, 197; Miguel Antonio Otero Jr., *The Real Billy the Kid*, 71, 73.
75 Frederick Nolan, *The West of Billy the Kid*, 229; Robert M. Utley, *Billy the Kid*, 136.
76 Robert M. Utley, *Billy the Kid*, 139, 140; Frederick Nolan, *The West of Billy the Kid*, 225.
77 Robert M. Utley, *Billy the Kid*, 140, 141; Frederick Nolan, *The West of Billy the Kid*, 233.
78 Robert M. Utley, *Billy the Kid*, 141.
79 Mark Lee Gardner, *To Hell on a Fast Horse*, 105; Frederick Nolan, *The West of Billy the Kid*, 234.
80 Mark Lee Gardner, *To Hell on a Fast Horse*, 105; Robert M. Utley, *Billy the Kid*, 142.
81 Mark Lee Gardner, *To Hell on a Fast Horse*, 106; Robert M. Utley, *Billy the Kid*, 142; Frederick Nolan, *The West of Billy the Kid*, 233.
82 Mark Lee Gardner, *To Hell on a Fast Horse*, 106; Robert M. Utley, *Billy the Kid*, 142; Frederick Nolan, *The West of Billy the Kid*, 234.
83 Mark Lee Gardner, *To Hell on a Fast Horse*, 107; Robert M. Utley, *Billy the Kid*, 142.
84 Mark Lee Gardner, *To Hell on a Fast Horse*, 108; Robert M. Utley, *Billy the Kid*, 143.
85 Mark Lee Gardner, *To Hell on a Fast Horse*, 109; Robert M. Utley, *Billy the Kid*, 143, 144.

86 Mark Lee Gardner, *To Hell on a Fast Horse*, 109; Robert M. Utley, *Billy the Kid*, 144.
87 Mark Lee Gardner, *To Hell on a Fast Horse*, 108, 109; Robert M. Utley, *Billy the Kid*, 145.
88 Mark Lee Gardner, *To Hell on a Fast Horse*, 109; Robert M. Utley, *Billy the Kid*, 145.
89 Henry F. Hoyt, *A Frontier Doctor*, xiv.
90 Henry F. Hoyt, *A Frontier Doctor*, 19, 109; Ted P. Yeatman, *Frank and Jesse James*, 186.
91 Henry F. Hoyt, *A Frontier Doctor*, 89, 91, 94, 108.
92 Henry F. Hoyt, *A Frontier Doctor*, 110; Frederick Nolan, *The West of Billy the Kid*, 208.
93 Ibid., 110–112.
94 Ibid., 111.
95 Ibid., 111–113.
96 Ibid., 113.

CHAPTER 12: TRIALS AND TRIBULATIONS

1 William A. Settle, *Jesse James Was His Name*, 184, 187; Ted P. Yeatman, *Frank and Jesse James*, 224.
2 Ted P. Yeatman, *Frank and Jesse James*, 227–229.
3 Ted P. Yeatman, *Frank and Jesse James*, 229, 230; T. J. Stiles, *Jesse James*, 359.
4 Ted P. Yeatman, *Frank and Jesse James*, 232, 233, 236; T. J. Stiles, *Jesse James*, 359.
5 T. J. Stiles, *Jesse James*, 359, 360; Ted P. Yeatman, *Frank and Jesse James*, 234–236.
6 Ted P. Yeatman, *Frank and Jesse James*, 238.
7 T. J. Stiles, *Jesse James*, 361.
8 T. J. Stiles, *Jesse James*, 360; Ted P. Yeatman, *Frank and Jesse James*, 240.
9 T. J. Stiles, *Jesse James*, 361; Ted P. Yeatman, *Frank and Jesse James*, 240.
10 Frederick Nolan, *The West of Billy the Kid*, 236, 238; Robert M. Utley, *Billy the Kid*, 145n16, 238.
11 Frederick Nolan, *The West of Billy the Kid*, 238; Robert M. Utley, *Billy the Kid*, 146, 147.
12 Robert M. Utley, *Billy the Kid*, 150–152.
13 Ibid., 153.
14 Frederick Nolan, *The West of Billy the Kid*, 242, 243; Robert M. Utley, *Billy the Kid*, 153, 154.
15 Pat Garrett, *The Authentic Life of Billy the Kid*, 90, 91; Miguel Antonio Otero Jr., *The Real Billy the Kid*, 73; Robert M. Utley, *Billy the Kid*, 155.
16 Pat Garrett, *The Authentic Life of Billy the Kid*, 91; Miguel Antonio Otero Jr., *The Real Billy the Kid*, 73; Robert M. Utley, *Billy the Kid*, 155, 156.

17 Pat Garrett, *The Authentic Life of Billy the Kid*, 91; Miguel Antonio Otero Jr., *The Real Billy the Kid*, 73; Robert M. Utley, *Billy the Kid*, 156.
18 Frederick Nolan, *The West of Billy the Kid*, 244; Robert M. Utley, *Billy the Kid*, 157.
19 Walter Noble Burns, *The Saga of Billy the Kid*, 210; Frederick Nolan, *The West of Billy the Kid*, 247; Pat Garrett, *The Authentic Life of Billy the Kid*, 94, 95; Robert M. Utley, *Billy the Kid*, 158.
20 Pat Garrett, *The Authentic Life of Billy the Kid*, 95; Robert M. Utley, *Billy the Kid*, 158.
21 Ibid.
22 Pat Garrett, *The Authentic Life of Billy the Kid*, 95; Robert M. Utley, *Billy the Kid*, 159.
23 Pat Garrett, *The Authentic Life of Billy the Kid*, 96; Robert M. Utley, *Billy the Kid*, 159.
24 Ibid.
25 Pat Garrett, *The Authentic Life of Billy the Kid*, 97; Robert M. Utley, *Billy the Kid*, 159.
26 Robert M. Utley, *Billy the Kid*, 160, 161; Frederick Nolan, *The West of Billy the Kid*, 248, 249.
27 Frederick Nolan, *The West of Billy the Kid*, 250; Robert M. Utley, *Billy the Kid*, 163.
28 Bill O'Neal, *Encyclopedia of Western Gunfighters*, 270; Robert M. Utley, *Billy the Kid*, 164, 165.
29 Robert M. Utley, *Billy the Kid*, 164; Frederick Nolan, *The West of Billy the Kid*, 250.
30 Ibid.
31 Robert M. Utley, *Billy the Kid*, 165.
32 Robert M. Utley, *Billy the Kid*, 165; Frederick Nolan, *The West of Billy the Kid*, 252.
33 Robert M. Utley, *Billy the Kid*, 165, 166.
34 Robert M. Utley, *Billy the Kid*, 166; Frederick Nolan, *The West of Billy the Kid*, 255.
35 Robert M. Utley, *Billy the Kid*, 166, 167.
36 Robert M. Utley, *Billy the Kid*, 167; Frederick Nolan, *The West of Billy the Kid*, 257.
37 Robert M. Utley, *Billy the Kid*, 168; Frederick Nolan, *The West of Billy the Kid*, 257, 258.
38 Robert M. Utley, *Billy the Kid*, 168; Frederick Nolan, *The West of Billy the Kid*, 258, 259.
39 Robert M. Utley, *Billy the Kid*, 169, 170; Frederick Nolan, *The West of Billy the Kid*, 259, 260.
40 Frederick Nolan, *The West of Billy the Kid*, 262; Robert M. Utley, *Billy the Kid*, 170.
41 Ibid.

42 Maurice Garland Fulton, *History of the Lincoln County War*, 371; Frederick Nolan, *The West of Billy the Kid*, 146, 215, 217.
43 Henry F. Hoyt, *A Frontier Doctor*, 170–172.
44 Frederick Nolan, *The West of Billy the Kid*, 262.
45 Ibid.
46 Frederick Nolan, *The West of Billy the Kid*, 264; Robert M. Utley, *Billy the Kid*, 172.
47 Frederick Nolan, *The West of Billy the Kid*, 261.
48 Frederick Nolan, *The West of Billy the Kid*, 264; Robert M. Utley, *Billy the Kid*, 172.
49 Robert M. Utley, *Billy the Kid*, 172; Frederick Nolan, *The West of Billy the Kid*, 264.
50 Robert M. Utley, *Billy the Kid*, 172, 173; Frederick Nolan, *The West of Billy the Kid*, 264, 265.
51 Frederick Nolan, *The West of Billy the Kid*, 265, 266.
52 Robert M. Utley, *Billy the Kid*, 174; Frederick Nolan, *The West of Billy the Kid*, 266.
53 Robert M. Utley, *Billy the Kid*, 174, 175; Frederick Nolan, *The West of Billy the Kid*, 266.
54 Robert M. Utley, *Billy the Kid*, 176–178; Frederick Nolan, *The West of Billy the Kid*, 266, 267.
55 Robert M. Utley, *Billy the Kid*, 178, 179; Frederick Nolan, *The West of Billy the Kid*, 267, 269.
56 Pat Garrett, *The Authentic Life of Billy the Kid*, 102; Frederick Nolan, *The West of Billy the Kid*, 269.
57 Frederick Nolan, *The West of Billy the Kid*, 269; Robert M. Utley, *Billy the Kid*, 179, 180.
58 Pat Garrett, *The Authentic Life of Billy the Kid*, 105; Frederick Nolan, *The West of Billy the Kid*, 269.
59 Frederick Nolan, *The West of Billy the Kid*, 261.
60 Robert M. Utley, *Billy the Kid*, 180; Frederick Nolan, *The West of Billy the Kid*, 269.
61 Pat Garrett, *The Authentic Life of Billy the Kid*, 103; Robert M. Utley, *Billy the Kid*, 180; Mark Lee Gardner, *To Hell on a Fast Horse*, 144.
62 Mark Lee Gardner, *To Hell on a Fast Horse*, 142; Robert M. Utley, *Billy the Kid*, 180.
63 Frederick Nolan, *The West of Billy the Kid*, 271.
64 Paul Andrew Hutton, "Billy the Kid's Final Escape," *Wild West Magazine*, December 2015; Pat Garrett, *The Authentic Life of Billy the Kid*, 103; Frederick Nolan, *The West of Billy the Kid*, 271, 273; Robert M. Utley, *Billy the Kid*, 180, 181.
65 Pat Garrett, *The Authentic Life of Billy the Kid*, 103; Mark Lee Gardner, *To Hell on a Fast Horse*, 145; Frederick Nolan, *The West of Billy the Kid*, 273.

66 Mark Lee Gardner, *To Hell on a Fast Horse*, 146; Pat Garrett, *The Authentic Life of Billy the Kid,* 103, 104. Robert M. Utley, *Billy the Kid*, 181.
67 Pat Garrett, *The Authentic Life of Billy the Kid*, 104.
68 Ibid.
69 Mark Lee Gardner, *To Hell on a Fast Horse*, 146; Frederick Nolan, *The West of Billy the Kid*, 275; Pat Garrett, *The Authentic Life of Billy the Kid*, 104.
70 Pat Garrett, *The Authentic Life of Billy the Kid*, 104.
71 Mark Lee Gardner, *To Hell on a Fast Horse*, 147; Robert M. Utley, *Billy the Kid*, 182.
72 Robert M. Utley, *Billy the Kid*, 182, 183.
73 Robert M. Utley, *Billy the Kid*, 183; Frederick Nolan, *The West of Billy the Kid*, 275; Pat Garrett, *The Authentic Life of Billy the Kid*, 104.
74 Mark Lee Gardner, *To Hell on a Fast Horse*, 148; Frederick Nolan, *The West of Billy the Kid*, 275.
75 Ben Ray Redman, introduction to *Ben-Hur: A Tale of the Christ*, by Lew Wallace (Norwalk, CT: Heritage Press, 1960), v.
76 Ibid., xiv.
77 Ibid., vi, viii.
78 The Heritage Club, "Ben-Hur," *Sandglass* (Norwalk, CT: Heritage Press, 1960), 2.
79 Ben Ray Redman, introduction to *Ben-Hur: A Tale of the Christ*, ix; The Heritage Club, "Ben-Hur," 3.
80 The Heritage Club, "Ben-Hur," 3, 4; Wikipedia, *Ben-Hur: A Tale of the Christ*, accessed November 29, 2018, https://en.wikipedia.org/wiki/Ben-Hur:_A_Tale_of_the_Christ.

Chapter 13: Billy the Kid's End

1 Frederick Nolan, *The West of Billy the Kid*, 276, 277; Robert M. Utley, *Billy the Kid*, 186, 187.
2 Robert M. Utley, *Billy the Kid*, 187; Frederick Nolan, *The West of Billy the Kid*, 277.
3 Frederick Nolan, *The West of Billy the Kid*, 277; Robert M. Utley, *Billy the Kid*, 187.
4 Robert M. Utley, *Billy the Kid*, 188.
5 Robert M. Utley, *Billy the* Kid, 184; Pat Garrett, *The Authentic Life of Billy the Kid*, 105, 106.
6 Robert M. Utley, *Billy the Kid*, 189; Pat Garrett, *The Authentic Life of Billy the Kid*, 107; Frederick Nolan, *The West of Billy the Kid*, 277, 278.
7 Pat Garrett, *The Authentic Life of Billy the Kid*, 107; Frederick Nolan, *The West of Billy the Kid*, 278.
8 Pat Garrett, *The Authentic Life of Billy the Kid*, 107, 108; Robert M. Utley, *Billy the* Kid, 189, 190.
9 Pat Garrett, *The Authentic Life of Billy the Kid*, 108.

10 Ibid.
11 Robert M. Utley, *Billy the Kid*, 190, 191; Pat Garrett, *The Authentic Life of Billy the Kid*, 108.
12 Frederick Nolan, *The West of Billy the Kid*, 279–281; Pat Garrett, *The Authentic Life of Billy the Kid*, 108.
13 Pat Garrett, *The Authentic Life of Billy the Kid*, 108, 109; Robert M. Utley, *Billy the Kid*, 191, 192.
14 Pat Garrett, *The Authentic Life of Billy the Kid*, 109; Robert M. Utley, *Billy the Kid*, 192; Frederick Nolan, *The West of Billy the Kid*, 282, 283.
15 Pat Garrett, *The Authentic Life of Billy the Kid*, 109.
16 Mark Lee Gardner, *To Hell on a Fast Horse*, 169, 170.
17 Ibid., 170.
18 Pat Garrett, *The Authentic Life of Billy, the Kid*, 109, 110; Robert M. Utley, *Billy the Kid*, 193, 194.
19 Robert M. Utley, *Billy the Kid*, 194.
20 Mark Lee Gardner, *To Hell on a Fast Horse*, 173, 174.
21 Ibid., 174.
22 Ibid., 178.
23 Walter Noble Burns, *The Saga of Billy the Kid*, 288, 289; Mark Lee Gardner, *To Hell on a Fast Horse*, 175; Pat Garrett, *The Authentic Life of Billy the Kid*, 111.
24 W. C. Jameson, *Billy the Kid: Beyond the Grave* (Lanham, MD: Taylor Trade Publishing, 2005), 16, 17.
25 Ibid., 17, 18.
26 Ibid., 41, 42.
27 Mark Lee Gardner, *To Hell on a Fast Horse*, 254.
28 W. C. Jameson, *Billy the Kid: Beyond the Grave*, 87, 103–106; Joe Nickell, *Camera Clues: A Handbook for Photographic Investigation* (Lexington: University Press of Kentucky, 2005), 88, 89.
29 Mark Boardman, "The Lunacy of Billy the Kid: You Can't Make This Stuff Up!" *True West Magazine*, July 2010, accessed December 8, 2018, https://truewestmagazine.com/the-lunacy-of-billy-the-kid/; Mark Lee Gardner, *To Hell on a Fast Horse*, 254–256; W. C. Jameson, *Billy the Kid: Beyond the Grave*, 81, 82.

Chapter 14: Jesse James's End

1 T. J. Stiles, *Jesse James*, 361; Ted P. Yeatman, *Frank and Jesse James*, 240.
2 Ted P. Yeatman, *Frank and Jesse James*, 242, 244, 245.
3 Ted P. Yeatman, *Frank and Jesse James*, 246, 248; T. J. Stiles, *Jesse James*, 361.
4 William A. Settle, *Jesse James Was His Name*, 184, 186, 187; Ted P. Yeatman, *Frank and Jesse James*, 251.
5 Ted P. Yeatman, *Frank and Jesse James*, 248; T. J. Stiles, *Jesse James*, 364.
6 William A. Settle, *Jesse James Was His Name*, 108; Ted P. Yeatman, *Frank and Jesse James*, 249.

7 William A. Settle, *Jesse James Was His Name*, 108; Ted P. Yeatman, *Frank and Jesse James*, 249; T. J. Stiles, *Jesse James*, 364, 365.
8 Ted P. Yeatman, *Frank and Jesse James*, 249.
9 Ibid., 249, 250
10 T. J. Stiles, *Jesse James*, 364; Ted P. Yeatman, *Frank and Jesse James*, 250.
11 William A. Settle, *Jesse James Was His Name*, 108; Ted P. Yeatman, *Frank and Jesse James*, 251.
12 William A. Settle, *Jesse James Was His Name*, 110, 111; Ted P. Yeatman, *Frank and Jesse James*, 250, 252; T. J. Stiles, *Jesse James*, 367.
13 T. J. Stiles, *Jesse James*, 367.
14 Ted P. Yeatman, *Frank and Jesse James*, 253, 254; William A. Settle, *Jesse James Was His Name*, 111; T. J. Stiles, *Jesse James*, 368.
15 Ted P. Yeatman, *Frank and Jesse James*, 253; William A. Settle, *Jesse James Was His Name*, 111.
16 Carl W. Breihan, *Saga of Jesse James*, 111; Ted P. Yeatman, *Frank and Jesse James*, 254.
17 William A. Settle, *Jesse James Was His Name*, 111, 112; Ted P. Yeatman, *Frank and Jesse James*, 254, 255; Carl W. Breihan, *Saga of Jesse James*, 112; T. J. Stiles, *Jesse James*, 368.
18 Ted P. Yeatman, *Frank and Jesse James*, 255; Carl W. Breihan, *Saga of Jesse James*, 111.
19 Carl W. Breihan, *Saga of Jesse James*, 111; T. J. Stiles, *Jesse James*, 369.
20 Carl W. Breihan, *Saga of Jesse James*, 112.
21 Ted P. Yeatman, *Frank and Jesse James*, 256.
22 William A. Settle, *Jesse James Was His Name*, 113.
23 Robertus Love, *The Rise and Fall of Jesse James*, 325, 326; William A. Settle, *Jesse James Was His Name*, 113, 114; Ted P. Yeatman, *Frank and Jesse James*, 257.
24 Robertus Love, *The Rise and Fall of Jesse James*, 327, 328; William A. Settle, *Jesse James Was His Name*, 113, 114.
25 Ted P. Yeatman, *Frank and Jesse James*, 260, 263, 264.
26 Ibid., 260–262.
27 Ibid., 261.
28 Carl W. Breihan, *Saga of Jesse James*, 113; T. J. Stiles, *Jesse James*, 371; Ted P. Yeatman, *Frank and Jesse James*, 261.
29 Carl W. Breihan, *Saga of Jesse James*, 119; Ted P. Yeatman, *Frank and Jesse James*, 264; T. J. Stiles, *Jesse James*, 373.
30 Ted P. Yeatman, *Frank and Jesse James*, 262; Carl W. Breihan, *Saga of Jesse James*, 113.
31 Carl W. Breihan, *Saga of Jesse James*, 113, 114; Ted P. Yeatman, *Frank and Jesse James*, 262; William A. Settle, *Jesse James Was His Name*, 116.
32 Ted P. Yeatman, *Frank and Jesse James*, 262; William A. Settle, *Jesse James Was His Name*, 116; Carl W. Breihan, *Saga of Jesse James*, 114.
33 T. J. Stiles, *Jesse James*, 373; Ted P. Yeatman, *Frank and Jesse James*, 265.
34 Ted P. Yeatman, *Frank and Jesse James*, 266; T. J. Stiles, *Jesse James*, 373, 374.

35 T. J. Stiles, *Jesse James*, 372; Carl W. Breihan, *Saga of Jesse James*, 120, 121.
36 T. J. Stiles, *Jesse James*, 372.
37 T. J. Stiles, *Jesse James*, 372; Ted P. Yeatman, *Frank and Jesse James*, 266.
38 William A. Settle, *Jesse James Was His Name*, 116; Ted P. Yeatman, *Frank and Jesse James*, 266.
39 William A. Settle, *Jesse James Was His Name*, 115; T. J. Stiles, *Jesse James*, 372, 373; Ted P. Yeatman, *Frank and Jesse James*, 266, 267.
40 T. J. Stiles, *Jesse James*, 374; Ted P. Yeatman, *Frank and Jesse James*, 267.
41 Ted P. Yeatman, *Frank and Jesse James*, 267.
42 Frank Triplett, *Jesse James*, 288, 289; T. J. Stiles, *Jesse James*, 374; Ted P. Yeatman, *Frank and Jesse James*, 267, 268.
43 Frank Triplett, *Jesse James*, 286; T. J. Stiles, *Jesse James*, 374; Carl W. Breihan, *Saga of Jesse James*, 124.
44 Carl W. Breihan, *Saga of Jesse James*, 123; William A. Settle, *Jesse James Was His Name*, 116.
45 T. J. Stiles, *Jesse James*, 375; Ted P. Yeatman, *Frank and Jesse James*, 268.
46 Carl W. Breihan, *Saga of Jesse James*, 123, 124; Frank Triplett, *Jesse James*, 288.
47 Carl W. Breihan, *Saga of Jesse James*, 124.
48 Ibid.
49 Ted P. Yeatman, *Frank and Jesse James*, 269; Frank Triplett, *Jesse James*, 289, 290; Robertus Love, *The Rise and Fall of Jesse James*, 343; Carl W. Breihan, *Saga of Jesse James*, 124.
50 Carl W. Breihan, *Saga of Jesse James*, 124–127; Ted P. Yeatman, *Frank and Jesse James*, 268, 269.
51 Carl W. Breihan, *Saga of Jesse James*, 126.
52 Carl W. Breihan, *Saga of Jesse James*, 126; Ted P. Yeatman, *Frank and Jesse James*, 269.
53 Carl W. Breihan, *Saga of Jesse James*, 128, 131.
54 Ibid., 129, 130.
55 Ibid., 131.
56 Ibid.
57 Ibid.
58 Ibid.
59 Carl W. Breihan, *Saga of Jesse James*, 131, 132.
60 Ted P. Yeatman, *Frank and Jesse James*, 269; Carl W. Breihan, *Saga of Jesse James*, 133.
61 Carl W. Breihan, *Saga of Jesse James*, 134, 135; T. J. Stiles, *Jesse James*, 377.
62 Ted P. Yeatman, *Frank and Jesse James*, 323, 324; William A. Settle, *Jesse James Was His Name*, 170.
63 Ted P. Yeatman, *Frank and Jesse James*, 323, 324.
64 Ibid., 324.
65 William A. Settle, *Jesse James Was His Name*, 170; Ted P. Yeatman, *Frank and Jesse James*, 324.

66 William A. Settle, *Jesse James Was His Name*, 170, 171; Ted P. Yeatman, *Frank and Jesse James*, 328.
67 Ted P. Yeatman, *Frank and Jesse James*, 328.
68 Ibid., 329.
69 Ibid., 329, 331, 332.
70 Ibid., 335–337, 375.
71 Ibid., 371, 374.

Chapter 15: End of the Trail

1 Mark Lee Gardner, *Shot All to Hell*, 222, 223; Ted P. Yeatman, *Frank and Jesse James*, 277–279.
2 Ted P. Yeatman, *Frank and Jesse James*, 279–289; Carl W. Breihan, *Saga of Jesse James*, 144.
3 Ted P. Yeatman, *Frank and Jesse James*, 292; Carl W. Breihan, *Saga of Jesse James*, 144.
4 Ted P. Yeatman, *Frank and Jesse James*, 290, 301.
5 Ibid., 301–311.
6 Ibid., 319.
7 Carl W. Breihan, *Saga of Jesse James*, 144; Ted P. Yeatman, *Frank and Jesse James*, 275, 276.
8 Ted P. Yeatman, *Frank and Jesse James*, 296; Find a Grave, "Jesse James," accessed December 18, 2018, https://www.findagrave.com/memorial/539/jesse-james.
9 Ted P. Yeatman, *Frank and Jesse James*, 294–296, 315.
10 William A. Settle, *Jesse James Was His Name*, 119; Ted P. Yeatman, *Frank and Jesse James*, 275.
11 Carl W. Breihan, *Saga of Jesse James*, 139; Ted P. Yeatman, *Frank and Jesse James*, 291.
12 Carl W. Breihan, *Saga of Jesse James*, 141; Ted P. Yeatman, *Frank and Jesse James*, 292.
13 Robert M. Utley, *Billy the Kid*, 198, 199; Frederick Nolan, *The West of Billy the Kid*, 293, 295.
14 Bill O'Neal, *Encyclopedia of Western Gunfighters*, 116, 118, 119.
15 Richard Weddle, "Chisum: 'Cattle King of the Pecos'"; Maurice Garland Fulton, *History of the Lincoln County War*, 410.
16 Maurice Garland Fulton, *History of the Lincoln County War*, 419–421.
17 Frederick Nolan, *The West of Billy the Kid*, 154.
18 Maurice Garland Fulton, *History of the Lincoln County War*, 415.
19 Wikipedia, "Thomas B. Catron," accessed December 19, 2018, https://en.wikipedia.org/wiki/Thomas_B._Catron.
20 Wikipedia, "John Kinney (Outlaw)," accessed December 19, 2018, https://en.wikipedia.org/wiki/John_Kinney_(outlaw).
21 Bill O'Neal, *Encyclopedia of Western Gunfighters*, 105, 106.

AFTERWORD

1 Bill Markley, "Tracking Roosevelt's River Pirates," *True West Magazine*, June 2011, 51, 53.
2 Bob Boze Bell, "Overkill! Bonnie & Clyde vs Frank Hamer and His Posse," *True West Magazine*, January 2019, 44.
3 Ted P. Yeatman, *Frank and Jesse James*, 297.
4 Wikipedia, "Jesse James (Folk Song)," accessed December 19, 2018, https://en.wikipedia.org/wiki/Jesse_James_(folk_song).
5 Johnny Boggs, personal e-mail communication to Bill Markley, December 20, 2018.

BIBLIOGRAPHY

MANUSCRIPTS AND PRIMARY RESOURCES

Boggs, Johnny, author of *Jesse James and the Movies* and *Billy the Kid on Film*, personal e-mail communication to Bill Markley, December 20, 2018.

Clark, Jim, manager of operations, James Clark & Company Railroad Motion Pictures Services, personal communication, July 26, 2018 and August 22, 2018.

DeVore, Brenda, director, Prairie Trails Museum of Wayne County, Corydon, IA, personal e-mail communication to Bill Markley, June 4, 2018.

BOOKS

Ball, Eve. *Ma'am Jones of the Pecos*. Tucson: University of Arizona Press, 1969.

Biographical and Historical Record of Wayne and Appanoose Counties, Iowa. Chicago: Interstate Publishing Co., 1886.

Brant, Marley. *Jesse James: The Man and the Myth*. New York: Berkley Books, 1998.

Brassington, William Salt. *Shakespeare's Homeland: Sketches of Stratford-upon-Avon, the Forest of Arden, and the Avon Valley*. London: J. M. Dent & Co., 1903.

Breihan, Carl W. *Saga of Jesse James*. Caldwell, ID: Caxton Printers, 1991.

Burns, Walter Noble. *The Saga of Billy the Kid: The Thrilling Life of America's Original Outlaw*. Reprint. New York: Skyhorse Publishing, 2014.

Christensen, Lawrence O., William E. Foley, and Gary Kremer, eds. *Dictionary of Missouri Biography*. Columbia: University of Missouri Press, 1999.

Dacus, J. A. *Life and Adventures of Frank and Jesse James, the Noted Western Outlaws*. St. Louis: N. D. Thompson & Co., 1881.

Dworkin, Mark J. *American Mythmaker: Walter Noble Burns and the Legends of Billy the Kid, Wyatt Earp, and Joaquin Murrieta*. Norman: University of Oklahoma Press, 2015.

Eakin, Sue, and Manie Culbertson. *Louisiana: The Land and Its People*. Gretna, LA: Pelican Publishing, 1998.

Edwards Brothers. *An Illustrated Historical Atlas of Clay County, Missouri*. Philadelphia: Edwards Brothers of Missouri, 1877.

Edwards, John N. *Noted Guerrillas, or the Warfare of the Border*. St. Louis, MO: Bryan Brand & Co., 1877.

Enss, Chris. *The Pinks: The First Women Detectives, Operatives, and Spies with the Pinkerton National Detective Agency*. Guilford, CT: Globe Pequot, 2017.

Fanebust, Wayne. *Chasing Frank and Jesse James: The Bungled Northfield Bank Robbery and the Long Manhunt*. Jefferson, NC: McFarland & Co., 2018.

Fulton, Maurice Garland. Edited by Robert N. Mullin. *History of the Lincoln County War*. Tucson: University of Arizona Press, 1968.

Gannett, Henry. *The Origin of Certain Place Names in the United States*. Washington, DC: US Government Printing Office, 1905.

Gardner, Mark Lee. *Shot All to Hell: Jesse James, the Northfield Raid, and the Wild West's Greatest Escape*. New York: HarperCollins Publishers, 2013.

—— *To Hell on a Fast Horse: Billy the Kid, Pat Garrett, and the Epic Chase to Justice in the Old West*. New York: HarperCollins Publishers, 2010.

Garrett, Pat. *The Authentic Life of Billy the Kid, the Noted Desperado of the Southwest, Whose Deeds of Daring and Blood Made His Name a Terror in New Mexico, Arizona and Northern Mexico.* Santa Fe: New Mexico Printing and Publishing Co., 1882.

History of Boone County, Missouri. St. Louis, MO: Western Historical Co., 1882.

History of Clay and Platte Counties, Missouri. St. Louis, MO: National Historical Co., 1885.

History of Ray County, Missouri. St. Louis: Missouri Historical Co., 1881.

Hoyt, Henry F. *A Frontier Doctor*. Reprint. New York: Houghton Mifflin Co., 1929.

James, Jesse, Jr. *Jesse James, My Father*. Cleveland: Buckeye Publishing Co., 1899.

Jameson, W. C. *Billy the Kid: Beyond the Grave*. Lanham, MD: Taylor Trade Publishing, 2005.

Koblas, John. *Faithful unto Death: The James-Younger Raid on the First National Bank, Northfield, Minnesota, September 7, 1876*. Northfield, MN: Northfield Historical Society Press, 2001.

Long, E. B. *The Civil War Day by Day: An Almanac 1861–1865*. Garden City, NY: Doubleday & Co., 1971.

Love, Robertus. *The Rise and Fall of Jesse James*. Lincoln: University of Nebraska Press, 1925.

Markley, Bill, and Kellen Cutsforth. *Old West Showdown: Two Authors Wrangle over the Truth about the Mythic Old West*. Guilford, CT: Rowman & Littlefield, 2018.

McPherson, James M. *Battle Cry of Freedom: The Civil War Era*. New York: Ballantine Books, 1988.

Nevin, David. *The Expressmen*. Alexandria, VA: Time-Life Books, 1974.

Nickell, Joe. *Camera Clues: A Handbook for Photographic Investigation*. Lexington: University Press of Kentucky, 2005.

Nolan, Frederick. *The West of Billy the Kid*. Norman: University of Oklahoma Press, 1998.

The Northfield Bank Raid. Reprinted in 2008 by *The Northfield News* from *The Northfield News*, August 27, September 3, 10, and 17, 1926, 10th edition.

O'Hara, S. Paul. *Inventing the Pinkertons or Spies, Sleuths, Mercenaries, and Thugs*. Baltimore, MD: Johns Hopkins University Press, 2016.

O'Neal, Bill. *Encyclopedia of Western Gunfighters*. Norman: University of Oklahoma Press, 1979.

Orgel, Stephen, and A. R. Braunmuller, eds. *William Shakespeare: The Complete Works*. New York, NY: Penguin Books, 2002.

Otero, Miguel Antonio, Jr. *The Real Billy the Kid: With New Light on the Lincoln County War*. Houston, TX: Arte Publico Press, 1998.

Pinkerton, William Allan. *Train Robberies, Train Robbers and the "Holdup" Men*. Reprint. Andesite Press, 1907.

Redman, Ben Ray. Introduction to *Ben-Hur: A Tale of the Christ*, by Lew Wallace. Norwalk, CT: Heritage Press, 1960.

Robison, Ken. *Yankees & Rebels on the Upper Missouri: Steamboats, Gold and Peace*. Charleston, SC: History Press, 2016.

Ross, James R. *I, Jesse James*. Thousand Oaks, CA: Dragon Books, 1989.

Sandburg, Carl. *Abraham Lincoln: The War Years*, vol. 1. New York: Harcourt, Brace & World, 1939.

Settle, William A., Jr., *Jesse James Was His Name or, Fact and Fiction Concerning the Careers of the Notorious James Brothers of Missouri*. Lincoln: University of Nebraska Press, 1966.

Siringo, Charles. *Riata and Spurs: The Story of a Lifetime Spent in the Saddle as Cowboy and Detective*. Reprint. New York: Cosimo Classics, 1927.

Stiles, T. J. *Jesse James: Last Rebel of the Civil War*. New York: Random House, 2002.

Trefousse, Hans Louis. *Ben Butler: The South Called Him Beast!* New York: Twayne Publishers, 1957.

The Trial of Frank James for Murder. Kansas City: George Miller Jr., 1898.

Triplett, Frank. *Jesse James: The Life, Times, and Treacherous Death of the Most Infamous Outlaw of All Time*. Reprint. New York: Skyhorse Publishing, 2013.

Utley, Robert M. *Billy the Kid: A Short and Violent Life*. Lincoln: University of Nebraska Press, 1989.

Wallis, Michael. *Billy the Kid: The Endless Ride*. New York: W. W. Norton & Co., 2007.

Ward, Geoffrey C. *The Civil War: An Illustrated History*. New York: Alfred A. Knopf, 1990.

Waters, Richard. *The Defeat of the James-Younger Gang in Northfield, Minnesota*. Northfield, MN: Northfield Historical Society, 2016.

Yeatman, Ted P. *Frank and Jesse James: The Story behind the Legend*. Naperville, IL: Sourcebooks, 2000.

Younger, Thomas Coleman. *The Story of Cole Younger, By Himself*. Reprint. St. Paul, MN: Minnesota Historical Society, 2000.

Periodicals

Aiello, Jeff. "The Claim." *True West Magazine*, February 2016.
Bell, Bob Boze. "Overkill! Bonnie & Clyde vs. Frank Hamer and His Posse." *True West Magazine*, January 2019.
———. "Cole Younger, American Outlaw." *True West Magazine*, September 2018.
Bell, Bob Boze, and various contributors. "What If Everything We Know about Billy the Kid Is Wrong?" *True West Magazine*, June 2015.
"The Billy the Kid Wannabe Yearbook." *True West Magazine*, June 2015.
Boardman, Mark. "The Croquet Kid." *True West Magazine*, February 2016.
———. "The Holy Grail for Sale." *True West Magazine*, June 2011.
Breihan, Carl W. "Did Cole Younger Rob the Bank at Corinth?" *Real West Magazine*, vol. XIV, no. 98, November 1971.
DeVore, Brenda. "The Trial of Clelland Miller." *Newsletter of the Wayne County Historical Society*, Corydon, IA, December 2012.
Eaton, David Wolfe. "How Missouri Counties, Towns and Streams Were Named." *Missouri Historical Review*, vol. 10, no. 3, April 1916.
The Heritage Club. "Ben-Hur." *Sandglass*, Norwalk, CT: Heritage Press, 1960.
Hutton, Paul Andrew. "Billy the Kid's Final Escape." *Wild West Magazine*, December 2015.
Koblas, John. "Robbing the Yankees: The James Brothers and Their Gang Were the Right Bandits for Their Time." *True West Magazine*, March 2007.
Markley, Bill. "Tracking Roosevelt's River Pirates." *True West Magazine*, June 2011.
Smith, Robert Barr. "The James Boys Go to War." *Civil War Times Illustrated Magazine*, January/February 1994.
Weddle, Richard. "Chisum: 'Cattle King of the Pecos.'" *Wild West Magazine*, August 2014.
Yeatman, Ted P., "Two Great Myths about Jesse James: Setting the Record Straight." *True West Magazine*, August 2002.

Internet Resources

Adams Funds. Accessed August 3, 2018, https://www.adamsfunds.com/about/history/.
American Experience. "Jesse James Primary Source Newspaper Accounts." Public Broadcasting Service. Accessed June 3, 2018, https://www.pbs.org/wgbh/americanexperience/features/james-newspapers/.
American Experience. "William 'Bloody Bill' Anderson." Accessed May 14, 2018, http://www.pbs.org/wgbh/americanexperience/features/james-anderson/.
Ancestry.com. 1880 United States Federal Census. Accessed April 17, 2018, https://www.ancestry.com/interactive/6742/4242010-00881?pid=15438484&backurl=https://search.ancestry.com/cgi-bin/sse.dll?indiv%3D1%26dbid%3D6742%26h%3D15438484%26tid%3D%26pid%3D%26usePUB%3

Dtrue%26_phsrc%3DuBu3%26_phstart%3DsuccessSource&treeid=&personid=&hintid=&usePUB=true&_phsrc=uBu3&_phstart=successSource&usePUBJs=true.

"Bank Robbery; Particulars of the Daylight Outrage in Ste. Genevieve, Mo.." *New York Times Archives*, May 31, 1873. Accessed June 3, 2018, https://timesmachine.nytimes.com/timesmachine/1873/05/31/82408551.pdf.

Bloom, Joseph, "Molly MacGuires in Pennsylvania Coal Regions." *American History Magazine*, June 12, 2006, HistoryNet. Accessed August 3, 2018, http://www.historynet.com/molly-macguires-in-pennsylvania-coal-regions.htm.

Boardman, Mark. "The Lunacy of Billy the Kid: You Can't Make This Stuff Up!" *True West Magazine*, July 2010. Accessed December 8, 2018, https://truewestmagazine.com/the-lunacy-of-billy-the-kid/.

Emley, Linda. "Postcards: Word of Mouth, Local Lore Add to Bank Robbery Story." *Richmond Daily News*, 2013. Accessed May 23, 2018, https://www.richmond-dailynews.com/2013/08/postcards-word-of-mouth-local-lore-add-to-bank-robbery-story/.

Find a Grave. "Jesse James." Accessed December 18, 2018,. https://www.findagrave.com/memorial/539/jesse-james.

Find a Grave. "Susan Lavenia James Parmer." Accessed April 16, 2018, https://www.findagrave.com/memorial/10700891/susan-lavenia-parmer.

Ganis, Ralph. "A Knight with the Widow Benton: Did the Robin Hood-Bandit Save a Widow's Home?" *True West Magazine*, August 1, 2002. Accessed October 14, 2018, https://truewestmagazine.com/a-knight-with-the-widow-benton/.

Kansaspedia. "Thomas W. Barber." Kansas Historical Society. Accessed May 17, 2018, https://www.kshs.org/kansapedia/thomas-w-barber/11730.

Middlecamp, David. "Paso Robles' Founders: A Vigilante, a Capitalist and Jesse James' Uncle." *The Tribune*. Accessed May 25, 2018, http://www.sanluisobispo.com/news/local/news-columns-blogs/photos-from-the-vault/article39472611.html.

Minnesota Department of Natural Resources. "Big Woods Subsection." Accessed August 22, 2018, https://www.dnr.state.mn.us/ecs/222Mb/index.html.

"The Ste. Genevieve, Missouri Robbery." *Civil War St. Louis*. Accessed June 3, 2018, http://www.civilwarstlouis.com/History/jamesstegenevieve.htm.

Stewart, Phil. "History of the James Farm." Friends of the James Farm website, 2. Accessed April 16, 2018, http://n.b5z.net/i/u/10126339/f/ArticleArchive/stewart_article.pdf.

Ward, Stephanie Francis. "The Lawyer Who Took on Jesse James . . . and Won." *American Bar Association Journal*, March 2008. Accessed June 1, 2018, http://www.abajournal.com/magazine/article/the_lawyer_who_took_on_jesse_james_and_won/.

Wells Fargo Today, 3rd Quarter 2018, Quarterly Fact Sheet. Accessed January 2, 2019, https://www08.wellsfargomedia.com/assets/pdf/about/corporate/wells-fargo-today.pdf.

Wikipedia. "Adams Express Company." Accessed January 2, 2019, https://en.wikipedia.org/wiki/Adams_Express_Company.

Wikipedia. "*Ben-Hur: A Tale of the Christ.*" Accessed November 29, 2018, https://en.wikipedia.org/wiki/Ben-Hur:_A_Tale_of_the_Christ.

Wikipedia. "Benjamin Butler." Accessed August 13, 2018, https://en.wikipedia.org/wiki/Benjamin_Butler.

Wikipedia. "Big Woods." Accessed August 22, 2018, https://en.wikipedia.org/wiki/Big_Woods.

Wikipedia. "Centennial Exposition." Accessed August 11, 2018, https://en.wikipedia.org/wiki/Centennial_Exposition.

Wikipedia. "Jesse James (Folk Song)." Accessed December 19, 2018, https://en.wikipedia.org/wiki/Jesse_James_(Folk_Song).

Wikipedia. "John Kinney (Outlaw)." Accessed December 19, 2018, https://en.wikipedia.org/wiki/John_Kinney_(Outlaw).

Wikipedia, "Thomas B. Catron." Accessed December 19, 2018, https://en.wikipedia.org/wiki/Thomas_B._Catron.

INDEX

ABOUT THE AUTHOR

Bill Markley is a member of Western Writers of America (WWA) and is a staff writer for WWA's *Roundup* magazine. He also writes for *True West*, *Wild West*, and *South Dakota* magazines. His latest book, *Wyatt Earp and Bat Masterson: Lawmen of the Legendary West*, examines the lives of these two well-known Old West characters. His book, written with coauthor Kellen Cutsforth, *Old West Showdown: Two Authors Wrangle over the Truth about the Mythic Old West*, explores differing viewpoints on ten Old West characters and events. Bill has written three additional nonfiction books: *Dakota Epic: Experiences of a Reenactor during the Filming of Dances with Wolves*; *Up the Missouri River with Lewis and Clark*; and *American Pilgrim: A Post-September 11th Bus Trip and Other Tales of the Road*. His first historical novel, *Deadwood Dead Men*, was selected by Western Fictioneers as a finalist for its 2014 Peacemaker Award in the category Best First Western Novel. Bill wrote the "Military Establishment" chapter and thirty entries for the *Encyclopedia of Western Expansion*. He was a member of Toastmasters International for twenty years. He earned a bachelor's degree in biology and a master's degree in environmental sciences and engineering at Virginia Tech, worked on two Antarctic field teams, and worked forty years with the South Dakota Department of Environment and Natural Resources. Raised on a farm near Valley Forge, Pennsylvania, Bill has always loved history. He reenacts Civil War infantry and frontier cavalry and has participated in the films *Dances with Wolves*, *Son of the Morning Star*, *Far and Away*, *Gettysburg*, and *Crazy Horse*. Bill and his wife Liz live in Pierre, South Dakota, where they have raised two children, now grown.

ABOUT THE ILLUSTRATOR

Jim Hatzell is a graduate of the American Academy of Art in Chicago, Illinois, with a degree in advertising and design, and in illustration. Jim has also been in the motion picture business since 1989, when he and Bill first met on the set of *Dances with Wolves*. Jim created the illustrations for Bill's book *Wyatt Earp and Bat Masterson: Lawmen of the Legendary West*. Jim and his wife, Jacqui, make their home in Rapid City, South Dakota.